Principles of Accounting

Principles of Accounting

Heather Murphy

CLANRYE INTERNATIONAL
www.clanryeinternational.com

Clanrye International,
750 Third Avenue, 9th Floor,
New York, NY 10017, USA

ISBN: 978-1-63240-901-0

Cataloging-in-Publication Data

Principles of accounting / Heather Murphy.
p. cm.
Includes bibliographical references and index.
ISBN 978-1-63240-901-0
1. Accounting. 2. Bookkeeping. 3. Financial statements.
I. Murphy, Heather.
HF5636 .P75 2019
657--dc23

For information on all Clanrye International publications
visit our website at www.clanryeinternational.com

CLANRYE INTERNATIONAL

Contents

Preface

Accounting refers to the processing, measurement and communication of financial data of businesses and corporations. The information gathered is communicated to investors, creditors and regulators in the form of financial reports and statements. Financial statements are developed on a set of generally accepted accounting principles. Auditing, financial accounting, tax accounting, management accounting, etc. are some of the subfields of accounting. Accounting information systems play a crucial role in reducing the costs of storing, accumulating and reporting of managerial accounting information. This book is compiled in such a manner, that it will provide in-depth knowledge about the theory and practice of accounting. The topics included in this book are of utmost significance and bound to provide incredible insights to readers. It will serve as a valuable source of reference for anyone interested in this field.

A short introduction to every chapter is written below to provide an overview of the content of the book:

Chapter 1- Accounting refers to the processing, measurement and communication of financial information. This field has many significant subfields such as management accounting, financial accounting, accrual-based accounting, tax accounting and fund accounting, among others. This is an introductory chapter, which will introduce briefly all the central aspects of accounting as well as its different types; **Chapter 2**- An accounting ratio is a standard ratio used within a firm for comparing the strengths and weaknesses in the company. Many accounting ratios are used for quantifying the different aspects of a business, such as financial ratio, debt ratio, debt-to-equity ratio, P/B ratio, liquidity ratio, etc. which have been discussed in great detail in this chapter; **Chapter 3**- A financial statement is a record of the financial transactions and activities of a business, person or entity. It may include a statement of financial position, an income statement, an equity statement and a cash flow statement. These topics have been elaborated in this chapter to provide a better perspective about the different formal records of financial activities; **Chapter 4**- Bookkeeping refers to the process of recording financial transactions in a business, such as purchases, sales and payments. This chapter closely examines the key concepts of bookkeeping to provide an extensive understanding of the recording of financial transactions such as accounting period, bank reconciliation, trial balance and adjusting entries as well as the ways to keep a general journal or a ledger; **Chapter 5**- An audit refers to a systematic examination and evaluation of an organization's financial statements and non-financial disclosures to fairly judge whether the records represent an accurate picture of the claims that they make. All the diverse aspects of auditing, such as audit management, internal audit, cost auditing, continuous auditing, auditor's report and internal audit, have been carefully analyzed in this chapter.

Finally, I would like to thank my fellow scholars who gave constructive feedback and my family members who supported me at every step.

Heather Murphy

1

Accounting and its Types

Accounting refers to the processing, measurement and communication of financial information. This field has many significant subfields such as management accounting, financial accounting, accrual-based accounting, tax accounting and fund accounting, among others. This is an introductory chapter, which will introduce briefly all the central aspects of accounting as well as its different types.

Accounting

Accounting is the systematic and comprehensive recording of financial transactions pertaining to a business. Accounting also refers to the process of summarizing, analyzing and reporting these transactions to oversight agencies, regulators and tax collection entities. The financial statements that summarize a large company's operations, financial position and cash flows over a particular period are a concise summary of hundreds of thousands of financial transactions it may have entered into over this period.

Let us try and understand the components of accounting to understand what it really means:

Recording

The primary function of accounting is to make records of all the transactions that the firm enters into. Recognizing what qualifies as a transaction and making a record of the same is called bookkeeping. Bookkeeping is narrower in scope than accounting and concerns only the recording part. For the purpose of recording, accountants maintain a set of books. Their procedures are very systematic. Nowadays, computers have been deployed to automatically account for transactions as they happen.

Summarizing

Recording for transactions creates raw data. Pages and pages of raw data are of little use to an organization for decision making. For this reason, accountants classify data into categories. These categories are defined in the chart of accounts. As and when transactions occur, two things happen, firstly an individual record is made and secondly the summary record is updated.

For instance a sale to Mr. X for Rs 100 would appear as:

- Sale to Mr. X for Rs 100
- Increase the total sales (summary) from 500 to 600

Reporting

Management is answerable to the investors about the company's state of affairs. The owners need to be periodically updated about the operations that are being financed with their money. For this reason, there are periodic reports which are sent to them. Usually the frequency of these reports is quarterly and there is one annual report which summarizes the performance of all four quarters. Reporting is usually done in the form of financial statements. These financial statements are regulated by government bodies to ensure that there is no misleading financial reporting.

Analyzing

Lastly, accounting entails conducting an analysis of the results. After results have been summarized and reported, meaningful conclusions need to be drawn. Management must find out its positive and negative points. Accounting helps in doing so by means of comparison. It is common practice to compare profits, cash, sales, assets, etc with each other to analyze the performance of the business.

Accounting is one of the key functions for almost any business. It may be handled by a bookkeeper or an accountant at a small firm, or by sizable finance departments with dozens of employees at larger companies. The reports generated by various streams of accounting, such as cost accounting and management accounting, are invaluable in helping management make informed business decisions. While basic accounting functions can be handled by a bookkeeper, advanced accounting is typically handled by qualified accountants who possess designations such as Certified Public Accountant (CPA) in the United States, or Chartered Accountant (CA), Certified General Accountant (CGA) or Certified Management Accountant (CMA) in Canada.

Creating Financial Statements

The financial statements that summarize a large company's operations, financial position and cash flows over a particular period are concise statements based on thousands of financial transactions. As a result, all accounting designations are the culmination of years of study and rigorous examinations combined with a minimum number of years of practical accounting experience.

Generally Accepted Accounting Principles

In most cases, accountants use generally accepted accounting principles (GAAP) when preparing financial statements. GAAP is a set of standards related to balance sheet identification, outstanding share measurements and other accounting issues, and its standards are based on double-entry accounting, a method which enters each expense or incoming revenue in two places on a company's balance sheet.

Example of Double Entry Accounting

To illustrate double-entry accounting, imagine a business issues an invoice to one of its clients. An accountant using the double-entry method enters a credit under the accounts receivables column and a debit under the balance sheet's revenue column. When the client pays the invoice, the accountant debits accounts receivables and credits revenue. Double-entry accounting is also called balancing the books, as all of the accounting entries are balanced against each other. If the entries aren't balanced, the accountant knows there must be a mistake somewhere in the ledger.

Financial Accounting vs. Management Accounting

Financial accounting refers to the processes accountants use to generate the annual accounting statements of a firm. Management accounting uses much of the same processes but utilizes information in different ways. Namely, in management accounting, an accountant generates monthly or quarterly reports that a business's management team can use to make decisions about how the business operates.

Financial Accounting vs. Cost Accounting

Just as management accounting helps businesses make decisions about management, cost accounting helps businesses make decisions about costing. Essentially, cost accounting considers all of the costs related to producing a product. Analysts, managers, business owners and accountants use this information to determine what their products should cost. In cost accounting, money is cast as an economic factor in production, whereas in financial accounting, money is considered to be a measure of a company's economic performance.

Financial Accounting

Financial accounting is a specialized branch of accounting that keeps track of a company's financial transactions. Using standardized guidelines, the transactions are recorded, summarized, and presented in a financial report or financial statement such as an income statement or a balance sheet.

Companies issue financial statements on a routine schedule. The statements are considered *external* because they are given to people outside of the company, with the primary recipients being owners/stockholders, as well as certain lenders. If a corporation's stock is publicly traded, however, its financial statements (and other financial reportings) tend to be widely circulated, and information will likely reach secondary recipients such as competitors, customers, employees, labor organizations, and investment analysts.

It's important to point out that the purpose of financial accounting is not to report the value of a company. Rather, its purpose is to provide enough information for others to assess the value of a company for themselves.

Double Entry and the Accrual Basis of Accounting

At the heart of financial accounting is the system known as double entry bookkeeping (or "double entry accounting"). Each financial transaction that a company makes is recorded by using this system.

The term "double entry" means that every transaction affects at least two accounts. For example, if a company borrows $50,000 from its bank, the company's Cash account increases, and the company's Notes Payable account increases. Double entry also means that one of the accounts must have an amount entered as a debit, and one of the accounts must have an amount entered as a credit. For any given transaction, the debit amount must equal the credit amount.

The advantage of double entry accounting is this: at any given time, the balance of a company's asset accounts will equal the balance of its liability and stockholders' (or owner's) equity accounts.

Financial accounting is required to follow the accrual basis of accounting (as opposed to the "cash basis" of accounting). Under the accrual basis, revenues are reported when they are earned, not when the money is received. Similarly, expenses are reported when they are *incurred*, not when they are paid. For example, although a magazine publisher receives a $24 check from a customer for an annual subscription, the publisher reports as revenue a monthly amount of $2 (one-twelfth of the annual subscription amount). In the same way, it reports its property tax expense each month as one-twelfth of the annual property tax bill.

By following the accrual basis of accounting, a company's profitability, assets, liabilities and other financial information is more in line with economic reality.

Accounting Principles

If financial accounting is going to be useful, a company's reports need to be credible, easy to understand, and comparable to those of other companies. To this end, financial accounting follows a set of common rules known as accounting standards or generally accepted accounting principles (GAAP, pronounced "gap").

GAAP is based on some basic underlying principles and concepts such as the cost principle, matching principle, full disclosure, going concern, economic entity, conservatism, relevance, and reliability.

GAAP, however, is not static. It includes some very complex standards that were issued in response to some very complicated business transactions. GAAP also addresses accounting practices that may be unique to particular industries, such as utility, banking, and insurance. Often these practices are a response to changes in government regulations of the industry.

GAAP includes many specific pronouncements as issued by the Financial Accounting Standards Board (FASB, pronounced "fas-bee"). The FASB is a non-government group that researches current needs and develops accounting rules to meet those needs.

In addition to following the provisions of GAAP, any corporation whose stock is publicly traded is also subject to the reporting requirements of the Securities and Exchange Commission (SEC), an agency of the U.S. government. These requirements mandate an annual report to stockholders as well as an annual report to the SEC. The annual report to the SEC requires that independent certified public accountants audit a company's financial statements, thus giving assurance that the company has followed GAAP.

Financial Statements

Financial accounting generates the following general-purpose, external, financial statements:

1. Income statement (sometimes referred to as "results of operations" or "earnings statement" or "profit and loss [P&L] statement")
2. Balance sheet (sometimes referred to as "statement of financial position")
3. Statement of cash flows (sometimes referred to as "cash flow statement")
4. Statement of stockholders' equity

Income Statement

The income statement reports a company's profitability during a specified period of time. The period of time could be one year, one month, three months, 13 weeks, or any other time interval chosen by the company.

The main components of the income statement are revenues, expenses, gains, and losses. Revenues include such things as sales, service revenues, and interest revenue. Expenses include the cost of goods sold, operating expenses (such as salaries, rent, utilities, advertising), and nonoperating expenses (such as interest expense). If a corporation's stock is publicly traded, the earnings per share of its common stock are reported on the income statement.

Balance Sheet

The balance sheet is organized into three parts: (1) assets, (2) liabilities, and (3) stockholders' equity at a specified date (typically, this date is the last day of an accounting period).

The first section of the balance sheet reports the company's *assets* and includes such things as cash, accounts receivable, inventory, prepaid insurance, buildings, and equipment. The next section reports the company's *liabilities*; these are obligations that are due at the date of the balance sheet and often include the word "payable" in their title (Notes Payable, Accounts Payable, Wages Payable, and Interest Payable). The final section is *stockholders' equity*, defined as the difference between the amount of assets and the amount of liabilities.

Statement of Cash Flows

The statement of cash flows explains the change in a company's cash (and cash equivalents) during the time interval indicated in the heading of the statement. The change is divided into three parts: (1) operating activities, (2) investing activities, and (3) financing activities.

The *operating activities* section explains how a company's cash (and cash equivalents) have changed due to operations. *Investing activities* refer to amounts spent or received in transactions involving long-term assets. The *financing activities* section reports such things as cash received through the issuance of long-term debt, the issuance of stock, or money spent to retire long-term liabilities.

Statement of Stockholders' Equity

The statement of stockholders' (or shareholders') equity lists the changes in stockholders' equity for the same period as the income statement and the cash flow statement. The changes will include items such as net income, other comprehensive income, dividends, the repurchase of common stock, and the exercise of stock options.

Accrual Method Vs. Cash Method

Financial accounting may be performed using either the accrual method, cash method or a combination of the two. Accrual accounting entails recording transactions when the transactions have occurred and the revenue is recognizable. Cash accounting entails recording transactions only upon the exchange of cash. Revenue is only recorded upon the receipt of payment, and expenses are only recorded upon the payment of the obligation.

Financial Accounting Reporting

Financial reporting occurs through the use of financial statements. The financial statements present the five main classifications of financial data: revenues, expenses, assets, liabilities and equity. Revenues and expenses are accounted for and reported on the income statement. Financial accounting results in the determination of net income at the bottom of the income statement. Assets, liabilities and equity accounts are reported on the balance sheet. The balance sheet utilizes financial accounting to report ownership of the company's future economic benefits.

Financial Accounting Vs. Managerial Accounting

The key difference between financial and managerial accounting is that financial accounting aims at providing information to parties outside the organization, whereas managerial accounting information is aimed at helping managers within the organization make decisions. Financial statement preparation using accounting principles is most relevant to regulatory organizations and financial institutions. Because there are numerous accounting rules that do not translate well into business operation management, different accounting rules and procedures are utilized by internal management for internal business analysis.

Accounting Certifications

The most common accounting designation demonstrating an ability to perform financial accounting within the United States is the Certified Public Accountant (CPA) license. Outside of the United States, holders of the Chartered Accountant (CA) license demonstrate the ability as well. The Certified Management Accountant (CMA) designation is more demonstrative of an ability to perform internal management functions than financial accounting.

Tax Accounting

Tax accounting refers to the rules used to generate tax assets and liabilities in the accounting records of a business or individual. Tax accounting is derived from the Internal Revenue Code (IRC), rather than one of the accounting frameworks, such as GAAP or IFRS. Tax accounting may result in the generation of a taxable income figure that varies from the income figure reported on an entity's income statement. The reason for the difference is that tax rules may accelerate or delay the recognition of certain expenses that would normally be recognized in a reporting period. These differences are temporary, since the assets will eventually be recovered and the liabilities settled, at which point the differences will be terminated.

A difference that results in a taxable amount in a later period is called a taxable temporary difference, while a difference that results in a deductible amount in a later period is called a deductible temporary difference. Examples of temporary differences are:

- Revenues or gains that are taxable either prior to or after they are recognized in the financial statements. For example, an allowance for doubtful accounts may not be immediately tax deductible, but instead must be deferred until specific receivables are declared bad debts.
- Expenses or losses that are tax deductible either prior to or after they are recognized in the financial statements. For example, some fixed assets are tax deductible at once, but can only be recognized through long-term depreciation in the financial statements.
- Assets whose tax basis is reduced by investment tax credits.

The essential tax accounting is derived from the need to recognize two items, which are:

- Current year. The recognition of a tax liability or tax asset, based on the estimated amount of income taxes payable or refundable for the current year.
- Future years. The recognition of a deferred tax liability or tax asset, based on the estimated effects in future years of carryforwards and temporary differences.

Based on the preceding points, the general accounting for income taxes is:

1. Create a tax liability for estimated taxes payable, and/or create a tax asset for tax refunds, that relate to the current or prior years.
2. Create a deferred tax liability for estimated future taxes payable, and/or create a deferred tax asset for estimated future tax refunds, that can be attributed to temporary differences and carryforwards.
3. Calculate the total income tax expense in the period.

Tax Principles vs. GAAP

Under GAAP, companies must follow a common set of accounting principles, standards and procedures when they compile their financial statements by accounting for any and all financial transactions. Balance sheet items can be accounted for differently when preparing financial statements and tax payables. For example, companies can prepare their financial statements implementing the first-in-first-out (FIFO) method to record their inventory for financial purposes, yet they can implement the last-in-first-out (LIFO) approach for tax purposes. The latter procedure reduces the current year's taxes payable.

While accounting encompasses all financial transactions to some degree, tax accounting focuses solely on those transactions that affect an entity's tax burden, and how those items relate to proper tax calculation and tax document preparation. Tax accounting is regulated by the Internal Revenue Service (IRS) to ensure that all associated tax laws are adhered to by tax accounting professionals and individual taxpayers. The IRS also requires the use of specific documents and forms to properly submit tax information as required by law.

Tax Accounting for an Individual

For an individual taxpayer, tax accounting focuses solely on items such as income, qualifying deductions, investment gains or losses, and other transactions that affect the individual's tax burden. This limits the amount of information that is necessary for an individual to manage an annual tax return, and while a tax accountant can be used by an individual, it is not a legal requirement.

Meanwhile, general accounting would involve the tracking of all funds coming in and out of the persons' possession regardless of the purpose, including personal expenses that have no tax implications.

Tax Accounting for a Business

From a business perspective, more information must be analyzed as part of the tax accounting process. While the company's earnings, or incoming funds, must be tracked just as they are for the individual, there is an additional level of complexity regarding any outgoing funds directed towards certain business obligations. This can include funds directed towards specific business expenses as well as funds directed towards shareholders.

While it is also not required that a business use a tax accountant to perform these duties, it is fairly common in larger organizations due to the complexity of the records involved.

Tax Accounting for a Tax-Exempt Organization

Even in instances where an organization is tax-exempt, tax accounting is necessary. This is due to the fact that all organizations must file annual returns. They must provide information regarding any incoming funds, such as grants or donations, as well as how the funds are used during the organization's operation. This helps ensure that the organization adheres to all laws and regulations governing the proper operation of a tax-exempt entity.

Cost Accounting

Cost accounting is an accounting method that aims to capture a company's costs of production by assessing the input costs of each step of production as well as fixed costs, such as depreciation of capital equipment. Cost accounting will first measure and record these costs individually, then compare input results to output or actual results to aid company management in measuring financial performance.

While cost accounting is often used within a company to aid in decision making, financial accounting is what the outside investor community typically sees. Financial accounting is a different representation of costs and financial performance that includes a company's assets and liabilities. Cost accounting can be most beneficial as a tool for management in budgeting and in setting up cost control programs, which can improve net margins for the company in the future.

One key difference between cost accounting and financial accounting is that while in financial accounting the cost is classified depending on the type of transaction, cost accounting classifies costs according to information needs of the management. Cost accounting, because it is used as an internal tool by management, does not have to meet any specific standard set by the Generally Accepted Accounting Principles (GAAP) and, as a result, varies in use from company to company or from department to department.

Features of Cost Accounting

1. It is a process of accounting for costs.
2. It records income and expenditure relating to production of goods and services.
3. It provides statistical data on the basis of which future estimates are prepared and quotations are submitted.
4. It is concerned with cost ascertainment, cost control and cost reduction.
5. It establishes budgets and standards so that actual cost may be compared to find out deviations or variances.
6. It involves the presentation of right information to the right person at the right time so that it may be helpful to management for planning, evaluation of performance, control and decision making.

Objectives of Cost Accounting:

Objectives of cost accounting are ascertainment of cost, fixation of selling price, proper recording and presentation of cost data to management for measuring efficiency and for cost control and cost reduction, ascertaining the profit of each activity, assisting management in decision making and determination of break-even point.

The aim is to know the methods by which expenditure on materials, wages and overheads is recorded, classified and allocated so that the cost of products and services may be accurately ascertained; these costs may be related to sales and profitability may be determined. Yet with the development of business and industry, its objectives are changing day by day.

Following are the Main Objectives of Cost Accounting:

1. To ascertain the cost per unit of the different products manufactured by a business concern;
2. To provide a correct analysis of cost both by process or operations and by different elements of cost;
3. To disclose sources of wastage whether of material, time or expense or in the use of machinery, equipment and tools and to prepare such reports which may be necessary to control such wastage;
4. To provide requisite data and serve as a guide for fixing prices of products manufactured or services rendered;
5. To ascertain the profitability of each of the products and advise management as to how these profits can be maximised;
6. To exercise effective control if stocks of raw materials, work-in-progress, consumable stores and finished goods in order to minimise the capital locked up in these stocks;
7. To reveal sources of economy by installing and implementing a system of cost control for materials, labour and overheads;
8. To advise management on future expansion policies and proposed capital projects;
9. To present and interpret data for management planning, evaluation of performance and control;
10. To help in the preparation of budgets and implementation of budgetary control;
11. To organise an effective information system so that different levels of management may get the required information at the right time in right form for carrying out their individual responsibilities in an efficient manner;
12. To guide management in the formulation and implementation of incentive bonus plans based on productivity and cost savings;
13. To supply useful data to management for taking various financial decisions such as introduction of new products, replacement of labour by machine etc.;
14. To help in supervising the working of punched card accounting or data processing through computers;
15. To organise the internal audit system to ensure effective working of different departments;

16. To organise cost reduction programmes with the help of different departmental managers;

17. To provide specialised services of cost audit in order to prevent the errors and frauds and to facilitate prompt and reliable information to management; and

18. To find out costing profit or loss by identifying with revenues the costs of those products or services by selling which the revenues have resulted.

Broadly speaking, the above objectives can be re-grouped under the following three heads:

(1) Ascertainment and analysis of cost and income by product, function and responsibility.

(2) Accumulation and utilisation of cost data for control purposes to have the minimum possible cost consistent with maintenance of quality. This objective is achieved through fixation of targets, ascertainment of actuals, comparison of actuals with targets, analysis of reasons of deviations between actuals and targets and reporting deviations to management for taking corrective action.

(3) Providing useful data to management for taking decisions.

Principles of Cost Accounting

1. Cause-Effect Relationship:

Cause-effect relationship should be established for each item of cost. Each item of cost should be related to its cause as minutely as possible and the effect of the same on the various departments should be ascertained. A cost should be shared only by those units which pass through the departments for which such cost has been incurred.

2. Charge of Cost Only after its Incurrence:

Unit cost should include only those costs which have been actually incurred. For example unit cost should not be charged with selling cost while it is still in factory.

3. Past Costs Should not Form Part of Future Costs:

Past costs (which could not be recovered in past) should not be recovered from future costs as it will not only affect the true results of future period but will also distort other statements.

4. Exclusion of Abnormal Costs from Cost Accounts:

All costs incurred because of abnormal reasons (like theft, negligence) should not be taken into consideration while computing the unit cost. If done so, it will distort the cost figures and mislead management resulting in wrong decisions.

5. Principles of Double Entry Should be Followed Preferably:

To lessen the chances of any mistake or error, cost ledgers and cost control accounts, as far as possible, should be maintained on double entry principles. This will ensure the correctness of cost sheets and cost statements which are prepared for cost ascertainment and cost control.

Types of Cost Accounting

- Standard Cost Accounting

This type of cost accounting uses ratios to compare efficient uses of labor and materials to produce goods or services under standard conditions. Assessing these differences is called a variance analysis. Traditional cost accounting essentially allocates cost based on one measure, labor or machine hours. Due to the fact that overhead cost has risen proportionate to labor cost since the genesis of standard cost accounting, allocating overhead cost as an overall cost has ended up producing occasionally misleading insights.

Some of the issues associated with cost accounting is that this type of accounting emphasizes labor efficiency despite the fact that it makes up a comparatively small amount of the costs for modern companies.

- Activity Based Costing

The Charter Institute of Management Accountants defines activity based accounting as, "an approach to the costing and monitoring of activities which involves tracing resource consumption and costing final outputs, resources assigned to activities, and activities to cost objects based on consumption estimates. The latter utilize cost drivers to attach activity costs to outputs."

Activity based costing accumulates the overheads from each department and assigns them to specific cost objects like services, customers, or products. The way these costs are assigned to cost objects are first decided in an activity analysis, where appropriate output measures are cost drivers. As a result, activity based costing tends to be much more accurate and helpful when it comes to helping managers understand the cost and profitability of their company's specific services or products. Accountants using activity based costing will pass out a survey to employees who will then account for the amount of time they spend on different tasks. This gives management a better idea of where their time and money is being spent.

- Lean Accounting

Lean accounting is an extension of the philosophy of lean manufacturing and production developed by Japanese companies in the 1980s. Most accounting practices for manufacturing work off the assumption that whatever is being produced is done in a large scale. Instead of using standard costing, activity based costing, cost-plus pricing, or other management accounting systems, when using lean accounting those methods are replaced by value-based pricing and lean-focused performance measurements, for example, using a box score to facilitate decision making and create simplified and digestible financial reports.

- Marginal Costing

Considered a simplified model of cost accounting, marginal costing (sometimes called cost-volume-profit analysis) is an analysis of the relationship between a product's or service's sales price, the volume of sales, the amount produced, expenses, costs, and profits. That specific relationship is called the contribution margin. The contribution margin is calculated by dividing revenue minus variable cost by revenue. This type of analysis can be used by management to gain insight on potential profits as impacted by changing costs, what types of sales prices to establish, and types of marketing campaigns.

Types of Costs

- Fixed Costs are costs that don't vary depending on the amount of work a company is doing. These are usually things like the payment on a building, or a piece of equipment that is depreciating at a fixed monthly rate.
- Variable costs are tied to a company's level of production. An example could be a coffee roaster, which after receiving a large order of beans from a far-away locale, has to pay a higher rate for both shipping, packaging, and processing.
- Operating costs are costs associated with the day-to-day operations of a business. These costs can be either fixed or variable depending.
- Direct costs are the costs related to producing a product. If a coffee roaster spends 5 hours roasting coffee, the direct costs of the finished product include the labor hours of the roaster, and the cost of the coffee green. The energy cost to heat the roaster would be indirect because they're inexact, hard to trace.

Objections Against Cost Accounting:

A number of objections are generally raised against the introduction of costing on various grounds.

Following are some of the important objections usually raised:

1. Want of Necessity:

It has been argued that costing is of recent origin and that industries prospered in the past and are still prospering without the aid of costing and, therefore, expenditure incurred in installing a costing system would be an unnecessary expenditure.

This argument overlooks the fact that modern industries are running under highly competitive conditions and that every manufacturer should know the actual cost of production to decide how far he can reduce the selling price. Many industrial failure.' in the past may be attributed to the lack of knowledge on the part of manufacturer of actual cost of production and, therefore, selling products below cost.

2. *Inapplicability:*

It is argued that modern methods of costing are inapplicable to many types of industries. It is true that costing cannot be applied with advantage to trading concerns and concerns of small size. But in many cases some methods of costing can always be devised to suit the requirements of the business.

It should be clearly understood that there is no stereotyped system of costing which can be applied to all types of industries. The system of costing should be so devised as to suit the business but not the business to suit the system.

3. *Failure in Many Cases:*

It is argued that the adoption of costing system failed to produce the desired results in many cases and, therefore, the system is defective. The failure of a system may be due to several causes such as apathy or indifference of management, lack of adequate facilities, non-co-operation or opposition from the employees. So it is hasty to find fault with the system, if it fails to produce the desired results.

4. *Mere Matter of Forms and Rulings:*

It is argued that after some time, a costing system degenerates into a matter of forms and rulings. This is not the fault of the system. It is the fault of the way in which the system is maintained. Forms and rulings are essential for a costing system but they must be revised and brought up-to-date in the light of altered conditions. If this is not done, the system is bound to degenerate into a mere matter of forms and rulings.

5. *Expensive:*

It is said that the cost involved in installing and working a cost system is out of all proportions to the benefits derived therefrom. It may be stated in this connection that a costing system must be a profitable investment and should produce benefits commensurate with the expenditure incurred on the system. If care is taken to devise a costing system to suit the requirements of the industry and avoid unnecessary elaboration, expenditure incurred in installing and operating the system will be a profitable investment and will bring adequate return.

Fund Accounting

Fund accounting is a type of accounting method or strategy that puts an emphasis on accountability rather than on tracking the generation of profits. It is used by organisations that exist to achieve a specific mission or purpose other than to make a profit. These entities are called non-profits or not-for-profit organisations, such as government agencies, churches or other religious affiliations, hospitals, schools and the like. Fund accounting as a methodology is unique to non-profits.

What is a Fund?

Funds are defined as a self-balancing set of accounts, wherein each fund represents the amount of money that has been set aside to achieve a specific goal within an organization. These areas need to be tracked separately from other expenses.

Fund Categories

Those involved with fund accounting are usually tasked with identifying and keeping track of a number of separate funds. Each fund will have certain characteristics that will dictate how it's to be used. There are six main categories that can be used to identify most funds:

1. Current Unrestricted Funds: Funds that fall into this category are used for the general operating expenses of the organization or governmental entity. These funds do not contain restrictions on the use of the assets that they contain. This allows an organization's board of directors to use these funds in essentially any way that they see fit so long as the funds are being used to carry out the purposes for which the organization was founded.

2. Board-Designated Funds: These funds are created when an organization's board of directors transfers assets from a current unrestricted fund into a new fund that is designated for a particular purpose. With board-designated funds the board rather than the donor determines the use of the fund.

3. Current Restricted Funds: A restricted fund holds donated assets with the expectation that they'll be used for a particular purpose. The restriction applies to the use of the money only. For example, a donor may give $1,000 and specify that it must be used to purchase books for a library. The organization's board may then only use those funds to pay for books; they may not use the funds to pay for building an addition onto the library.

4. Endowment Funds: An endowment fund holds assets that earn additional income. Organizations are generally allowed to use the income generated by endowment assets, so long as they don't touch the principal. Endowment fund

income may be placed in either a restricted or unrestricted account depending on the donor's instructions. In some cases, endowment income must be placed back into the endowment fund to continue earning interest for a number of years before excess income can be placed in an alternative fund.

5. Fixed Asset Funds: Monetary assets that are placed in fixed asset funds are generally used to pay for the organization's long-term assets such as land, buildings and equipment. These items are usually paid for in fixed installments over time. The main purpose of this type of fund is to prevent money for fixed payments from being withdrawn from the unrestricted fund. This allows the organization to get a clearer picture of the current activities of the organization by comparing and contrasting discretionary spending from year to year.

6. Specialized Fund Groupings: As an example, some universities establish scholarship funds for exceptional students or for those who have demonstrated financial hardship. Essentially, specialized funds can be established for any purpose, but money donated to a specialized fund must be used towards the purpose for which the fund was established.

Reason Why Fund Accounting uses Several General Ledgers

To show a detailed account of how and where the money is spent, several general ledgers are maintained instead of a single general ledger, as opposed to a single ledger which is used by for-profit businesses. As previously mentioned, one way to distinguish this accounting methodology from profit-oriented businesses is in the way it uses its ledger: fund accounting uses multiple general ledgers or a set of self-balancing accounts that are segregated for specific purposes among various funds.

Reason Why Nonprofits Need Fund Accounting

Fund accounting is unique to nonprofits. It is a method that allows both donor and recipient to keep track of the resources and ensure that such resources go towards achieving their designated purpose. Here are the main reasons why fund accounting is the best method to be used by non-profits.

1. Transparency

By keeping each fund separate under specific categories, the inflows of donations, endowments and resources can be tagged appropriately. Using fund accounting methods will also show how the funds earmarked for a specific project is used.

2. Compliance

Nonprofits enjoy special privileges in the form of tax breaks and other government concessions, but they can only continue to benefit from it for as long as they remain compliant. They must abide by the rules stipulated in forming their organisation; otherwise, such privileges will be removed.

3. Measure Progress

Applying fund accounting principles in a non-profit setting allows those who are managing it with a systematic method that shows how goals are being met. By identifying the revenue coming in and immediately investing it towards the fund it was earmarked for, it's easier to track how close they are to meeting a specific purpose.

4. Funding Sources

Funds can come from various sources, and each one must be properly categorized before being placed in its correct fund. Designating the inflows of resources from the get-go lessens the chances of making accounting mistakes as well as ensure that no compliance issues or problems are encountered.

The main sources of income are the following: Donations and gifts, grants, equity capital and loan financing, contracts, and trading.

5. Donations and Gifts

These funds are sourced from any of the following entities: individuals, companies, charitable trusts, foundations, fundraising events, or other philanthropists who want to leave a legacy after they pass away. These funds in general can be applied in any way a non-profit chooses to use it, unless it was given in response to a specific purpose or campaign. It is also a good way to receive tax breaks and other privileges to reduce overhead.

6. Grants

These types of funds usually come from the public sector such as charitable trusts and foundations, and the money coming from these sources do not have to be repaid. Grants are also typically tax exempt, and usually come with a list of conditions before it can be applied. Such conditions are those related to following specific results or outputs, achieving previously agreed milestones, returning unspent funds, and strict reporting requirements that show how the funds are used and how the project is progressing.

7. Equity Capital

The source of these funds come from external investors who require a permanent stake in the organization. Typically used by social enterprises, an equity investor shares in the rewards of an organisation once it achieves some measure of success. Investors of this type don't always make monetary contributions; they might also choose to provide services or expertise as a form of donation.

8. Debt Financing

Debt or loan financing is used by organisations that borrow money from various lenders in order to fund their projects. These loans have to be repaid, usually with interest. Some lenders might also require collateral for secured loans, although unsecured debt financing can also be granted, usually with higher interest.

9. Contracts

This fund source is secured through a formal written agreement between two parties. Both parties are bound by the terms covered by the contract and by contract law. If either one fails to do what is included in the contract, then they must abide by the consequences that is written on the document.

A contract is considered to be a commercial agreement, and as such the income from it may be subject to Value Added Tax (VAT) or other taxes.

10. Trading

Nonprofits can also choose to engage in business-like activities to raise funding. They can do so by selling goods and services to the public or other organisations. Trading provides organisations with the most flexibility and freedom as to how funds are used and appropriated, because the source does not come from a benefactor or grant with a list of conditions attached to it.

Basic Principles of Fund Accounting

To retain a nonprofit's integrity and the donor's confidence, the basic principles of fund accounting focus on the recording and reporting of activities as prescribed by the Financial Accounting Standards Board (FASB). Following these guidelines assures donors that endowments received are disbursed properly and are aligned with any agreed upon conditions and limitations, including the nonprofit's overall mission.

1. The nonprofit receives donations or gifts on an unconditional and non-reciprocal basis.
2. A grant that includes a donor-imposed condition or restriction will have a set of requirements on how the funds can be applied. Such conditions must be agreed upon by both parties and its limitations followed for the grant to be valid.
3. Funding received by a nonprofit are technically considered to be revenue, and will be booked as Contributions Received.
4. All Contributions Received are recorded at their fair value or the current asking or selling price in the market. Otherwise, other available valuation techniques will be used.
5. If a fair valuation for a donated object is not established based on available valuation techniques, it will not be recognized as an asset.
6. Income generated from a donation will be recognized as part of that donation received from the donor.
7. Donations or gifts without donor-imposed conditions are booked as Contributions Received-Unrestricted Support. Donations of long-lived assets will also be booked under Unrestricted Support, unless the nonprofit has an existing policy on how these types of assets will be recognized and use for.
8. The nonprofit must maintain consistent and accurate financial reports.
9. Donation pledges that are due in the future are booked under Restricted Support. These fund sources cannot be used in the current year's activities without explicit permission from the donor.
10. Any donated assets that are not recorded in the books of account will be recorded as Contributions Received, not capitalized asset.
11. All expiring donations that occur within donor-imposed restrictions are booked within the same accounting period as the lapsed date; expenses accrued but paid after expiration will still be borne by the donor.
12. Donations in the form of skills or professional expertise must abide the regulations outlined under FASB 116.
13. Accrual method is used for booking disbursements.

14. Any expenses incurred must be clearly defined and matched to the project or program the cost falls under.
15. Operating costs must be proportionately matched with contributions received when presenting separate reports to donors.

Assets and Liabilities in Fund Accounting

Because nonprofit organizations are not profit-oriented businesses, these entities do not use capital. Any funds acquired fall either assets or liabilities, and are shown in the balance sheet.

Assets are bought by the nonprofit organization with money from funds acquired from donations and other sources. It may either be liquid assets (i.e. cash) or fixed assets such as land, building, machinery, and the like.

Liabilities are financial obligations that may be in the form of loans or collected but unused funds.

Expenses and Revenue in Fund Accounting

All expenses and revenues are used towards the operating costs of achieving a specific nonprofit's mission or purpose. Both are recorded and placed into the segregated funds to which each have been assigned. Excess revenue are booked as surplus to fund new projects, and will be recorded as liabilities in the accounting books.

Benefits of Fund Accounting

Due to their unique corporate set-up, nonprofit organisations are required to create detailed reports about how and where donations are disbursed. It can be challenging to keep track of all the funding sources, which is why fund accounting helps nonprofits to properly manage funds while remaining compliant. Some of the benefits include:

1. Uncomplicated auditing

Fund accounting makes it easier to retrieve data quickly. Instead of having to go through various receipts to deliver the required reports, all these pieces of information can be referred to in the books. All data can be accessed in one place, making the auditing process faster and easier.

2. Better Compliance

Nonprofits are typically exempt from income and property taxes, but some areas impose a threshold so that any excess needs to filed as taxable income. Using fund accounting methods will help accountants keep track of expenditures and inflows, making it easier to trace any excesses and do the proper filing as needed.

3. Easier fund planning

Seeing how and where funds are going makes it easier to decide what the next course of action will be. This makes it easier to create strategies for the next fund raising event or other programs in the pipeline.

4. Increased Efficiency

When all data points are recorded properly, disbursements are implemented faster. Programs can be finished at a faster pace and within the projected timelines.

5. Clearer Accountability

Clear programs and clear descriptions allows both donors and nonprofits to see how and where funds are going. Fund accounting also allows everyone to see how a specific project is progressing, and implement counter-measures to correct mistakes, if any.

How Technology Helps Nonprofits in Fund Accounting

Profit oriented enterprises have long embraced the numerous advantages that technology has done to increase efficiency in business. Such benefits can be applied for nonprofit organisations as well. Here's how.

Fund Accounting Software Provides a Competitive Advantage when Applying for Grants

Nonprofits that invest in fund accounting software will have the ability to provide the necessary reporting required when applying for grants. Grant donors that provide additional conditions or limitations may need specific reports that can easily be created with the right software system. A reliable accounting system also assures the funder that the nonprofit is able to report in a fast, efficient manner once funds are given.

Online Fundraising Systems Widens the Avenues for Sourcing Funds

Donors want an easy way to give, and what could be simpler than giving donations through mobile devices and smartphones? Mobile-giving increases your donor base and allows nonprofits to meet funding raising goals in a timely manner.

Mobile Devices Allow Real-Time Access to Important Information Anytime, Anywhere

Those who work for nonprofits now have the ability to access their fund accounting software on their mobile devices. This means that they can update vital information on their fund raising activities, access, edit and verify data for reporting purposes, and share documents with others within the organization.

Mobile Apps and Software Increase Efficiency

Instead of being bogged down by countless data and numerous paperwork, the latest technologies frees up time and resources so that more of it can be delegated toward important fund-raising and mission-related tasks.

Going Paperless Reduces Overall Cost

Using online systems reduces paper, ink, and labor costs. It also promotes efficiency by streamlining documents and processes into a single software system that is available to anyone who needs it.

In conclusion fund accounting principles allow nonprofit organisations to properly manage donations in an efficient, transparent manner. Funds can come from a variety of sources, and it's important to keep track of each one to ensure that donations are used appropriately. As such, it has unique identification and reporting challenges that will help prevent the co-mingling of funds. It is a critical method for easier and better institutional and managerial reporting, one that will streamline operations and help nonprofits achieve their overall mission.

Management Accounting

Management accounting, also called managerial accounting or cost accounting, is the process of analyzing business costs and operations to prepare internal financial report, records, and account to aid managers' decision making process in achieving business goals. In other words, it is the act of making sense of financial and costing data and translating that data into useful information for management and officers within an organization.

What Does Management Accounting Mean?

Management accountants (also called managerial accountants) look at the events that happen in and around a business while considering the needs of the business. From this, data and estimates emerge. Cost accounting is the process of translating these estimates and data into knowledge that will ultimately be used to guide decision-making.

The main difference between financial and managerial accounting is whether there is an internal or external focus. Financial accounting focuses on creating and evaluating financial statements that will be reported externally, like creditors and investors. In contrast, managerial accounting analyses and results are kept in-house for business leaders to use to drive decision-making and run the company more effectively. Managerial accountants handle many facets of accounting. These include margins, constraints, capital budgeting, trends and forecasting, valuation and product costing.

Example

Anderson is the CEO of a small consulting firm. He wants to hire a management accountant and a financial accountant. He has come up with a list of job tasks and he needs to break them up into those that should be performed by the managerial accountant and those that should be performed by the financial accountant. Here is the list of tasks that Anderson has come up with:

1. Preparing cash flow statements
2. Income statement reporting
3. Budgeting
4. Calculating changes in stockholder equity
5. Preparing taxes for the organization

In this example, the only tasks that would be assigned to the management accountant are budgeting and taxes. The financial accountant would handle the other tasks.

Functions and Objects of Management Accounting

The primary object of Management Accounting is to present the accounting information to the management.

The Objects are:

1. To Assist in Planning:

Management Accounting assists the management in planning as well as to formulate policies by making forecasts about the production, the selling, the inflow and outflow of cash etc., i.e., in planning a very wide range of activities of the business.

Not only that, it may also forecast how much may be needed for alternative courses of action or the expected rate of return therefrom and, at the same time, decide upon the programme of activities to be undertaken.

2. To Assist in Organising:

By preparing budgets and ascertaining specific cost centre, it delivers the resources to each centre and delegates the respective responsibilities to ensure their proper utilisation. As a result, an inter-relationship grows among different parts of the enterprise.

3. To Assist in Motivating:

By setting goals, planning the best and economical courses of action and also by measuring the performances of the employees, it tries to increase their efficiency and, ultimately, motivate the organisation as a whole.

4. To Coordinate:

It helps the management in coordinating the activities of the enterprise, firstly, by preparing the functional budgets, then coordinating the whole activity by integrating all functional budgets into one which goes by the name of 'Master Budget'. In this way it helps the management by coordinating the different parts of the enterprise. Besides, overall coordination is not at all possible without 'Budgetary Control'.

5. To Control:

The actual work done can be compared with 'Standards' to enable the management to control the performances effectively.

6. To Communicate:

It helps the management in communicating the financial information about the enterprise. For taking decisions as well as for evaluating business performances, management needs information. Now, this information is available with the help of reports and statements which form an integral part of Management Accounting.

7. To Interpret Financial Information:

It is not possible for all concerned to understand clearly the different treatments of accounting until and unless the users have acquired a sufficient knowledge about the subject since accounting is a highly technical subject.

And, for the same reason, management may not understand the implications of the accounting information in its raw form. But this problem does not arise in the case of Management Accounting as it presents the required information in an intelligible and non-technical way. This leads the management to interpret financial data, evaluate alternative courses of action and to take correct decisions.

Miscellaneous:

(a) To provide necessary help while evaluating the efficiency and effectiveness of different policies;

(b) To provide necessary help in locating uneconomic as well as inefficient place of business activities;

(c) To provide necessary help in solving business problems, e.g., to expand the existing business unit or not, etc.

Nature or Characteristics of Management Accounting

The very purpose of Management Accounting is to serve the needs of the management by presenting relevant information so that the business may be conducted in a better way. Here, information—both economic and financial—is collected from internal as well as external sources.

The information so collected is analysed and processed accordingly in the prescribed manner. The results thus obtained are presented to the management for taking decisions. It may also be called an information system since it is concerned with the getting and giving of information.

Management Accounting deals with the forecasts about the future. It helps the management to take decisions as well as to draw plans for future courses of action.

Secondly, it adopts a selective technique. Its technique is not in the nature of collecting and then sorting the data.

Thirdly, it is analytical, i.e., it explains the reason why the profit or loss increases or decreases in comparison with the past periods. Besides, it tries to examine and analyse the effect of different variables on profit and profitability and thereby helps the management to adopt future plans of action.

Fourthly, it does not provide information in a prescribed format like Financial Accounting. It provides information to the management in such a way that it may be more useful to them.

Lastly, it does not take any decision but helps the management in taking decision by supplying necessary data and information, i.e., it can recommend but cannot prescribe.

Things which can be found in the Report

The information found in management accounting is vastly different than financial accounting in a number of ways. While financial accounting reports tend to be based on historical data, management reports are primarily forward-looking.

Management accounting reports are also usually confidential and for internal use only, as opposed to financial accounting statements, which are publically reported.

Also, instead of being calculated based on generally accepted accounting practices, they are calculated based on management's informational needs.

Tools of Management Accounting

Management accounting employs various tools to forecast business trends:

- Ratios
- Skills and ability to read and analyze financial statements
- Management information systems (MIS)
- Key performance indicators (KPIs)
- Simulations
- Financial modeling
- Game theory
- Balance scorecards, and any other set of data that the company can produce can be used to complete the analysis.

Management accounting uses activity-based costing to decide what to produce, how much to spend on a product, how much it will cost to service a customer, and what customers and products are profitable. They find the answers to these integral questions so that senior management can focus on maximizing revenue.

Information deluge has transformed how companies operate. Companies can no longer take vital decisions without considering the implications and outcomes. They can use intelligent analysis and management accounting to invest smartly, and at the same time prepare quickly for events that might impact them negatively.

Budgeting and Variance Analysis

In the organizations, budgets are prepared for every year. They are based on the long-term planning of the organizations and hence assist in achieving long-term goals of an organization. Variance analysis is the comparison of standard budgets and actual outputs. This comparison enables managers to know about the deviations from the plans. The deviations can be good or bad. Positive deviations are called favorable variance and negative deviations are called unfavorable variance.

Cost-Volume-Profit Analysis

CVP analysis assists managers in finding out the level of output at which cost and revenue are equal. It is a 'no profit – no loss' situation also known as the breakeven point.

Most of the cost accounting techniques are used by management accountants. Other important techniques are incremental analysis, cost behavior analysis, economic order quantity (EOQ) and economic batch quantity (EBQ), return on investment analysis, safety stock, lead time, segment reporting etc.

Limitations of Management Accounting

1) Management Accounting is based on financial and cost accounting, in which historical data is used to make future decisions. Thus, strength and weakness of the managerial decisions are based on the strength and weakness of the accounting records.

2) Management Accounting is useful only to those people who are in the decision making process.

3) Tools and techniques used in management accounting only provide information and not ready made decision. Thus, it is only a supplementary service.

4) In Management Accounting, decision is based on the manager's institution as management try to avoid lengthy courses of scientific decision making.

5) Personal prejudices and bias affect the decisions as the interpretation of financial information is based on personal judgment of the interpreter.

Forensic Accounting

Whenever there is fraud, it is human nature to respond since nobody wants to be bamboozled or deceived. Fraud constitutes four essential features: misrepresentation or omission of an important matter; scanter or awareness of misrepresentation; reliance on the individual who obtains or acquires the misrepresented information relied upon; and damages or the sustained financial consequences.

Types of Fraud

There are numerous kinds of frauds and a lot of ways to classify them. But the ones that are closely related to accounting professionals are Employee Fraud or Misappropriation of Assets and Financial Statement Fraud.

- Employee Fraud or Misappropriation of Assets

Also referred to as retail fraud, employee fraud is the most typical kind of fraud. It is associated with skimming revenues, theft of cash or inventory, embezzlement, and payroll fraud. Employee fraud also involves employees assisting and instigating individuals outside the organization to either dupe or swindle third parties.

- *Financial Statement Fraud*

Financial statement fraud or wholesale fraud is described with deliberate misrepresentations or omissions of important information in financial reporting to mislead or delude the users of the financial statement. This type of fraud is associated with abusing the accounting standards and guidelines on purpose in order to manipulate the outcome.

Forensic Accounting

Forensic accounting utilizes accounting, auditing and investigative skills to conduct an examination into a company's financial statements. Forensic accounting provides an accounting analysis suitable for court. Forensic accountants are trained to look beyond the numbers and deal with the business reality of a situation. They are frequently used in fraud cases.

Forensic accountants analyze, interpret and summarize complex financial and business matters. They may be employed by insurance companies, banks, police forces, government agencies or public accounting firms. Forensic accountants compile financial evidence, develop computer applications to manage the information collected and communicate their findings in the form of reports or presentations.

Along with testifying in court, a forensic accountant may be asked to prepare visual aids to support trial evidence. For business investigations, forensic accounting entails the use of tracing funds, asset identification, asset recovery and due diligence reviews. Forensic accountants may seek out additional training in alternative dispute resolution (ADR) due to their high involvement in legal issues and familiarity with the judicial system.

Components of Forensic Accounting

Litigation Support

Forensic accounting is utilized in litigation when quantification of damages is needed. Parties involved in legal disputes use the quantifications to assist in resolving disputes via settlements or court decisions. For example, this may arise due to compensation and benefit disputes. The forensic accountant may be utilized as an expert witness if the dispute escalates to a court decision.

Investigation

Forensic accounting also encompasses the determination of whether criminal matters occurred. Such crimes may include employee theft, securities fraud, falsification of financial statement information, identify theft or insurance fraud. Forensic accountants may assist in searching for hidden assets in divorce cases or provide their services for other civil matters such as breach of contracts, tort, disagreements relating to company acquisitions, breaches of warranty or business valuation disputes.

Forensic accounting assignments include investigating construction claims, expropriations, product liability claims or trademark or patent infringements. Forensic accounting can be used to determine the economic results of the breach of a nondisclosure or noncompetition agreement.

Computer forensics is also a large part of forensic accounting. With the aid of technology, it has become a lot easier to perpetrate and hide fraud. However, forensic accounting has brought about innovative technology that can detect even the most encrypted fraud, ensuring that every dollar that companies earn is accounted for.

Objectives of Forensic Accounting

Forensic accounting aims to determine the probability and/or extent of the occurrence of fraud. By analyzing definite financial and non-financial information, checking public records, and administering fact-finding and admission-seeking questioning and evaluation, suspicions or accusations will be resolved and refuted.

Forensic Accounting in the Insurance Industry

A forensic accountant may be asked to quantify the economic damages arising from a vehicle accident or a case of medical malpractice. The accountant must be knowledgeable about the legislative process relating to these cases. Forensic accounting encompasses the review of insurance policies to determine coverage issues and methods of calculating potential losses. Forensic accounting may be utilized for either the insured or insurer's case.

Accrual-based Accounting

Accrual accounting is an accounting method that measures the performance and position of a company by recognizing economic events regardless of when cash transactions occur. The general idea is that economic events are recognized by matching revenues to expenses (the matching principle) at the time in which the transaction occurs rather than when payment is made (or received). This method allows the current cash inflows/outflows to be combined with future expected cash inflows/outflows to give a more accurate picture of a company's current financial condition.

Accrual accounting is considered to be the standard accounting practice for most companies, with the exception of very small businesses. This method provides a more accurate picture of the company's current condition, but its relative complexity makes it more expensive to implement.

The need for this method arose out of the increasing complexity of business transactions and a desire for more accurate financial information. Selling on credit and projects that provide revenue streams over a long period of time affect the company's financial condition at the point of the transaction. Therefore, it makes sense that such events should also be reflected on the financial statements during the same reporting period that these transactions occur.

Accrual accounting is the opposite of cash accounting, which recognizes transactions only when there is an exchange of cash. For example, consider a consulting company that provides a $5,000 service to a client on October 30th. The client receives the bill for services rendered and makes her cash payment on November 25th. The entry of this transaction will be recorded differently under the cash and accrual methods. The revenue generated by the consulting services will only be recognized under the cash method when the money is received by the company. A company that uses the cash accounting method will record $5,000 revenue on November 25th.

Accrual accounting, however, says that the cash method isn't accurate because it is likely, if not certain, that the company will receive the cash at some point in the future because the services have been provided. The accrual method recognizes revenue when the services provided for the client are concluded even though cash isn't yet in the bank. Revenue will be recognized as earned on October 30th. The sale is booked to an account known as accounts receivable, found in the current assets section of the balance sheet.

A company that incurs an expense that it is yet to pay for will recognize the business expense on the day the expense arises. Under the accrual method of accounting, the company receiving goods or services on credit must report the liability no later than the date they were received. The accrued expense will be recorded as an accounts payable under the current liabilities section of the balance sheet, and also as an expense in the income statement. On the general ledger, when the bill is paid, the accounts payable account is debited and the cash account is credited.

Under accrual accounting, firms have an immediate feedback of their expected cash inflows and outflows, which makes it easier for businesses to better manage their current resources and plan effectively for the future.

Limitations of Accrual-based Accounting

A significant failing of the accrual basis of accounting is that it can indicate the presence of profits, even though the associated cash inflows have not yet occurred. The result can be a supposedly profitable entity that is starved for cash, and which may therefore go bankrupt despite its reported level of profitability. Consequently, you should pay attention to the statement of cash flows of a business, which indicates the flows of cash into and out of a business.

Accrual

Accruals are earned revenues and incurred expenses that have an overall impact on an income statement. They also affect the balance sheet, which represents liabilities and non-cash-based assets used in accrual-based accounting. These accounts include, among many others, accounts payable, accounts receivable, goodwill, future tax liabilities and future interest expenses.

The use of accrual accounts has greatly increased the amount of information on accounting statements. Before the use of accruals, accountants only recorded cash transactions on these statements. But cash transactions don't give information about other important business activities, such as revenue based on credit and future liabilities. By recording accruals, a company can measure what it owes in the short-term and also what cash revenue it expects to receive. It also allows a company to show assets that do not have a cash value, such as goodwill.

Using the accrual method, an accountant makes adjustments for revenue that has been earned but is not yet recorded in the accounts, and expenses that have been incurred but are not yet recorded in the accounts. The accruals must be added via adjusting journal entries, so that the financial statements report these amounts.

In double-entry bookkeeping, the offset to an accrued expense is an accrued liability account, which appears in the balance sheet. The offset to accrued revenue is an accrued asset account, which also appears in the balance sheet. Therefore, an accrual entry will impact the balance sheet and the income statement.

Accruals are revenues and expenses that are incurred during an accounting period for which no invoices or payments were received or made. Accruals are, therefore, estimated figures since the invoice, when received, may have different numbers. When invoice has been received, a company records the amount under the accounts payable (for money owing suppliers and vendors) or accounts receivable account (for money to be collected from customers) in the balance sheet.

Examples

Let's look at an example of an accrual regarding revenue that involves an electric utility company. The utility company generated electricity that customers received in December. However, the utility does not bill the electric customers until the following month. To have the proper amounts on the utility's financial statements, there needs to be an adjusting entry to report revenue that was earned in December, which reflects the receivables that the utility has a right to as of December 31. The following month, when the cash is received, the receivables will go down, and the cash account will increase.

An example of an accrual involving an expense is employee bonuses that were earned in 2016, but will not be paid until 2017. The 2016 financial statements need to reflect the bonus expense and the bonus liability. Therefore, prior to issuing the 2016 financial statements, an adjusting entry records this accrual. The accountant increases an expense and creates a liability. Once the payment has been made in the new year, the liability will be eliminated, and the cash will be reduced.

Another expense accrual occurs for interest. For instance, a company with a bond will accrue interest expense. Interest on bonds is typically paid semi-annually, but the interest expense will be recorded as the amount that has accrued as of the date of the financial statement. A corresponding interest liability will be recorded on the balance sheet.

Accruals in Accounting

For example, a company delivers a product to a customer who will pay for it 30 days later in the next fiscal year, which starts a week after the delivery. The company recognizes the proceeds as a revenue in its current income statement still for the fiscal year of the delivery, even though it will not get paid until the following accounting period. The proceeds are also an accrued income (asset) on the balance sheet for the delivery fiscal year, but not for the next fiscal year when cash is received.

Similarly, a salesperson, who sold the product, earned a commission at the moment of sale (or delivery). The company will recognize the commission as an expense in its current income statement, even though the salesperson will actually get paid at the end of the following week in the next accounting period. The commission is also an accrued liability on the balance sheet for the delivery period, but not for the next period when the commission (cash) is paid out to the salesperson.

The term *accrual* is also often used as an abbreviation for the terms accrued expense and accrued revenue that share the common name word, but they have the opposite economic/accounting characteristics.

- Accrued revenue: revenue is recognized before cash is received.
- Accrued expense: expense is recognized before cash is paid out.

Accrued Revenue

Accrued revenue (or accrued assets) is an asset, such as unpaid proceeds from a delivery of goods or services, when such income is earned and a related revenue item is recognized, while cash is to be received in a later period, when the amount is deducted from *accrued revenues*.

In the rental industry, there are specialized revenue accruals for rental income which crosses month end boundaries. These are normally utilized by rental companies who charge in arrears, based on an anniversary of a contract date. For example, a rental contract which began on 15 January, being invoiced on a recurring monthly basis will not generate its first invoice until 14 February. Therefore, at the end of the January financial period an accrual must be raised for sixteen days' worth of the monthly charge. This may be a simple prorate basis (e.g. 16/31 of the monthly charge) or may be more complex if only week days are being charged or a standardized month is being used (e.g. 28 days, 30 days etc.)

Accrued Expense

Accrued expense is a liability whose timing or amount is uncertain by virtue of the fact that an invoice has not yet been received. The uncertainty of the accrued expense is not significant enough to qualify it as a provision. An example of an accrued expense is a pending obligation to pay for goods or services received from a counterpart, while cash is to be paid out in a later accounting period when the amount is deducted from *accrued expenses*.

Under International Financial Reporting Standards, this difference is best summarized by IAS 37 which states:

> "11 Provisions can be distinguished from other liabilities such as trade payables and accruals because there is uncertainty about the timing or amount of the future expenditure required in settlement. By contrast:
>
> "(a) trade payables are liabilities to pay for goods or services that have been received or supplied and have been invoiced or formally agreed with the supplier; and
>
> "(b) accruals are liabilities to pay for goods or services that have been received or supplied but have not been paid, invoiced or formally agreed with the supplier, including amounts due to employees (for example, amounts relating to accrued vacation pay). Although it is sometimes necessary to estimate the amount or timing of accruals, the uncertainty is generally much less than for provisions.
>
> "Accruals are often reported as part of trade and other payables, whereas provisions are reported separately."

To add to the confusion, some legalistic accounting systems take a simplistic view of 'accrued revenue' and 'accrued expenses", defining each as revenue or expense that has not been formally invoiced. This is primarily due to tax considerations, since in some countries, the act of issuing an invoice creates taxable revenue, even if the customer does not ultimately pay and the related receivable becomes noncollectable.

Accruals in Payroll

In payroll, a common benefit that an employer will provide for employees is a vacation or sick accrual. This means that as time passes, an employee accumulates additional sick leave or vacation time and this time is placed into a bank. Once the time is accumulated, the employer or the employer's payroll provider will track the amount of time used for sick or vacation.

Length of Service

For most employers, a time-off policy is published and followed with regard to benefit accruals. These guidelines ensure that all employees are treated fairly with regard to the distribution and use of sick and vacation time.

Within these guidelines, the rate at which the employee will accumulate the vacation or sick time is often determined by length of service (the amount of time the employee has worked for the employers).

Trial Period

In many cases, these guidelines indicate there is a trial period (usually 30 to 90 days) where no time is awarded to the employee. This does not prevent an employee from calling in sick immediately after being hired, but it does mean that they will not get paid for this time off. However, it does prevent an employee, for example, scheduling a vacation for the second week of work. After this trial period, the award of time may begin or it may be retroactive, back to the date of hire.

Rollover/Carry Over

Some accrual policies have the ability to carry over or roll over some or all unused time that has been accrued into the next year. If the accrual policy does not have any type of rollover, any accrued time that is in the bank is usually lost at the end of the employer's calendar year.

Deferral

In accounting, a deferral refers to the delay in recognition of an accounting transaction. This can arise with either a revenue or expense transaction. For example, if a customer were to pay in advance for goods or services not yet delivered, then the recipient should defer recognition of the payment as revenue until such time as it delivers the related goods or services. In regard to expenses, a company may pay a supplier in advance, but should defer recognition of the related expense until such time as it receives and consumes the item for which it paid. In the case of the deferral of a revenue transaction, you would credit a liability account instead of the revenue account. In the case of the deferral of an expense transaction, you would debit an asset account instead of an expense account.

For example, ABC International receives a $10,000 advance payment from a customer. ABC debits the cash account and credits the unearned revenue liability account, both for $10,000. ABC delivers the related goods in the following month, and credits the revenue account for $10,000 and debits the unearned revenue liability account for the same amount. Thus, the unearned revenue liability account was effectively a holding account until ABC could complete the shipment to the customer.

For example, ABC International pays $24,000 of insurance in advance to a supplier for its full-year D&O insurance. ABC records this as a credit to its cash account and a debit to its prepaid expenses asset account. After one month, it has consumed 1/12th of the prepaid asset and records a debit to the insurance expense account for $2,000 and a credit to the prepaid expenses asset account for the same amount.

Deferred Charge

Deferred charge (or deferral) is cost that is accounted-for in latter accounting period for its anticipated future benefit, or to comply with the requirement of matching costs with revenues. *Deferred charges* include costs of starting up, obtaining long-term debt, advertising campaigns, etc., and are carried as a non-current asset on the balance sheet pending amortization. *Deferred charges* often extend over five years or more and occur infrequently unlike prepaid expenses, e.g. insurance, interest, rent. Financial ratios are based on the total assets excluding *deferred charges* since they have no physical substance (cash realization) and cannot be used in reducing total liabilities.

Deferred Expense

A Deferred expense or prepayment, prepaid expense, plural often prepaids, is an asset representing cash paid out to a counterpart for goods or services to be received in a later accounting period. For example, if a service contract is paid quarterly in advance, at the end of the first month of the period two months remain as a deferred expense. In the deferred expense the early payment is accompanied by a related recognized expense in the subsequent accounting period, and the same amount is deducted from the prepayment. The deferred expense shares characteristics with accrued revenue (or *accrued assets*) with the difference that an asset to be covered later are proceeds from a delivery of goods or services, at which such income item is earned and the related revenue item is recognized, while cash for them is to be received in a later period, when its amount is deducted from *accrued revenues*.

For example, when the accounting periods are monthly, an 11/12 portion of an annually paid insurance cost is added to *prepaid expenses*, which are decreased by 1/12 of the cost in each subsequent period when the same fraction is recognized as an expense, rather than all in the month in which such cost is billed. The not-yet-recognized portion of such costs remains as *prepayments* (assets) to prevent such cost from turning into a fictitious loss in the monthly period it is billed, and into a fictitious profit in any other monthly period.

Similarly, cash paid out for (the cost of) goods and services not received by the end of the accounting period is added to the *prepayments* to prevent it from turning into a fictitious loss in the period cash was paid out, and into a fictitious profit in the period of their reception. Such cost is not recognized in the income statement (*profit and loss* or P&L) as the expense incurred in the period of payment, but in the period of their reception when such costs are recognized as expenses in P&L and deducted from prepayments (assets) on balance sheets.

Deferred Revenue

Deferred revenue (or deferred income) is a liability, such as cash received from a counterpart for goods or services that are to be delivered in a later accounting period. When such income item is earned, the related revenue item is recognized, and the *deferred revenue* is reduced. It shares characteristics with *accrued expense* with the difference that a liability to be covered later is an obligation to pay for goods or services received from a counterpart, while cash for them is to be paid out in a later period when its amount is deducted from *accrued expenses*.

For example, a company receives an annual software license fee paid out by a customer upfront on the January 1. However, the company's fiscal year ends on May 31. So, the company using accrual accounting adds only five months' worth (5/12) of the fee to its revenues in profit and loss for the fiscal year the fee was received. The rest is added to *deferred income* (liability) on the balance sheet for that year.

Matching Principle

The matching principle states that expenses should be recognized and recorded when those expenses can be matched with the revenues those expenses helped to generate. In other words, expenses shouldn't be recorded when they are paid. Expenses should be recorded as the corresponding revenues are recorded. This matches the revenues and expenses in a period. In this sense, the matching principle recognizes expenses as the revenue recognition principle recognizes income.

In general, there are two types of costs: product and period costs. Product costs can be tied directly to products and in turn revenues. Period costs, on the other hand, cannot.

Period costs do not have corresponding revenues. Administrative salaries, for example, cannot be matched to any specific revenue stream. These expenses are recorded in the current period.

The matching principle also states that expenses should be recognized in a "rational and systematic" manner. This is the key concept behind depreciation where an asset's cost is recognized over many periods.

In short, the matching principle states that where expenses can be matched with revenues, we should do so because the benefits of an asset or revenue should be linked to the costs of that asset or revenue.

Examples

– Angle Machining, Inc. buys a new piece of equipment for $100,000 in 2015. This machine has a useful life of 10 years. This means that the machine will produce products for at least 10 years into the future. According to the matching principle, the machine cost should be matched with the revenues it creates. Thus, the machine is depreciated over its 10-year useful life instead of being fully expensed in 2015.

– Bajor Art Studio produces picture frames and sells them to wholesalers like Michaels and Hobby Lobby. Bajor pays its employees $20 an hour and sells every frame produced by its employees. Since the payroll costs can be directly linked back to revenue generated in the period, the payroll costs are expensed in the current period.

– Big Appliance has sold kitchen appliances for 30 years in a small town. It purchases a large appliance from wholesalers for $5,000 and resells it to a local restaurant for $8,000. At the end of the period, Big Appliance should match the $5,000 cost with the $8,000 revenue.

Expense vs. cash Timing

Two types of balancing accounts exist to avoid fictitious profits and losses that might otherwise occur when cash is paid out not in the same accounting periods as expenses are recognized, because expenses are recognized when obligations are incurred regardless when cash is paid out according to the matching principle in accrual accounting. Cash can be paid out in an earlier or later period than obligations are incurred (when goods or services are received) and related expenses are recognized that results in the following two types of accounts:

- Accrued expense: Expense is recognized before cash is paid out.
- Deferred expense: Expense is recognized after cash is paid out.

Accrued expenses is a liability with an uncertain timing or amount, but where the uncertainty is not significant enough to qualify it as a provision. An example is an obligation to pay for goods or services received from a counterpart, while cash for them is to be paid out in a later accounting period when its amount is deducted from *accrued expenses*. It shares characteristics with deferred income (or *deferred revenue*) with the difference that a liability to be covered latter is cash received from a counterpart, while goods or services are to be delivered in a latter period, when such income item is earned, the related revenue item is recognized, and the same amount is deducted from *deferred revenues*.

Deferred expenses (or prepaid expenses or prepayment) is an asset, such as cash paid out TO a counterpart for goods or services to be received in a latter accounting period when fulfilling the promise to pay is actually acknowledged, the related expense item is recognized, and the same amount is deducted from *prepayments*. It shares characteristics with accrued revenue (or *accrued assets*) with the difference that an asset to be covered latter are proceeds from a delivery of goods or services, at which such income item is earned and the related revenue item is recognized, while cash for them is to be received in a later period, when its amount is deducted from *accrued revenues*.

Examples

- Accrued expense allows one to match future costs of products with the proceeds from their sales prior to paying out such costs.
- Deferred expense (prepaid expense) allows one to match costs of products paid out and not received yet.
- Depreciation matches the cost of purchasing fixed assets with revenues generated by them by spreading such costs over their expected life.

Accrued Expenses

For example, goods supplied by a vendor in one accounting period, but paying for them in a later period results in an *accrued expense* that prevents a fictitious increase in the receiving company's value equal to the increase in its inventory (assets) by the cost of the goods received, but unpaid. Without such *accrued expense,* a sale of such goods in the period they were supplied would cause that the unpaid inventory (recognized as an expense fictitiously incurred) would effectively offset the sale proceeds (revenue) resulting in a fictitious profit in the period of sale, and in a fictitious loss in the latter period of payment, both equal to the cost of goods sold.

Period costs, such as office salaries or selling expenses, are immediately recognized as expenses (and offset against revenues of the accounting period) also when employees are paid in the next period. Unpaid period costs are *accrued expenses* (liabilities) to avoid such costs (as expenses fictitiously incurred) to offset period revenues that would result in a fictitious profit. An example is a commission earned at the moment of sale (or delivery) by a sales representative who is compensated at the end of the following week, in the next accounting period. The company recognizes the commission as an expense incurred immediately in its current income statement to match the sale proceeds (revenue), so the commission is also added to *accrued expenses* in the sale period to prevent it from otherwise becoming a fictitious profit, and it is deducted from *accrued expenses* in the next period to prevent it from otherwise becoming a fictitious loss, when the rep is compensated.

Deferred Expenses

A Deferred expense (*prepaid expenses* or *prepayment*) is an asset used to costs paid out and not recognized as expenses according to the matching principle.

For example, when the accounting periods are monthly, an 11/12 portion of an annually paid insurance cost is added to *prepaid expenses*, which are decreased by 1/12 of the cost in each subsequent period when the same fraction is recognized as an expense, rather than all in the month in which such cost is billed. The not-yet-recognized portion of such costs remains as *prepayments* (assets) to prevent such cost from turning into a fictitious loss in the monthly period it is billed, and into a fictitious profit in any other monthly period.

Similarly, cash paid out for (the cost of) goods and services not received by the end of the accounting period is added to the *prepayments* to prevent it from turning into a fictitious loss in the period cash was paid out, and into a fictitious profit in the period of their reception. Such cost is not recognized in the income statement (*profit and loss* or P&L) as the expense incurred in the period of payment, but in the period of their reception when such costs are recognized as expenses in P&L and deducted from prepayments (assets) on balance sheets.

Depreciation

Depreciation is used to distribute the cost of the asset over its expected life span according to the matching principle. If a machine is bought for $100,000, has a life span of 10 years, and can produce the same amount of goods each year, then $10,000 of the cost (i.e. $100,000/10 years) of the machine is matched to each year, rather than charging $100,000 in the first year and nothing in the next 9 years. So, the cost of the machine is offset against the sales in that year. This matches costs to sales and therefore gives a more accurate representation of the business, but results in a temporary discrepancy between profit/loss and the cash position of the business.

Revenue Recognition

Revenue recognition is a generally accepted accounting principle (GAAP) that determines the specific conditions in which revenue is recognized or accounted for. Generally, revenue is recognized only when a critical event has occurred, and the amount of revenue is measurable. However, there are several situations in which exceptions may apply.

Revenue is at the heart of business performance. Everything hinges on the sale. As such, regulators know how tempting it is for companies to push the limits on what qualifies as revenue, especially when not all revenue is collected when the work is done. Attorneys often bill clients in billable hours and present the invoice after work is completed. Construction managers often bill clients on a percentage-of-completion method. As a result, analysts like to know that revenue recognition policies for a company are relatively standard for the industry. This also helps to ensure an apples-to-apples comparison is made between metrics using line items from the income statement.

Revenue Recognition Requirements

The revenue recognition principle, a combination of accrual accounting and the matching principle, stipulates that revenues are recognized when realized and earned, not necessarily when received. Realizable means that goods and/or services have been received, but payment for the product/service is expected later. Earned revenue accounts for goods and/or services that have been provided or performed, respectively. In addition, the revenue generating activity must be fully or primarily complete to include its revenue during the respective accounting period, and there must be a reasonable level of certainty that earned revenue will be received. Lastly, according to the matching principle, the revenue and its associated costs must be reported in the same accounting period.

GAAP Changes to Revenue Recognition Policies

On May 28, 2014, the Financial Accounting Standards Board (FASB) and International Accounting Standards Board (IASB) jointly issued Accounting Standards Codification (ASC) 606, regarding revenue from contracts with customers. ASC 606 provides a uniform framework for recognizing revenue from contracts with customers. The old guidance was based on industry-specific guidance, which created a system of fragmented policies. The new guidance is industry-neutral and therefore more transparent. The core principle of ASC 606 is that revenue is recognized when the delivery of promised goods or services matches the amount of consideration expected in exchange for the goods and services. There are five steps that allow the recognition of revenue under that core principle:

1. Identify the contract
2. Identify the contractual performance obligations
3. Determine the amount of consideration/price for the transaction
4. Allocate the determined amount of consideration/price to the contractual obligations
5. Recognize revenue when or as the performing party satisfies a performance obligation.

2

Accounting Ratios

An accounting ratio is a standard ratio used within a firm for comparing the strengths and weaknesses in the company. Many accounting ratios are used for quantifying the different aspects of a business, such as financial ratio, debt ratio, debt-to-equity ratio, P/B ratio, liquidity ratio, etc. which have been discussed in great detail in this chapter.

Financial Ratio

Financial ratios are relationships determined from a company's financial information and used for comparison purposes. Examples include such often referred to measures as return on investment (ROI), return on assets (ROA), and debt-to-equity, to name just three. These ratios are the result of dividing one account balance or financial measurement with another. Usually these measurements or account balances are found on one of the company's financial statements—balance sheet, income statement, cashflow statement, and/or statement of changes in owner's equity. Financial ratios can provide small business owners and managers with a valuable tool with which to measure their progress against predetermined internal goals, a certain competitor, or the overall industry. In addition, tracking various ratios over time is a powerful means of identifying trends in their early stages. Ratios are also used by bankers, investors, and business analysts to assess a company's financial status.

Ratios are calculated by dividing one number by another, total sales divided by number of employees, for example. Ratios enable business owners to examine the relationships between items and measure that relationship. They are simple to calculate, easy to use, and provide business owners with insight into what is happening within their business, insights that are not always apparent upon review of the financial statements alone. Ratios are aids to judgment and cannot take the place of experience. But experience with reading ratios and tracking them over time will make any manager a better manager. Ratios can help to pinpoint areas that need attention before the looming problem within the area is easily visible.

Virtually any financial statistics can be compared using a ratio. In reality, however, small business owners and managers only need to be concerned with a small set of ratios in order to identify where improvements are needed.

It is important to keep in mind that financial ratios are time sensitive; they can only present a picture of the business at the time that the underlying figures were prepared.

For example, a retailer calculating ratios before and after the Christmas season would get very different results. In addition, ratios can be misleading when taken singly, though they can be quite valuable when a small business tracks them over time or uses them as a basis for comparison against company goals or industry standards.

Perhaps the best way for small business owners to use financial ratios is to conduct a formal ratio analysis on a regular basis. The raw data used to compute the ratios should be recorded on a special form monthly. Then the relevant ratios should be computed, reviewed, and saved for future comparisons. Determining which ratios to compute depends on the type of business, the age of the business, the point in the business cycle, and any specific information sought. For example, if a small business depends on a large number of fixed assets, ratios that measure how efficiently these assets are being used may be the most significant. In general, financial ratios can be broken down into four main categories—1) profitability or return on investment; 2) liquidity; 3) leverage, and 4) operating or efficiency—with several specific ratio calculations prescribed within each.

Sources of Data

Values used in calculating financial ratios are taken from the balance sheet, income statement, statement of cash flows or (sometimes) the statement of changes in equity. These comprise the firm's "accounting statements" or financial statements. The statements' data is based on the accounting method and accounting standards used by the organisation.

Purpose and Types

Financial ratios quantify many aspects of a business and are an integral part of the financial statement analysis. Financial ratios are categorized according to the financial aspect of the business which the ratio measures. Liquidity ratios measure the availability of cash to pay debt. Activity ratios measure how quickly a firm converts non-cash assets to cash assets. Debt ratios measure the firm's ability to repay long-term debt. Profitability ratios measure the firm's use of its assets and control of its expenses to generate an acceptable rate of return. Market ratios measure investor response to owning a company's stock and also the cost of issuing stock. These are concerned with the return on investment for shareholders, and with the relationship between return and the value of an investment in company's shares.

Financial ratios allow for comparisons

- between companies
- between industries
- between different time periods for one company
- between a single company and its industry average

Ratios generally are not useful unless they are benchmarked against something else, like past performance or another company. Thus, the ratios of firms in different industries, which face different risks, capital requirements, and competition are usually hard to compare.

Accounting Methods and Principles

Financial ratios may not be directly comparable between companies that use different accounting methods or follow various standard accounting practices. Most public companies are required by law to use generally accepted accounting principles for their home countries, but private companies, partnerships and sole proprietorships may not use accrual basis accounting. Large multi-national corporations may use International Financial Reporting Standards to produce their financial statements, or they may use the generally accepted accounting principles of their home country.

There is no international standard for calculating the summary data presented in all financial statements, and the terminology is not always consistent between companies, industries, countries and time periods.

Abbreviations and Terminology

Various abbreviations may be used in financial statements, especially financial statements summarized on the Internet. Sales reported by a firm are usually net sales, which deduct returns, allowances, and early payment discounts from the charge on an invoice. Net income is always the amount *after* taxes, depreciation, amortization, and interest, unless otherwise stated. Otherwise, the amount would be EBIT, or EBITDA.

Companies that are primarily involved in providing services with labour do not generally report "Sales" based on hours. These companies tend to report "revenue" based on the monetary value of income that the services provide.

Note that Shareholders' Equity and Owner's Equity are *not* the same thing, Shareholder's Equity represents the total number of shares in the company multiplied by each share's book value; Owner's Equity represents the total number of shares that an individual shareholder owns (usually the owner with controlling interest), multiplied by each share's book value. It is important to make this distinction when calculating ratios.

Abbreviations

(*Note:* These are not ratios, but values in currency.)

- COGS = Cost of goods sold, or cost of sales.
- EBIT = Earnings before interest and taxes

- EBITDA = Earnings before interest, taxes, depreciation, and amortization
- EPS = Earnings per share

Ratios

Profitability Ratios

Profitability ratios measure the company's use of its assets and control of its expenses to generate an acceptable rate of return

Gross Margin, Gross Profit Margin or Gross Profit Rate

$$\frac{\text{Gross Profit}}{\text{Net Sales}} \;:::\text{OR}:::\; \frac{\text{Net Sales - - COGS}}{\text{Net Sales}}$$

Operating Margin, Operating Income Margin, Operating Profit Margin or Return on sales (ROS)

$$\frac{\text{Operating Income}}{\text{Net Sales}}$$

Note: Operating income is the difference between operating revenues and operating expenses, but it is also sometimes used as a synonym for EBIT and operating profit. This is true if the firm has no non-operating income. (Earnings before interest and taxes / Sales).

Profit Margin, Net Margin or Net Profit Margin

$$\frac{\text{Net Profit}}{\text{Net Sales}}$$

Return on equity (ROE)

$$\frac{\text{Net Income}}{\text{Average Shareholders Equity}}$$

Return on assets (ROA ratio or Du Pont Ratio)

$$\frac{\text{Net Income}}{\text{Average Total Assets}}$$

Return on assets (ROA)

$$\frac{\text{Net Income}}{\text{Total Assets}}$$

Return on assets Du Pont (ROA Du Pont)

$$\left(\frac{\text{Net Income}}{\text{Net Sales}}\right)\left(\frac{\text{Net Sales}}{\text{Total Assets}}\right)$$

Return on Equity Du Pont (ROE Du Pont)

$$\left(\frac{\text{Net Income}}{\text{Net Sales}}\right)\left(\frac{\text{Net Sales}}{\text{Average Assets}}\right)\left(\frac{\text{Average Assets}}{\text{Average Equity}}\right):$$

Return on net assets (RONA)

$$\frac{\text{Net Income}}{\text{Fixed Assets} + \text{Working Capital}}$$

Return on capital (ROC)

$$\frac{\text{EBIT(1 Tax Rate)}}{\text{Invested Capital}}$$

Risk adjusted return on capital (RAROC)

$$\frac{\text{Expected Return}}{\text{Economic Capital}} \text{:::OR:::} \frac{\text{Expected Return}}{\text{Value at Risk}}$$

Return on capital employed (ROCE)

$$\frac{\text{EBIT}}{\text{Capital Employed}}$$

Note: this is somewhat similar to (ROI), which calculates Net Income per Owner's Equity.

Cash flow return on investment (CFROI)

$$\frac{\text{Cash Flow}}{\text{Market Recapitalisation}}$$

Efficiency ratio

$$\frac{\text{Non-Interest expense}}{\text{Revenue}}$$

Net gearing

$$\frac{\text{Net debt}}{\text{Equity}}$$

Basic Earnings Power Ratio

$$\frac{\text{EBIT}}{\text{Total Assets}}$$

Liquidity Ratios

Liquidity ratios measure the availability of cash to pay debt.

Current ratio (Working Capital Ratio)

$$\frac{\text{Current Assets}}{\text{Current Liabilities}}$$

Acid-test ratio (Quick ratio)

$$\frac{\text{Current Assets} - - (\text{Inventories} + \text{Prepayments})}{\text{Current Liabilities}}$$

Cash ratio

$$\frac{\text{Cash and Marketable Securities}}{\text{Current Liabilities}}$$

Operating cash flow ratio

$$\frac{\text{Operating Cash Flow}}{\text{Total Debts}}$$

Activity Ratios (Efficiency Ratios)

Activity ratios measure the effectiveness of the firm's use of resources.

Average collection period

$$\frac{\text{Accounts Receivable}}{\text{Annual Credit Sales} \div 365 \text{ Days}}$$

Degree of Operating Leverage (DOL)

$$\frac{\text{Percent Change in Net Operating Income}}{\text{Percent Change in Sales}}$$

DSO Ratio.

$$\frac{\text{Accounts Receivable}}{\text{Total Annual Sales} \div \text{365 Days}}$$

Average payment period

$$\frac{\text{Accounts Payable}}{\text{Annual Credit Purchases} \div \text{365 Days}}$$

Asset turnover

$$\frac{\text{Net Sales}}{\text{Total Assets}}$$

Stock turnover ratio

$$\frac{\text{Cost of Goods Sold}}{\text{Average Inventory}}$$

Receivables Turnover Ratio

$$\frac{\text{Net Credit Sales}}{\text{Average Net Receivables}}$$

Inventory conversion ratio

$$\frac{\text{365 Days}}{\text{Inventory Turnover}}$$

Inventory conversion period

$$\left(\frac{\text{Inventory}}{\text{Cost of Goods Sold}}\right)\text{365 Days}$$

Receivables conversion period

$$\left(\frac{\text{Receivables}}{\text{Net Sales}}\right)\text{365 Days}$$

Payables conversion period

$$\left(\frac{\text{Accounts Payables}}{\text{Purchases}}\right)365\text{ Days}$$

Cash Conversion Cycle

Inventory Conversion Period + Receivables Conversion Period - Payables Conversion Period

Debt Ratios (Leveraging Ratios)

Debt ratios quantify the firm's ability to repay long-term debt. Debt ratios measure financial leverage.

Debt Ratio

$$\frac{\text{Total Liabilities}}{\text{Total Assets}}$$

Debt to equity ratio

$$\frac{\text{Long- term Debt} + \text{Value of Leases}}{\text{Average Shareholders Equity}}$$

Long-term Debt to equity (LT Debt to Equity)

$$\frac{\text{Long- term Debt}}{\text{Average Shareholders Equity}}$$

Times interest earned ratio (Interest Coverage Ratio)

$$\frac{\text{EBIT}}{\text{Annual Interest Expense}}$$

OR

$$\frac{\text{Net Income}}{\text{Annual Interest Expense}}$$

Debt service coverage ratio

$$\frac{\text{Net Operating Income}}{\text{Total Debt Service}}$$

Market Ratios

Market ratios measure investor response to owning a company's stock and also the cost of issuing stock. These are concerned with the return on investment for shareholders, and with the relationship between return and the value of an investment in company's shares.

Earnings per share (EPS)

$$\frac{\text{Net Earnings}}{\text{Number of Shares}}$$

Payout ratio

$$\frac{\text{Dividends}}{\text{Earnings}}$$

OR

$$\frac{\text{Dividends}}{\text{EPS}}$$

Dividend cover (the inverse of Payout Ratio)

$$\frac{\text{Earnings per Share}}{\text{Dividend per Share}}$$

P/E ratio

$$\frac{\text{Market Price per Share}}{\text{Diluted EPS}}$$

Dividend yield

$$\frac{\text{Dividend}}{\text{Current Market Price}}$$

Cash flow ratio or Price/cash flow ratio

$$\frac{\text{Market Price per Share}}{\text{Present Value of Cash Flow per Share}}$$

Price to book value ratio (P/B or PBV)

$$\frac{\text{Market Price per Share}}{\text{Balance Sheet Price per Share}}$$

Price/sales ratio

$$\frac{\text{Market Price per Share}}{\text{Gross Sales}}$$

PEG ratio

$$\frac{\text{Price per Earnings}}{\text{Annual EPS Growth}}$$

Other Market Ratios

EV/EBITDA

$$\frac{\text{Enterprise Value}}{\text{EBITDA}}$$

EV/Sales

$$\frac{\text{Enterprise Value}}{\text{Net Sales}}$$

Cost/Income ratio

Sector-specific ratios

EV/capacity

EV/output

Capital Budgeting Ratios

In addition to assisting management and owners in diagnosing the financial health of their company, ratios can also help managers make decisions about investments or projects that the company is considering to take, such as acquisitions, or expansion.

Many formal methods are used in capital budgeting, including the techniques such as

- Net present value
- Profitability index
- Internal rate of return
- Modified internal rate of return
- Equivalent annuity

Debt Ratio

The debt ratio is a financial ratio that measures the extent of a company's leverage. The debt ratio is defined as the ratio of total debt to total assets, expressed as a decimal or percentage. It can be interpreted as the proportion of a company's assets that are financed by debt.

$$Debt\ Ratio = \frac{TotalDebt}{TotalAssets}$$

The debt ratio is also referred to as the debt-to-assets ratio.

The higher the debt ratio, the more leveraged a company is, implying greater financial risk. At the same time, leverage is an important tool that companies use to grow, and many businesses find sustainable uses for debt.

Debt ratios vary widely across industries, with capital-intensive businesses such as utilities and pipelines having much higher debt ratios than other industries such as the technology sector. For example, if a company has total assets of $100 million and total debt of $30 million, its debt ratio is 30% or 0.30. Is this company in a better financial situation than one with a debt ratio of 40%? The answer depends on the industry.

A debt ratio of 30% may be too high for an industry with volatile cash flows, in which most businesses take on little debt. A company with a high debt ratio relative to its peers would probably find it expensive to borrow and could find itself in a crunch if circumstances change. The fracking industry, for example, experienced tough times beginning in the summer of 2014 due to high levels of debt and plummeting energy prices.

Conversely, a debt level of 40% may be easily manageable for a company in a sector such as utilities, where cash flows are stable and higher debt ratios are the norm.

A debt ratio greater than 100% tells you that a company has more debt than assets. Meanwhile, a debt ratio less than 100% indicates that a company has more assets than debt. Used in conjunction with other measures of financial health, the debt ratio can help investors determine a company's risk level.

Some sources define the debt ratio as total liabilities divided by total assets. This reflects a certain ambiguity between the terms "debt" and "liabilities" that depends on the circumstance. The debt-to-equity ratio, for example, is closely related to and more common than the debt ratio, but uses total liabilities in the numerator. In the case of the debt ratio, financial data providers calculate it using only long-term and short-term debt (including current portions of long-term debt), excluding liabilities such as accounts payable, negative goodwill and "other."

Examples of Debt Ratio

Let's look at a few examples from different industries to contextualize the debt ratio. Starbucks Corp. (SBUX) listed $0 in short-term and current portion of long-term debt on its balance sheet for the fiscal year ended October 1, 2017, and $3,932,600,000 in long-term debt. The company's total assets were $14,365,600,000. This gives us a debt ratio of $3,932,600,000 ÷ $14,365,600,000 = 0.2738, or 27.38%.

To assess whether this is high, we should consider the capital expenditures that go into opening a Starbucks: leasing commercial space, renovating it to fit a certain layout, and purchasing expensive specialty equipment, much of which is used infrequently. The company must also hire and train employees in an industry with exceptionally high employee turnover, adhere to food safety regulations, etc. for 23,768 locations, in 74 countries. Perhaps 27% isn't so bad after all, and indeed Morningstar gives the industry average as 40%. The result is that Starbucks has an easy time borrowing money; creditors trust that it is in a solid financial position and can be expected to pay them back in full.

What about a technology company? For the fiscal year ended December 31, 2016, Facebook Inc. (FB) reported its short-term and current portion of long-term debt as $280,000,000; its long-term debt was $5,767,000,000; its total assets were $64,961,000,000. Facebook's debt ratio can be calculated as ($280,000,000 + $5,767,000,000) ÷ $64,961,000,000 = 0.0931, or 9.31%. Facebook does not borrow on the corporate bond market. It has an easy enough time raising capital through stock.

Finally, let's look at a basic materials company, the St. Louis-based miner Arch Coal Inc. (ARCH). For the fiscal year ended December 31, 2016, the company posted short-term and current portions of long-term debt of $11,038,000, long-term debt of $351,841,000 and total assets of $2,136,597,000. Coal mining is extremely capital-intensive, so the industry is forgiving of leverage: the average debt ratio is 47%. Even in this cohort, Arch Coal's debt ratio of ($11,038,000 + $351,841,000) ÷ $2,136,597,000 = 16.98% is well below average.

In the consumer lending and mortgages business, two common debt ratios that are used to assess a borrower's ability to repay a loan or mortgage are the gross debt service ratio and the total debt service ratio. The gross debt ratio is defined as the ratio of monthly housing costs (including mortgage payments, home insurance, and property costs) to monthly income, while the total debt service ratio is the ratio of monthly housing costs plus other debt such as car payments and credit card borrowings to monthly income. Acceptable levels of the total debt service ratio, in percentage terms, range from the mid-30s to the low-40s.

Debt-to-equity Ratio

Debt/Equity (D/E) Ratio, calculated by dividing a company's total liabilities by its stockholders' equity, is a debt ratio used to measure a company's financial leverage.

The D/E ratio indicates how much debt a company is using to finance its assets relative to the value of shareholders' equity. The formula for calculating D/E ratios is:

Debt/Equity Ratio = Total Liabilities / Shareholders' Equity

The result can be expressed either as a number or as a percentage.

The debt/equity ratio is also referred to as a risk or gearing ratio

Debt/Equity Ratio for Corporate Fundamental Analysis

Given that the debt/equity ratio measures a company's debt relative to the total value of its stock, it is most often used to gauge the extent to which a company is taking on debt as a means of leveraging (attempting to increase its value by using borrowed money to fund various projects). A high debt/equity ratio generally means that a company has been aggressive in financing its growth with debt. Aggressive leveraging practices are often associated with high levels of risk. This may result in volatile earnings as a result of the additional interest expense.

Highest Debt/Equity Ratio Stocks in the S&P 500			
Add	**Symbol**	**D/E Ratio**	**Price**
	SPGI	51,000.00	209.76
	S&P Global Inc		
	MCO	2,757.94	176.69
	Moody's Corp		
	SEE	2,139.20	42.89
	Sealed Air Corp		

Lowest* Debt/Equity Ratio Stocks in the S&P 500			
Add	**Symbol**	**D/E Ratio**	**Price**
	RHI	0.07	66.34
	Robert Half International Inc		
	MNST	0.27	59.57
	Monster Beverage Corp		
	ACN	0.29	166.46
	Accenture PLC		

* excluding companies with no debt

For example, utility company Dominion Energy (NYSE:D), in its fiscal year ended 2016, listed its total liabilities as $54.77 billion and total shareholders' equity as $14.61 billion. It's D/E ratio is, therefore, $54.77 / $14.61 = 3.75, or 375%. For the same fiscal year, Alphabet, Inc. (Nasdaq:GOOG) recorded total liabilities of $27.13 billion and total equity of $120.33 billion. It's D/E ratio is $27.13 / $120.33 = 0.2255, or 22.55%. The ratios of both companies indicate that Dominion is taking on more debt than Alphabet relative to the equity value.

If a lot of debt is used to finance increased operations (high debt to equity), the company could potentially generate more earnings than it would have without this outside financing. If this were to increase earnings by a greater amount than the debt cost (interest), then the shareholders benefit as more earnings are being spread among the same number of shareholders. However, if the cost of debt financing ends up outweighing the returns that the company generates on the debt through investment and business activities, stakeholders' share values may take a hit. If the cost of debt becomes too much for the company to handle, it can even lead to bankruptcy, which could leave shareholders with nothing since creditors are paid first during liquidation proceedings.

Debt/Equity Ratio for Personal Finances

The Debt/Equity (D/E) ratio can be applied to personal financial statements as well, in which case it is also known as the Personal Debt/Equity Ratio. Here, "equity" refers not to the value of stakeholders' shares but rather to the difference between the total value of an individual's assets and the total value of his or her debt or liabilities. The formula for the personal D/E ratio, then, can be represented as:

D/E = Total Personal Debt / (Total Assets - Total Personal Debt)

The personal debt/equity ratio is often used in financing, as when an individual or small business is applying for a loan. This form of D/E essentially measures the dollar amount of debt an individual has for each dollar of equity they have. D/E is very important to a lender when considering a candidate for a loan, as it can greatly contribute to the lender's confidence (or lack thereof) in the candidate's financial stability.

A candidate with a high personal debt/equity ratio has a high amount of debt relative to their available equity, and will not likely instill much confidence in the lender that the candidate can repay the loan. On the other hand, a candidate with a low personal debt/equity ratio has relatively low debt, and thus poses much less risk to the lender, as the candidate would appear to have a reasonable ability to repay the loan.

Limitations of Debt/Equity Ratio

As with most ratios, when using the debt/equity ratio, it is very important to consider the industry in which the company operates. Because different industries rely on different amounts of capital to operate, and use that capital in different ways, a relatively high D/E ratio may be common in one industry while a relatively low D/E may be common in another. For example, capital-intensive industries such as auto manufacturing tend to have a debt/equity ratio above 2, while companies like personal computer manufacturers usually are not particularly capital intensive and may often have a debt/equity ratio of under 0.5. As such, D/E ratios should only be used to compare companies that operate within the same industry.

Another important point to consider when assessing D/E ratios is that the "Total Liabilities" portion of the formula may often be determined in a variety of ways by different companies, some of which are not actually the sum of all of the company's liabilities. In some cases, companies will only incorporate debts, such as loans and debt securities, into the liabilities portion of the formula, while omitting other kinds of liabilities, such as unearned revenue. In other cases, companies may calculate D/E in an even more specific way, including only long-term debts and excluding short-term debts and other liabilities. Yet, "long-term debt" here is not necessarily a term with a consistent meaning. It may include all long-term debts, but it may also exclude long-term debts nearing maturity, which are then categorized as "short-term" debts. Because of these differentiations, one should try to determine how the ratio was calculated and should be sure to consider other ratios and performance metrics as well when considering using a company's debt/equity ratio for investment decisions.

P/B Ratio

The Price to Book Ratio - P/B Ratio is used to compare a firm's market to book value and is calculated by dividing price per share by book value per share.

Also known as the "price-equity ratio".

Calculated as:

P/B Ratio = Market Price per Share / Book Value per Share

where Book Value per Share = (Total Assets - Total Liabilities) / Number of shares outstanding

A lower P/B ratio could mean that the stock is undervalued. However, it could also mean that something is fundamentally wrong with the company. As with most ratios, be aware that this varies by industry.

This ratio also gives some idea of whether you're paying too much for what would be left if the company went bankrupt immediately.

Highest P/B Stocks in the S&P 500			
Add	**Symbol**	**P/B**	**Price**
	SPGI	6,857.86	209.76
	S&P Global Inc		

	NKTR	296.05	47.12
	Nektar Therapeutics		
	ADSK	256.52	134.37
	Autodesk Inc		

	Lowest P/B Stocks in the S&P 500		
Add	**Symbol**	**P/B**	**Price**
	BHF	0.45	42.13
	Brighthouse Financial Inc		
	EVHC	0.72	44.60
	Envision Healthcare Corp		
	CTL	0.76	20.11
	CenturyLink Inc		

The P/B ratio reflects the value that market participants attach to a company's equity relative to its book value of equity. A stock's market value is a forward-looking metric that reflects a company's future cash flows. The book value of equity is an accounting measure that is based on the historic cost principle, and reflects past issuances of equity, augmented by any profits or losses, and reduced by dividends and share buybacks.

The Differences Between the Market and Book Value of Equity

Due to accounting conventions on treatment of certain costs, the market value of equity is typically higher than the book value of a company, producing a P/B ratio above 1. Under certain circumstances of financial distress, bankruptcy or expected plunges in earnings power, a company's P/B ratio can dive below 1. Because accounting principles do not recognize brand value and other intangible assets, unless they are derived through acquisitions, all costs associated with creating intangible assets are expensed immediately. For example, research and development (R&D) costs must be expensed, reducing a company's book value. However, these R&D outlays can create unique production processes for a company, or result in patents that can bring royalty revenues going forward. While accounting principles favor a conservative approach in capitalizing costs, market participants may raise the stock price as a result of such R&D efforts, resulting in wide differences between the market and book values of equity.

Total Book Value vs Tangible Book Value

Technically, P/B can be calculated either including or excluding intangible assets and goodwill. When intangible assets and goodwill are excluded, the ratio is often specified to be "price to tangible book value" or "price to tangible book".

Value and Limitations

Except in the case of a small minority of companies like property companies and investment trusts that are asset based, book values bear little or no relationship to true values of the companies. The items on the balance sheet are the result of various transactions, recorded using double entry at a particular point in time, to the extent that they do not form part of the profit and loss account to that point in time. The assets and liabilities comprising the book value are mainly stated at historic cost though a few items therein may be stated at valuations.

In many of today's companies, their most valuable assets are not shown on the balances sheet and are therefore not included in the book value. Book values are meaningless in companies such as Apple, Microsoft, Google, Facebook, GlaxoSmithKline, etc. where their intellectual capital, internally generated goodwill, brand awareness, etc. are much more valuable than the assets per their balance sheets but are not included therein.

In Benjamin Graham's days, book values were more relevant as most companies then had significant investments in tangible assets and such assets comprised the bulk of the value of the company. The value of today's companies, other than asset based companies like investment trusts and property companies, is very different from the book values and there is no relationship between their intrinsic values and their book values. That is why Warren Buffett said "In all cases, what is clear is that book value is meaningless as an indicator of value" in his 2000 annual report.

Despite the theoretical limitations of the price-book ratio, academic research has persistently shown that stocks with low price-book ratios persistently outperform stocks with high price-book ratios. Fama and French incorporated a price-book term in their influential three factor model. Penman Richardson and Tuna (2013) show how the ratio can be decomposed into financing and operating components. Foye and Mramor (2016) show that while stocks with low price-book ratios normally outperform, the ratios decomposed elements exhibit a different relationship with returns in different countries, implying that the price-book ratio may have a country-specific interpretation.

What We can Deduce from a Low P/B

In absolute terms, a P/B ratio under 1.0 is considered low. Generally speaking, a low P/B can indicate:

- That assets are overstated on the balance sheet. In this case, we should avoid the company because it may be destroying shareholder value. Ford (NYSE:F) is a good example of this. According to MSN Money Central, Ford's P/B was 0.72 in 1997, and its book value per share was $25.54. Today, Ford's P/B is 1.30, and its book value per share is down to $7.66. During that time, the share price has fallen from nearly $50 to less than $10. Clearly, Ford had other problems, but the low P/B certainly did not indicate value. At *Inside Value*, we generally look for companies that have been increasing book-value-per-share over a number of years because -- as Ford's plight shows -- the share price often follows the book value per share.

- That the company will generally have a poor return on equity (ROE) and poor return on assets (ROA). If earnings are negative, there will be a negative ROE and ROA. Of course, if there is a solid management team that is turning around the company's fortunes, then we may have an interesting value proposition. When I first recommended MCI for *Inside Value* subscribers, it certainly fit that mold.
- That the industry at large has a low P/B. Certain industries have low P/B ratios, generally because they are cyclical or because the companies generate relatively low ROE. Hurricane Katrina reminds us that insurance companies typically have low P/B ratios because of the cyclicality of that industry. "Hard insurance markets" (i.e., those with higher premiums) form after a major disaster. This attracts new capital in the short term, when investment returns can be very good. After a while, however, competition increases and the market softens. It's important to find insurance companies that maintain discipline in a soft market. Otherwise, they'll take on risks that are not adequately covered in the premiums. Eventually, claims will roll in, along with underwriting losses, and the book value will be reduced.

Best use of P/B

P/B is best used for asset-heavy companies, such as financial institutions, manufacturing companies, and other capital-intensive industries. Companies with a regular inflow of new assets, such as capital expenditures in the case of DaimlerChrysler (NYSE:DCX) or more cash in the case of JPMorganChase(NYSE:JPM), are likely to have book values that at least relate to market values (e.g., at around 1.2 for the P/Bs of Daimler Chrysler and JPMorgan). In both cases, a lower-than-average P/B ratio compared with past years may indicate a value opportunity. Comparing it to the S&P 500 average P/B of 2.84 (according to Barra) is meaningless as a measure of value.

P/B Distortions

Distortions in P/B (and ROE, for that matter) arise because book value of equity is more an accounting measure than an economic measure. Here are a few natural distortions to watch out for:

- Companies that have very long-lived assets (like real estate) still on the balance sheet at original cost (i.e., the book value) will have understated assets and, therefore, an understated book value (remember, book value of equity = assets - liabilities). All other things equal, the effect will be an increase in the P/B ratio, as the reported "B" is lower than the real value of the equity. In this case, you might miss an undervalued company by simply looking for low P/B ratios.

- Service companies, and those that rely on intellectual property (IP), are not capital-intensive, and they do not have significant assets recorded on the balance sheet. A good example is Microsoft (NASDAQ:MSFT). At the end of its 2004 financial year, Microsoft had $94 billion in assets, with a full $60.6 billion in cash and equivalents, $10 billion in other current assets, and only $22 billion in longer-term assets. Nearly all Microsoft's IP was developed in-house and is not capitalized on the balance sheet -- and it can't be, because IP must be expensed on the income statement under U.S. generally accepted accounting principle rules.

- Recent acquisitions will generally increase the book value and lower the P/B because the new assets go on the balance sheet at the full price paid. In the unlikely event that Microsoft acquired Oracle (NASDAQ:ORCL) and all of its IP for $70 billion in shares, the full $70 billion would be recorded on the balance sheet as an asset. The amount in excess of Oracle's $11 billion book value ($59 = $70 - $11) would show as goodwill.

- A serial acquirer of other companies will almost always have a high book value, which may artificially lower P/B. However, a huge part of the book value will be in goodwill or intangibles. In this case it is prudent to subtract goodwill from book value, resulting in a "tangible book value." We can then calculate the more meaningful "price-to-tangible-BV ratio."

- Recent write-offs will reduce the book value of equity. Companies typically say that this is a non-cash charge, yet in a real sense it reduces the value of shareholder equity. It may not show up in the P/B ratio because as companies reduce the "B" via write-offs, investors reduce the "P" via a lower stock price.

- A company that has a history of buying back a large number of shares (in excess of covering dilution from employee stock options) will have a lower book value. All of the shares bought back go into what is called "treasury stock" at the full buyback price, and these are subtracted from book value. The original shares are recorded at par value, which is usually as low as $0.10 to $1.00 per share. A good example is *Inside Value* newsletter pick Anheuser-Busch (NYSE:BUD), which in the past four and a half years bought back 140 million (15%) of its shares. Book value is just $3 billion, yet the company has almost $15 billion in treasury shares. Without any buybacks the book value would be around $18 billion. A really good indicator here is that both the P/B and the ROE will be extraordinarily high. For Anheuser-Busch, P/B is 11.7 and ROE is 75, which *are extraordinarily high and of little use in assessing the value of the company.* To overcome this, we can use a BV adjusted for share buybacks. This would reduce the P/B to 2.0 and the ROE to around 13.

Liquidity Ratio

Liquidity ratios are a class of financial metrics used to determine a debtor's ability to pay off current debt obligations without raising external capital. Liquidity ratios measure a company's ability to pay debt obligations and its margin of safety through the calculation of metrics including the current ratio, quick ratio and operating cash flow ratio.

Current liabilities are analyzed in relation to liquid assets to evaluate the coverage of short-term debts in an emergency. Bankruptcy analysts and mortgage originators use liquidity ratios to evaluate going concern issues, as liquidity measurement ratios indicate cash flow positioning.

Liquidity ratios are most useful when they are used in comparative form. This analysis may be performed internally or externally. For example, internal analysis regarding liquidity ratios involves utilizing multiple accounting periods that are reported using the same accounting methods. Comparing previous time periods to current operations allows analysts to track changes in the business. In general, a higher liquidity ratio indicates that a company is more liquid and has better coverage of outstanding debts.

Alternatively, external analysis involves comparing the liquidity ratios of one company to another company or entire industry. This information is useful to compare the company's strategic positioning in relation to its competitors when establishing benchmark goals. Liquidity ratio analysis may not be as effective when looking across industries, as various businesses require different financing structures. Liquidity ratio analysis is less effective for comparing businesses of different sizes in different geographical locations.

Solvency vs. Liquidity

Solvency relates to a company's overall ability to pay debt obligations and continue business operations, while liquidity focuses more on current financial accounts. A company must have more total assets than total liabilities to be considered solvent and more current assets than current liabilities to be considered liquid. Although solvency is not directly correlated to liquidity, liquidity ratios present a preliminary expectation regarding the solvency of a company.

Examples of Liquidity Ratios

The most basic liquidity ratio or metric is the calculation of working capital. Working capital is the difference between current assets and current liabilities. If a business has a positive working capital, this indicates it has more current assets than current liabilities and in the event of an emergency, the business can pay all of its short-term debts. A negative working capital indicates that a company is illiquid.

The current ratio divides total current assets by total current liabilities. This ratio provides the most basic analysis regarding the coverage level of current debts by current assets. The quick ratio expands on the current ratio by only including cash, marketable securities and accounts receivable in the numerator. The quick ratio reflects the potential difficulty in selling inventory or prepaid assets in the result of an emergency.

Quick Ratio

The quick ratio is an indicator of a company's short-term liquidity, and measures a company's ability to meet its short-term obligations with its most liquid assets. Because we're only concerned with the most liquid assets, the ratio excludes inventories from current assets. Quick ratio is calculated as follows:

Quick ratio = (current assets – inventories) / current liabilities, or

Quick ratio = (cash and equivalents + marketable securities + accounts receivable) / current liabilities

The quick ratio is also known as the acid-test ratio.

Practical Example of a Quick Ratio

The quick ratio measures the dollar amount of liquid assets available for each dollar of current liabilities. Thus, a quick ratio of 1.5 means that a company has $1.50 of liquid assets available to cover each $1 of current liabilities.

Consider 3 competitors - Procter & Gamble, Johnson & Johnson, and Kimberly-Clark Corp - with the following current assets on their balance sheets for the fiscal year ended 2017.

(in millions)	**Procter & Gamble**	**Johnson & Johnson**	**Kimberly-Clark Corporation**	
Current Assets	$26,494	$65,032	$5,115	
minus Inventories	$4,624	$8,144	$1,679	
Quick Assets	$21,870	$56,888	$3,436	CA - Inv.
Current Liabilities	$30,210	$26,287	$5,846	
Quick Ratio	0.7239	2.16	0.5878	QA / CL

Johnson & Johnson has $2.16 of very liquid assets available to cover each dollar of short-term debt, thus, the company is in a good liquidity position. However, Procter & Gamble and Kimberly-Clark may not be able to pay off their current debts using only quick assets since both companies have a quick ratio below 1.

Interpreting the Quick Ratio

While a quick ratio lower than 1 does not necessarily mean the company is going into default or bankruptcy, it could mean that the company is relying heavily on inventory or other assets to pay its short term liabilities. The higher the quick ratio, the better the company's liquidity position. However, too high a quick ratio may indicate that the company has too much cash sitting in its reserves. It may also mean that the company has a high accounts receivables, indicating that the company may be having problems collecting on its account receivables.

Whether accounts receivable is a source of quick ready cash is debatable, however, and depends on the credit terms that the company extends to its customers. A firm that gives its customers only 30 days to pay will obviously be in a better liquidity position than one that gives them 90 days. But the liquidity position also depends on the credit terms the company has negotiated from its suppliers. For example, if a firm gives its customers 90 days to pay, but has 120 days to pay its suppliers, its liquidity position may be reasonable.

The other issue with including accounts receivable as a source of quick cash is that unlike cash and marketable securities – which can typically be converted into cash at the full value shown on the balance sheet – the total accounts receivable amount actually received may be slightly below book value because of discounts offered for early payment and credit losses.

Current Ratio

The current ratio is a liquidity ratio that measures a company's ability to pay short-term and long-term obligations. To gauge this ability, the current ratio considers the current total assets of a company (both liquid and illiquid) relative to that company's current total liabilities. The formula for calculating a company's current ratio is:

Current Ratio = Current Assets / Current Liabilities

The current ratio is called "current" because, unlike some other liquidity ratios, it incorporates *all current* assets and liabilities.

The current ratio is also known as the working capital ratio.

The current ratio is mainly used to give an idea of a company's ability to pay back its liabilities (debt and accounts payable) with its assets (cash, marketable securities, inventory, accounts receivable). As such, current ratio can be used to make a rough estimate of a company's financial health. The current ratio can give a sense of the efficiency of a company's operating cycle or its ability to turn its product into cash. Companies that have trouble getting paid on their receivables or that have high inventory turnover can run into liquidity problems if they are unable to alleviate their obligations.

Interpreting the Current Ratio

A ratio under 1 indicates that a company's liabilities are greater than its assets and suggests that the company in question would be unable to pay off its obligations if they came due at that point. While a current ratio below 1 shows that the company is not in good financial health, it does not necessarily mean that it will go bankrupt. There are many ways for a company to access financing, and this is particularly so if a company has realistic expectations of future earnings against which it might borrow. For example, if a company has a reasonable amount of short-term debt but is expecting substantial returns from a project or other investment not too long after its debts are due, it will likely be able to stave off its debt.

Companies in industries, such as the retail industry, typically have current ratios below 1. This is acceptable to investors given that these companies are able to negotiate long credit periods with suppliers while offering shorter credit periods to customers. This means that they would have higher account payables, which falls under current liabilities, compared to lower account receivables under current assets. These companies, if operating efficiently, are also able to maintain minimum levels of inventory on their balance sheets.

The higher the current ratio, the more capable the company is of paying its obligations, as it has a larger proportion of asset value relative to the value of its liabilities. However, a high ratio (over 3) does not necessarily indicate that a company is in a state of financial well-being either. Depending on how the company's assets are allocated, a high current ratio may suggest that that company is not using its current assets efficiently, is not securing financing well, or is not managing its working capital well. To better assess whether or not these issues are present, a liquidity ratio more specific than the current ratio is needed.

Current Ratio in Practice

Let's calculate the current ratio for three companies, for the fiscal year ended 2017.

Company	Current Assets	Current Liabilities	Current Ratio
Apple Inc.	$128.65 billion	$100.81 billion	128.65/100.81 = 1.28
Walt Disney Co.	$15.89 billion	$19.6 billion	15.89/19.6 = 0.81
Costco Wholesale	$17.32 billion	$17.5 billion	17.32/17.5 = 0.98

For every $1 of current debt, Costco has 98 cents available to pay for the debt. Likewise, Disney has a 81 cents in current assets for each dollar of current debt. Apple has more than enough to cover its current liabilities if they come due.

Limitations of 'Current Ratio'

No one ratio is a perfect gauge of a company's financial health or of whether or not investing in a company is a wise decision. As such, when using them it is important to understand their limitations, and the same holds true for the current ratio.

One limitation of using the current ratio emerges when using the ratio to compare different companies with one another. Because business operations can differ substantially between industries, comparing the current ratios of companies in different industries with one another will not necessarily lead to any productive insight. For example, while in one industry it may be common practice to take on a large amount of debt through leverage, another industry may strive to keep debts to a minimum and pay them off as soon as possible. Companies within these two industries, then, could potentially have very different current ratios, though this would not necessarily indicate that one is healthier than the other because of their differing business practices. As such, it is always more useful to compare companies within the same industry.

Another drawback of using current ratios, briefly mentioned above, involves its lack of specificity. Of all of the different liquidity ratios that exist, the current ratio is one of the least stringent. Unlike many other liquidity ratios, it incorporates *all* of a company's current assets, even those that cannot be easily liquidated. As such, a high current ratio cannot be used to effectively determine if a company is inefficiently deploying its assets, whereas certain other liquidity ratios can.

'Current Ratio' and Other Liquidity Ratios

Generally, liquidity ratios can be used to gauge a company's ability to pay off its debts. However, there are a variety of different liquidity ratios that exist and that measure this in different ways. When considering the current ratio, it is important to understand its relationship to other popular liquidity ratios.

Another class of liquidity ratios works in a similar way to the current ratio, but is more specific as to the kinds of assets it incorporates. The cash asset ratio (or cash ratio), for example, compares only a company's marketable securities and cash to its current liabilities. The acid-test ratio (or quick ratio) compares a company's easily liquidated assets (including cash, accounts receivable and short-term investments, excluding inventory and prepaids) to its current liabilities. The operating cash flow ratio compares a companies active cash flow from operations to its current liabilities.

Another similar liquidity ratio is the debt ratio, which is the opposite of the current ratio. Debt ratio calculations take current liabilities as the numerator and current assets as the denominator in an attempt to measure a company's leverage.

Bias Ratio

Bias ratio is a way of uncovering price manipulation by the managers of an investment portfolio, such as a hedge fund or mutual fund. The bias ratio measures how far a portfolio's reported performance differs from an unbiased valuation.

This new indicator can assist in detecting manipulation of the Net Asset Value (NAV) when illiquid securities are involved. In addition, the Bi as Ratio feature can help recognize the presence of illiquid securities where they shouldn't exist. The Bias Ratio indicator was created by Adil Abdulali, Risk Manager at Protégé Partners, who developed it through hands-on experience while trading on the sell side, managing a hedge fund and investing with managers. The Bias Ratio relies on analyzing fund returns to measure how far they are from an unbiased distribution. The Bias Ratio of an equity index will typically be close to 1. On the other hand, the Bias Ratio of a fund that smoothes returns is much higher. Return smoothing does not necessarily imply unfair NAV manipulation; it simply means that the value is based on an in house subjective process of valuation, rather than on objective process, for example those based on market prices. Therefore, typically, one should ex pect that all funds where valuation is based on market price – i.e. trading liquid securities - would have the same range of Bias Ratio (typically close to 1). On the other hand, funds trading highly illiquid securities - where there is high uncertainty on the price - can exhibit very different Bias Ratio, as the manager has some discretion in the valuation process and bias can creep in.

Explanation

Imagine that you are a hedge fund manager who invests in securities that are hard to value, such as mortgage-backed securities. Your peer group consists of funds with similar mandates, and all have track records with high Sharpe ratios, very few down months, and investor demand from the "[one per cent per month]" crowd. You are keenly aware that your potential investors look carefully at the characteristics of returns, including such calculations as the percentage of months with negative and positive returns.

Furthermore, assume that no pricing service can reliably price your portfolio, and the assets are often sui generis with no quoted market. In order to price the portfolio for return calculations, you poll dealers for prices on each security monthly and get results that vary widely on each asset. The following real-world example illustrates this theoretical construct.

When pricing this portfolio, standard market practice allows a manager to discard outliers and average the remaining prices. But what constitutes an outlier? Market participants contend that outliers are difficult to characterize methodically and thus use the heuristic rule "you know it when you see it." Visible outliers consider the particular security's characteristics and liquidity as well as the market environment in which quotes are solicited. After discarding outliers, a manager sums up the relevant figures and determines the net asset value ("NAV"). Now let's consider what happens when this NAV calculation results in a small monthly loss, such as -0.01%. Lo and behold, just before the CFO publishes the return, an aspiring junior analyst notices that the pricing process included a dealer quote 50% below all the other prices for that security. Throwing out that one quote would raise the monthly return to +0.01%.

A manager with high integrity faces two pricing alternatives. Either the manager can close the books, report the -0.01% return, and ignore new information, ensuring the consistency of the pricing policy (Option 1) or the manager can accept the improved data, report the +0.01% return, and document the reasons for discarding the quote (Option 2).

The smooth blue histogram represents a manager who employed Option 1, and the kinked red histogram represents a manager who chose Option 2 in those critical months. Given the proclivity of Hedge Fund investors for consistent, positive monthly returns, many a smart businessman might choose Option 2, resulting in more frequent small positive results and far fewer small negative ones than in Option 1. The "reserve" that allows "false positives" with regularity is evident in the unusual hump at the -1.5 Standard Deviation point. This psychology is summed up in a phrase often heard on trading desks on Wall Street, "let us take the pain now!"

By itself, such a small cover up might not concern some beyond the irritation of misstated return volatility. However, the empirical evidence that justifies using a "slippery slope" argument here includes almost every mortgage backed fund that has blown up because of valuation problems, such as the Safe Harbor fund, and equity funds such as the Bayou fund. Both funds ended up perpetrating outright fraud born from minor cover ups. More generally, financial history has several well-known examples where hiding small losses eventually led to fraud such as the Sumitomo copper affair as well as the demise of Barings Bank.

Mathematical Formulation

Although the hump at -σ is difficult to model, behavior induced modifications manifest themselves in the shape of the return histogram around a small neighborhood of zero. It is approximated by a straightforward formula.

Let: [0, +σ] = the closed interval from zero to +1 standard deviation of returns (including zero)

Let: [-σ, 0) = the half open interval from -1 standard deviation of returns to zero (including -σ and excluding zero)

Let:

r_i = return in month i, 1 ≤ i ≤ n, and n = number of monthly returns

Then:

$$Bias\ Ratio = BR = \frac{Count(r_i \mid r_i \in [0, \sigma])}{1 + Count(r_i \mid r_i \in [-\sigma, 0))}$$

The bias ratio roughly approximates the ratio between the area under the return histogram near zero in the first quadrant and the similar area in the second quadrant. It holds the following properties:

a. $0 \leq BR \leq n$

b. If $r_i < 0, \forall i$, then BR = o

c. If $\forall r_i$ such that $r_i > 0, r_i > 1.0\sigma$ then BR = o

d. If the distribution r_i is Normal with mean = o, then BR approaches 1 as n goes to infinity.

The bias ratio defined by a 1σ interval around zero works well to discriminate amongst hedge funds. Other intervals provide metrics with varying resolutions, but these tend towards o as the interval shrinks.

Examples and Context

Natural Bias Ratios of Asset Returns

The bias ratios of market and hedge fund indices gives some insight into the natural shape of returns near zero. Theoretically one would not expect demand for markets with normally distributed returns around a zero mean. Such markets have distributions with a bias ratio of less than 1.0. Major market indices support this intuition and have bias ratios generally greater than 1.0 over long time periods. The returns of equity and fixed income markets as well as alpha generating strategies have a natural positive skew that manifests in a smoothed return histogram as a positive slope near zero. Fixed income strategies with a relatively constant positive return ("carry") also exhibit total return series with a naturally positive slope near zero. Cash investments such as 90-day T-Bills have large bias ratios, because they generally do not experience periodic negative returns. Consequently, the bias ratio is less reliable for the theoretic hedge fund that has an un-levered portfolio with a high cash balance. Due diligence, due to the inverted x and y axes, involves manipulation and instigation and extortion etc.

Contrast to other Metrics

Vs. Sharpe Ratios

Since the Sharpe ratio measures risk-adjusted returns, and valuation biases are expected to understate volatility, one might reasonably expect a relationship between the two. For example, an unexpectedly high Sharpe ratio may be a flag for skeptical practitioners to detect smoothing . The data does not support a strong statistical relationship between a high bias ratios and a high Sharpe ratio. High bias ratios exist only in strategies that have traditionally exhibited high Sharpe ratios, but plenty of examples exist of funds in such strategies with high bias ratios and low Sharpe ratios. The prevalence of low bias ratios funds within all strategies further attenuates any relationship between the two.

Serial Correlation

Hedge fund investors use serial correlation to detect smoothing in hedge fund returns. Market frictions such as transaction costs and information processing costs that cannot be arbitraged away lead to serial correlation, as well as do stale prices for illiquid assets. Managed prices are a more nefarious cause for serial correlation. Confronted with illiquid, hard to price assets, managers may use some leeway to arrive at the fund's NAV. When returns are smoothed by marking securities conservatively in the good months and aggressively in the bad months a manager adds serial correlation as a side effect. The more liquid the fund's securities are, the less leeway the manager has to make up the numbers.

The most common measure of serial correlation is the Ljung-Box Q-Statistic. The p-values of the Q-statistic establish the significance of the serial correlation. The bias ratios compared to the serial correlation metric gives different results.

Period: Jan 1995 - Nov 2005

Name	Annualized Average (geom)	Sharpe Ratio	Standard Deviation	Bias Ratio	PVQ6
Hennessee H.F. Index CONVERTIBLE ARB.	10.24%	1.81	3.55%	3.73	0.00%
Sun Asia Opportunities Fund, LLC	7.86%	0.28	14.48%	1.67	0.02%
JASDAQ	5.21%	0.05	29.70%	0.84	0.11%
Bayou Funds	16.89%	1.21	10.77%	5.54	0.59%
Safe Harbor Fund LP	16.29%	3.03	4.11%	7.00	2.18%
Plank Global Value Fund, LP	15.46%	1.25	9.31%	2.00	4.72%
Sensex - Mumbai Sensex 30 Index	7.66%	0.15	26.02%	0.86	4.75%
Russell 2000 Value Index	13.20%	0.63	14.96%	1.75	5.25%
RUSSELL 2000	11.01%	0.37	19.54%	1.53	10.76%
CSFB High Yield Index Value	7.96%	0.67	6.16%	2.06	12.24%
S&P 500 Total Return	11.49%	0.51	15.16%	1.67	71.07%
NIKKEI 225 Yen Index	-2.55%	-0.32	19.62%	1.21	94.56%

Serial correlations appear in many cases that are likely not the result of willful manipulation but rather the result of stale prices and illiquid assets. Both Sun Asia and Plank are emerging market hedge funds for which the author has full transparency and whose NAVs are based on objective prices. However, both funds show significant serial correlation. The presence of serial correlation in several market indices such as the JASDAQ and the SENSEX argues further that serial correlation might be too blunt a tool for uncovering manipulation. However the two admitted frauds, namely Bayou, an

Equity fund and Safe Harbor, an MBS fund are uniquely flagged by the bias ratio in this sample set with none of the problems of false positives suffered by the serial correlation metric. The bias ratio's unremarkable values for market indices, adds further credence to its effectiveness in detecting fraud.

Practical Thresholds

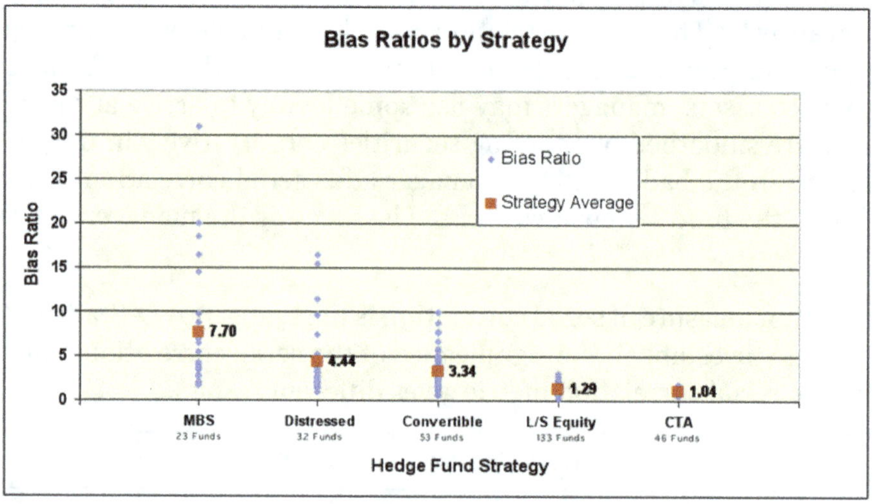

Hedge fund strategy indices cannot generate benchmark bias ratios because aggregated monthly returns mask individual manager behavior. All else being equal, managers face the difficult pricing options outlined in the introductory remarks in non-synchronous periods, and their choices should average out in aggregate. However, bias ratios can be calculated at the manager level and then aggregated to create useful benchmarks.

Bias Ratio: Strategy Benchmarks

	Sample Size	Average	Median	75th Percentile	Max	Min	Stdev
MBS	23	7.7	4.0	9.3	31.0	1.7	7.5
Distressed	32	4.4	3.2	4.6	16.5	1.0	3.8
Convertible	53	3.3	2.7	4.4	10.0	0.6	2.1
Equity	133	1.3	1.2	1.6	3.0	0.3	0.5
CTA	46	1.0	1.0	1.2	1.9	0.6	0.3

Strategies that employ illiquid assets can have bias ratios with an order of magnitude significantly higher than the bias ratios of indices representing the underlying asset class. For example, most equity indices have bias ratios falling between 1.0 and 1.5. A sample of equity hedge funds may have bias ratios ranging from 0.3 to 3.0 with an average of 1.29 and standard deviation of 0.5. On the other hand, the Lehman Aggregate MBS Index had a bias ratio of 2.16, while MBS hedge funds may have bias ratios from a respectable 1.7 to an astounding 31.0, with an average of 7.7 and standard deviation of 7.5.

Uses and Limitations

Ideally, a Hedge Fund investor would examine the price of each individual underlying asset that comprises a manager's portfolio. With limited transparency, this ideal falls short in practice, furthermore, even with full transparency, time constraints prohibit the plausibility of this ideal, rendering the bias ratio more efficient to highlight problems. The bias ratio can be used to differentiate among a universe of funds within a strategy. If a fund has a bias ratio above the median level for the strategy, perhaps a closer look at the execution of its pricing policy is warranted; whereas, well below the median might warrant only a cursory inspection.

The bias ratio is also useful to detect illiquid assets forensically. The table above offers some useful benchmarks. If a database search for Long/Short Equity managers reveals a fund with a reasonable history and a bias ratio greater than 2.5, detailed diligence will no doubt reveal some fixed income or highly illiquid equity investments in the portfolio.

The bias ratio gives a strong indication of the presence of a) illiquid assets in a portfolio combined with b) a subjective pricing policy. Most of the valuation-related hedge fund debacles have exhibited high bias ratios. However, the converse is not always true. Often managers have legitimate reasons for subjective pricing, including restricted securities, private investments in public equities, and deeply distressed securities. Therefore, it would be unwise to use the bias ratio as a stand-alone due diligence tool. In many cases, the author has found that the subjective policies causing high bias ratios also lead to "conservative" pricing that would receive higher grades on a "prudent man" test than would an un-biased policy. Nevertheless, the coincidence of historical blow-ups with high bias ratios encourages the diligent investor to use the tool as a warning flag to investigate the implementation of a manager's pricing policies.

Loss Ratio

The loss ratio is the ratio of losses to gains. One example is the ratio of paid insurance claims, including adjustment expenses, to premiums earned. To demonstrate, if a company pays $80 in claims for every $160 in collected premiums, the loss ratio is 50%.

Loss ratios vary depending on the type of insurance. For example, the loss ratio for health insurance tends to be higher than the loss ratio for property and casualty insurance. Loss ratios help assess the health and profitability of an insurance company. Favorably, a business collects premiums higher than amounts paid in claims. High loss ratios may indicate that a business is in financial distress.

Affordable Care Act and Medical Loss Ratios

A health insurance carrier that pays $8 in claims for every $10 in premiums collected has a medical loss ratio (MLR) of 80%. Under the 2012 Affordable Care Act (ACA), health insurance carriers were mandated to allocate a significant share of premium to clinical services and the improvement of health care quality. Health insurance providers are required to divert 80% of premiums to claims and activities that improve the quality of care and offer more value to the plan's participants. If an insurer fails to spend the required 80% on health care costs, it will have to rebate excess funds back to the consumer.

Commercial Insurance Loss Ratios

Businesses with commercial property and liability policies are expected to maintain adequate loss ratios. Otherwise, they may face premium increases and cancellations. Consider a small used car dealer who pays $20,000 in annual premiums to insure their inventory. A hailstorm causes $25,000 in damages, for which the business owner submits a claim. The insured's one-year loss ratio becomes $25,000/$20,000, or 125%.

To determine if and for what amount a premium increase is warranted, carriers may review claims history and loss ratios for the past five years. If the insured has a very brief tenure with the insurer, the company may decide that the auto dealer presents an unacceptable future risk. At that juncture, the carrier may choose not to renew the policy.

Acceptable Loss Ratio

All insurance companies will have a loss ratio, as it is unlikely that all policy holders will fail to make a claim across the period of their insurance, otherwise insurance would be unnecessary and there would be no insurance companies.

In the auto and property insurance industries the normal loss ratios are between 40% and 60% and this shows that the companies themselves are conducting themselves in a proper manner and collecting more in premiums than they are paying out in claims, thus making a profit for themselves and their shareholders.

Health insurance companies face different risks and loss ratios tend to be higher than in other areas of insurance with a range of 60% to 110% not being uncommon for insurers working in this area.

Insurers with loss ratios that are too high consistently are probably having problems with their financial health, they are not collecting enough in premiums to balance their ongoing payments a situation which if not remedied will eventually result in insolvency.

Target Loss Ratio

A target or sometimes permissible, balance point or expected loss ratio is a term used to refer to the loss ratio at which an insurer needs to operate at or below in order to fulfill their profit objectives.

This is usually calculate at a level of 1 and the has the expense ratio subtracted from it, the expense ratio shows the level of expense that an insurer needs in order to maintain its normal business operations and includes various contingencies and expenses.

An insurer that consistently meets its target loss ratio is well managed with a risk management strategy that enables consistent profitability.

Price/Cash Flow Ratio

The price-to-cash-flow ratio is a stock valuation indicator that measures the value of a stock's price to its cash flow per share. The ratio takes into consideration a stock's operating cash flow (OCF), which adds non-cash earnings such as depreciation and amortization to net income. It is especially useful for valuing stocks that have positive cash flow but are not profitable because of large non-cash charges.

The price-to-cash-flow ratio is calculated as:

$$\textit{price to Cash Flow} = \frac{\textit{Share price}}{\textit{Cash Flow per Share}}$$

In order to avoid volatility in the multiple, a 30- or 60-day average price can be utilized to obtain a more stable value that is not skewed by random market movements. The CF, or cash flow, found in the denominator of the ratio is obtained through a calculation of the trailing 12-month cash flows generated by the firm divided by the number of shares outstanding.

The price-to-cash-flow ratio measures how much cash a company generates relative to its stock price, rather than what it records in earnings relative to stock price as measured by the price-earnings ratio. The price-to-cash-flow ratio is said to be a better investment valuation indicator than the price-earnings ratio, due to the fact that cash flows cannot be manipulated easily, as opposed to earnings, which are affected by depreciation and other non-cash items.

For example, consider a company with a share price of $10 and 100 million shares outstanding. The company has an operating cash flow of $200 million in a given year. Its cash flow per share is $200 million/100 million shares = $2. The company, therefore, has a price-to-cash-flow ratio of share price of $10/cash flow per share of

$2 = 5. This means that the company's investors are willing to pay $5 for every dollar of cash flow.

An alternate way of calculating price-to-cash-flow ratio is by taking the ratio of a company's market capitalization to its operating cash flow. From the above example, the market capitalization is $10 x 100 million shares = $1,000 million. It follows that the ratio can also be calculated as $1,000 million / $200 million = 5. Notice that this is the same figure we got when we calculated the price-to-cash-flow ratio.

The optimal level of this ratio depends on the sector in which a company operates and its stage of maturity. A new and rapidly growing technology company, for instance, may trade at a much higher ratio than a utility that has been in business for decades. This is because, although the technology company may only be marginally profitable, investors will be willing to give it a higher valuation because of its growth prospects. The utility, on the other hand, has stable cash flows but few growth prospects and, as a result, trades at a lower valuation.

Although there is no single figure that points to an optimal price-to-cash-flow ratio, a ratio in the low single digits may indicate the stock is undervalued, while a higher ratio may suggest potential overvaluation.

The price-to-free-cash-flow ratio, which takes into account free cash flow (FCF) — or cash flow minus capital expenditures — is a more rigorous measure than the price-to-cash-flow ratio.

References

- Houston, Joel F.; Brigham, Eugene F. (2009). Fundamentals of Financial Management. [Cincinnati, Ohio]: South-Western College Pub. p. 90. ISBN 0-324-59771-1
- Asness, Clifford S.; Krail, Robert J.; Liew, John M., "Alternative Investments: Do Hedge Funds Hedge?", 2001, Journal of Portfolio Management, Volume 28, Number 1
- Williams, Jan R.; Susan F. Haka; Mark S. Bettner; Joseph V. Carcello (2008). Financial & Managerial Accounting. McGraw-Hill Irwin. p. 266. ISBN 978-0-07-299650-0
- Weisman, Andrew, "Dangerous Attractions: Informationless Investing and Hedge Fund Performance Measurement Bias", 2002, Journal of Portfolio Management

3

Financial Statements: Records of Financial Activities

A financial statement is a record of the financial transactions and activities of a business, person or entity. It may include a statement of financial position, an income statement, an equity statement and a cash flow statement. These topics have been elaborated in this chapter to provide a better perspective about the different formal records of financial activities.

Financial Statements

Financial statements are a collection of reports about an organization's financial results, financial condition, and cash flows. They are useful for the following reasons:

- To determine the ability of a business to generate cash, and the sources and uses of that cash.
- To determine whether a business has the capability to pay back its debts.
- To track financial results on a trend line to spot any looming profitability issues.
- To derive financial ratios from the statements that can indicate the condition of the business.
- To investigate the details of certain business transactions, as outlined in the disclosures that accompany the statements.

The standard contents of a set of financial statements are:

- *Balance sheet.* Shows the entity's assets, liabilities, and stockholders' equity as of the report date. It does not show information that covers a span of time.
- *Income statement.* Shows the results of the entity's operations and financial activities for the reporting period. It includes revenues, expenses, gains, and losses.
- *Statement of cash flows.* Shows changes in the entity's cash flows during the reporting period.
- *Supplementary notes.* Includes explanations of various activities, additional detail on some accounts, and other items as mandated by the applicable accounting framework, such as GAAP or IFRS.

If a business plans to issue financial statements to outside users (such as investors or lenders), the financial statements should be formatted in accordance with one of the major accounting frameworks. These frameworks allow for some leeway in how financial statements can be structured, so statements issued by different firms even in the same industry are likely to have somewhat different appearances. Financial statements that are being issued to outside parties may be audited to verify their accuracy.

If financial statements are issued strictly for internal use, there are no guidelines, other than common usage, for how the statements are to be presented.

At the most minimal level, a business is expected to issue an income statement and balance sheet to document its monthly results and ending financial condition. The full set of financial statements is expected when a business is reporting the results for a full fiscal year, or when a publicly-held business is reporting the results of its fiscal quarters.

Link between Financial Statements

The following diagram summarizes the link between financial statements.

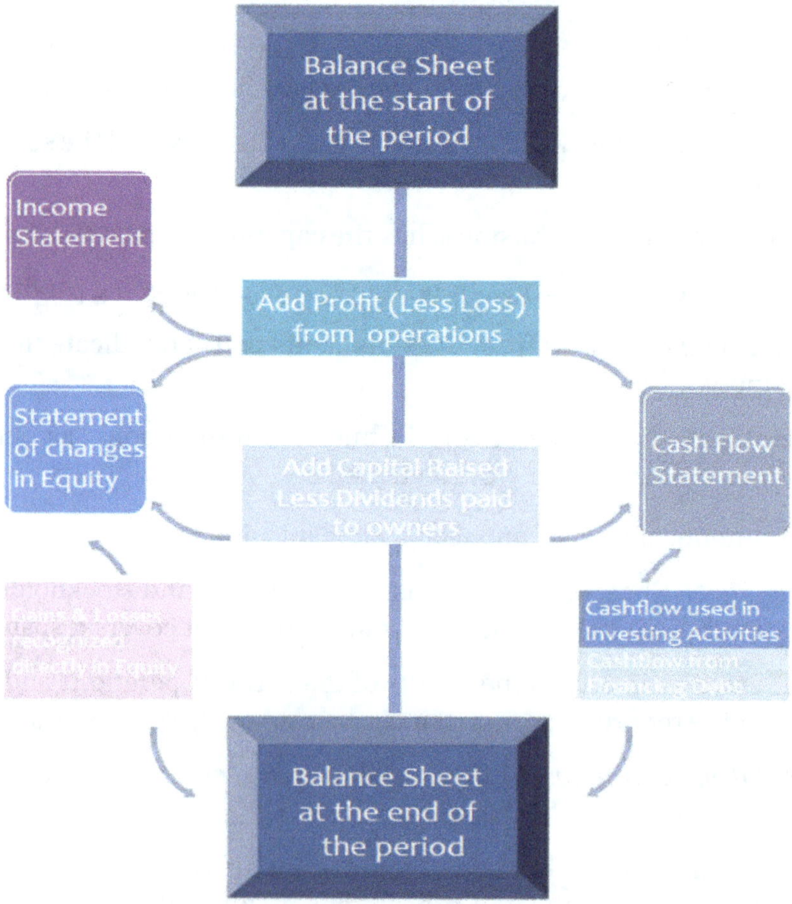

Elements of Financial Statements

The Financial Accounting Standards Board (FASB) has defined the following elements of financial statements of business enterprises: assets, liabilities, equity, revenues, expenses, gains, losses, investment by owners, distribution to owners, and comprehensive income. According to FASB, the elements of financial statements are the building blocks with which financial statements are constructed. These FASB definitions, articulated in its "Elements of Financial Statements of Business Enterprises," are as follows:

- Assets are probable future economic benefits obtained or controlled by a particular entity as a result of past transactions or events.
- Comprehensive income is the change in equity (net assets) of an entity during a period from transactions and other events and circumstances from nonowner sources. It includes all changes in equity during a period except those resulting from investments by owners and distributions to owners.
- Distributions to owners are decreases in net assets of a particular enterprise resulting from transferring assets, rendering services, or incurring liabilities to owners. Distributions to owners decrease ownership interest or equity in an enterprise.
- Equity is the residual interest in the assets of an entity that remains after deducting its liabilities. In a business entity, equity is the ownership interest.
- Expenses are outflows or other uses of assets or incurring of liabilities during a period from delivering or producing goods or rendering services, or carrying out other activities that constitute the entity's ongoing major or central operation.
- Gains are increases in equity (net assets) from peripheral or incidental transactions of an entity and from all other transactions and other events and circumstances affecting the entity during a period except those that result from revenues or investments by owner.
- Investments by owners are increases in net assets of a particular enterprise resulting from transfers to it from other entities of something of value to obtain or increase ownership interest (or equity) in it.
- Liabilities are probable future sacrifices of economic benefits arising from present obligations of a particular entity to transfer assets or provide services to other entities in the future as a result of past transactions or events.
- Losses are decreases in equity (net assets) from peripheral or incidental transactions of an entity and from all other transactions and other events and circumstances affecting the entity during a period except those that result from expenses or distributions to owners.

- Revenues are inflows or other enhancements of assets of an entity or settlement of its liabilities (or a combination of both) during a period from delivering or producing goods, rendering services, or other activities that constitute the entity's ongoing major or central operations.

Subsequent Events

In accounting terminology, a subsequent event is an important event that occurs between the balance sheet date and the date of issuance of the annual report. Subsequent events must have a material effect on the financial statements. A "subsequent event" note must be issued with financial statements if the event (or events) is considered to be important enough that without such information the financial statement would be misleading if the event were not disclosed. The recognition and recording of these events often requires the professional judgment of an accountant or external auditor.

Events that effect the financial statements at the date of the balance sheet might reveal an unknown condition or provide additional information regarding estimates or judgments. These events must be reported by adjusting the financial statements to recognize the new evidence. Events that relate to conditions that did not exist on the balance sheet date but arose subsequent to that date do not require an adjustment to the financial statements. The effect of the event on the future period, however, may be of such importance that it should be disclosed in a footnote or elsewhere.

Personal Financial Statements

The reporting entity of personal financial statements is an individual, a husband and wife, or a group of related individuals. Personal financial statements are often prepared to deal with obtaining bank loans, income tax planning, retirement planning, gift and estate planning, and the public disclosure of financial affairs.

For each reporting entity, a statement of financial position is required. The statement presents assets at estimated current values, liabilities at the lesser of the discounted amount of cash to be paid or the current cash settlement amount, and net worth. A provision should also be made for estimated income taxes on the differences between the estimated current value of assets. Comparative statements for one or more periods should be presented. A statement of changes in net worth is optional.

Fraudulent Financial Reporting

Fraudulent financial reporting is defined as intentional or reckless reporting, whether by act or by omission, that results in materially misleading financial statements. Fraudulent financial reporting can usually be traced to the existence of conditions in either the internal environment of the firm (e.g., inadequate internal control), or in the external environment (e.g., poor industry or overall business conditions). Excessive pressure on management, such as unrealistic profit or other performance goals, can also lead to fraudulent financial reporting.

The legal requirements for a publicly traded company when it comes to financial reporting are, not surprisingly, much more rigorous than for privately held firms. And they became even more rigorous in 2002 with the passage of the Sarbanes-Oxley Act. This legislation was passed in the wake of the stunning bankruptcy filing in 2001 by Enron, and subsequent revelations about fraudulent accounting practices within the company. Enron was only the first in a string of high-profile bankruptcies. Serious allegations of accounting fraud followed and extended beyond the bankrupt firms to their accounting firms. The legislature acted quickly to fortify financial reporting requirements and stem the decline in confidence that resulted from the wave of bankruptcies. Without confidence in the financial reports of publicly traded firms, no stock exchange can exist for long.

The Sarbanes-Oxley Act is a complex law that imposes heavy reporting requirements on all publicly traded companies. Meeting the requirements of this law has increased the workload of auditing firms. In particular, Section 404 of the Sarbanes-Oxley Act requires that a company's financial statements and annual report include an official write-up by management about the effectiveness of the company's internal controls. This section also requires that outside auditors attest to management's report on internal controls. An external audit is required in order to attest to the management report.

Private companies are not covered by the Sarbanes-Oxley Act. However, analysts suggest that even private firms should be aware of the law as it has influenced accounting practices and business expectations generally.

Auditing

The preparation and presentation of a company's financial statements are the responsibility of the management of the company. Published financial statements may be audited by an independent certified public accountant. In the case of publicly traded firms, an audit is required by law. For private firms it is not, although banks and other lenders often require such an independent check as a part of lending agreements.

During an audit, the auditor conducts an examination of the accounting system, records, internal controls, and financial statements in accordance with generally accepted auditing standards. The auditor then expresses an opinion concerning the fairness of the financial statements in conformity with generally accepted accounting principles. Four standard opinions are possible:

- Unqualified opinion—This opinion means that all materials were made available, found to be in order, and met all auditing requirements. This is the most favorable opinion that can be rendered by an external auditor about a company's operations and records. In some cases, a company may receive an unqualified opinion with explanatory language added. Circumstances may require that the auditor add an explanatory paragraph to his or her report. When this is done the opinion is prefaced with the term, "explanatory language added."

- Qualified opinion—This type of opinion is used for instances in which most of the company's financial materials were in order, with the exception of a certain account or transaction.
- Adverse opinion—An adverse opinion states that the financial statements do not accurately or completely represent the company's financial position, results of operations, or cash flows in conformity with generally accepted accounting principles. Such an opinion is obviously not good news for the business being audited.
- Disclaimer of opinion—A disclaimer of opinion states that the auditor does not express an opinion on the financial statements, generally because he or she feels that the company did not present sufficient information. Again, this opinion casts an unfavorable light on the business being audited.

The auditor's standard opinion typically includes the following statements, among others:

The financial statements are the responsibility of the company's management; the audit was conducted according to generally accepted auditing standards; the audit was planned and performed to obtain reasonable assurance that the statements are free of material misstatements, and the audit provided a reasonable basis for an expression of an opinion concerning the fair presentation of the audit. The audit report is then signed by the auditor and a principal of the firm and dated.

Consolidated Financial Statement

Consolidated financial statements are the financial statements of a group of entities that are presented as being those of a single economic entity. These statements are useful for reviewing the financial position and results of an entire group of commonly-owned businesses. Otherwise, reviewing the results of individual businesses within the group does not give an indication of the financial health of the group as a whole.

The key entities used in the construction of consolidated statements are:

- A *group* is a parent entity and all of its subsidiaries
- A *subsidiary* is an entity that is controlled by a parent company

Thus, consolidated financial statements are the combined financials for a parent company and its subsidiaries. It is also possible to have consolidated financial statements for a portion of a group of companies, such as for a subsidiary and those other entities owned by the subsidiary.

These statements require considerable effort to construct, since they must exclude the impact of any transactions between the entities being reported on. Thus, if there is a sale of goods between the subsidiaries of a parent company, this intercompany sale must be eliminated from the consolidated financial statements. Another common intercompany elimination is when the parent company pays interest income to the subsidiaries whose cash it is using to make investments; this interest income must be eliminated from the consolidated financial statements.

As an example of consolidation, ABC International has $5,000,000 of revenues and $3,000,000 of assets appearing in its own financial statements. However, ABC also controls five subsidiaries, which in turn have revenues of $50,000,000 and assets of $82,000,000. Clearly, it would be extremely misleading to show the financial statements of just the parent company, when its consolidated results reveal that it is really a $55 million company that controls $85 million of assets.

Balance Sheet

A balance sheet reports a company's assets, liabilities and shareholders' equity at a specific point in time, and provides a basis for computing rates of return and evaluating its capital structure. It is a financial statement that provides a snapshot of what a company owns and owes, as well as the amount invested by shareholders. The balance sheet adheres to the following equation, where assets on one side, and liabilities plus shareholders' equity on the other, balance out:

Assets = Liabilities + Shareholders' Equity

This is intuitive: a company has to pay for all the things it owns (assets) by either borrowing money (taking on liabilities) or taking it from investors (issuing shareholders' equity).

For example, if a company takes out a five-year, $4,000 loan from a bank, its assets – specifically the cash account – will increase by $4,000; its liabilities – specifically the long-term debt account – will also increase by $4,000, balancing the two sides of the equation. If the company takes $8,000 from investors, its assets will increase by that amount, as will its shareholders' equity. All revenues the company generates in excess of its liabilities will go into the shareholders' equity account, representing the net assets held by the owners. These revenues will be balanced on the assets side, appearing as cash, investments, inventory, or some other asset.

Assets, liabilities and shareholders' equity are each comprised of several smaller accounts that break down the specifics of a company's finances. These accounts vary widely by industry, and the same terms can have different implications depending on the nature of the business. Broadly, however, there are a few common components investors are likely to come across.

Types

A balance sheet summarizes an organization or individual's assets, equity and liabilities at a specific point in time. Two forms of balance sheet exist. They are the report form and the account form. Individuals and small businesses tend to have simple balance sheets. Larger businesses tend to have more complex balance sheets, and these are presented in the organization's annual report. Large businesses also may prepare balance sheets for segments of their businesses. A balance sheet is often presented alongside one for a different point in time (typically the previous year) for comparison.

Personal

A personal balance sheet lists current assets such as cash in checking accounts and savings accounts, long-term assets such as common stock and real estate, current liabilities such as loan debt and mortgage debt due, or overdue, long-term liabilities such as mortgage and other loan debt. Securities and real estate values are listed at market value rather than at historical cost or cost basis. Personal net worth is the difference between an individual's total assets and total liabilities.

Us Small Business

Sample Small Business Balance Sheet				
Assets (current)		**Liabilities and Owners' Equity**		
Cash	$6,600	Liabilities		
Accounts Receivable	$6,200	Notes Payable	$5,000	
Assets (non-current)		Accounts Payable $25,000		
Tools and equipment	$25,000	*Total liabilities*		$30,000
		Owners' equity		
		Capital Stock	$7,000	
		Retained Earnings	$800	
		Total owners' equity		$7,800
Total	$37,800	*Total*		$37,800

A small business balance sheet lists current assets such as cash, accounts receivable, and inventory, fixed assets such as land, buildings, and equipment, intangible assets such as patents, and liabilities such as accounts payable, accrued expenses, and long-term debt. Contingent liabilities such as warranties are noted in the footnotes to the balance sheet. The small business's equity is the difference between total assets and total liabilities.

Public Business Entities Structure

Guidelines for balance sheets of public business entities are given by the International Accounting Standards Board and numerous country-specific organizations/ companies. The standard used by companies in the USA adhere to U.S. Generally Accepted Accounting Principles (GAAP). The Federal Accounting Standards Advisory Board (FASAB) is a United States federal advisory committee whose mission is to develop generally accepted accounting principles (GAAP) for federal financial reporting entities.

Balance sheet account names and usage depend on the organization's country and the type of organization. Government organizations do not generally follow standards established for individuals or businesses.

If applicable to the business, summary values for the following items should be included in the balance sheet: Assets are all the things the business owns. This will include property, tools, vehicles, furniture, machinery, and so on.

Assets

- Current assets
    1. Accounts receivable
    2. Cash and cash equivalents
    3. Inventories
    4. Cash at bank, Petty Cash, Cash On Hand
    5. Prepaid expenses for future services that will be used within a year
    6. Revenue Earned In Arrears (Accrued Revenue) for services done but not yet received for the year
    7. Loan To (Less than one financial period)
- Non-current Assets (Fixed assets)
    1. Property, plant and equipment
    2. Investment property, such as real estate held for investment purposes
    3. Intangible assets such as (patents, copyrights and goodwill)
    4. Financial assets (excluding investments accounted for using the equity method, accounts receivables, and cash and cash equivalents), such as notes receivables
    5. Investments accounted for using the equity method

6. Biological assets, which are living plants or animals. Bearer biological assets are plants or animals which bear agricultural produce for harvest, such as apple trees grown to produce apples and sheep raised to produce wool.
7. Loan To (More than one financial period).

Liabilities

1. Accounts payable
2. Provisions for warranties or court decisions (contingent liabilities that are both probable and measurable)
3. Financial liabilities (excluding provisions and accounts payables), such as promissory notes and corporate bonds
4. Liabilities and assets for current tax
5. Deferred tax liabilities and deferred tax assets
6. Unearned revenue for services paid for by customers but not yet provided
7. Interests on loan stock

Equity/Capital

The net assets shown by the balance sheet equals the third part of the balance sheet, which is known as the shareholders' equity. It comprises:

1. Issued capital and reserves attributable to equity holders of the parent company (controlling interest)
2. Non-controlling interest in equity

Formally, shareholders' equity is part of the company's liabilities: they are funds "owing" to shareholders (after payment of all other liabilities); usually, however, "liabilities" is used in the more restrictive sense of liabilities excluding shareholders' equity. The balance of assets and liabilities (including shareholders' equity) is not a coincidence. Records of the values of each account in the balance sheet are maintained using a system of accounting known as double-entry bookkeeping. In this sense, shareholders' equity by construction must equal assets minus liabilities, and thus the shareholders' equity is considered to be a residual.

Regarding the items in equity section, the following disclosures are required:

1. Numbers of shares authorized, issued and fully paid, and issued but not fully paid

2. Par value of shares
3. Reconciliation of shares outstanding at the beginning and the end of the period
4. Description of rights, preferences, and restrictions of shares
5. Treasury shares, including shares held by subsidiaries and associates
6. Shares reserved for issuance under options and contracts
7. A description of the nature and purpose of each reserve within owners' equity

Substantiation

Balance sheet substantiation is the accounting process conducted by businesses on a regular basis to confirm that the balances held in the primary accounting system of record (e.g. SAP, Oracle, other ERP system's General Ledger) are reconciled (in balance with) with the balance and transaction records held in the same or supporting sub-systems.

Balance sheet substantiation includes multiple processes including reconciliation (at a transactional or at a balance level) of the account, a process of review of the reconciliation and any pertinent supporting documentation and a formal certification (sign-off) of the account in a predetermined form driven by corporate policy.

Balance sheet substantiation is an important process that is typically carried out on a monthly, quarterly and year-end basis. The results help to drive the regulatory balance sheet reporting obligations of the organization.

Historically, balance sheet substantiation has been a wholly manual process, driven by spreadsheets, email and manual monitoring and reporting. In recent years software solutions have been developed to bring a level of process automation, standardization and enhanced control to the balance sheet substantiation or account certification process. These solutions are suitable for organizations with a high volume of accounts and/or personnel involved in the Balance Sheet Substantiation process and can be used to drive efficiencies, improve transparency and help to reduce risk.

Sample

The following balance sheet is a very brief example prepared in accordance with IFRS. It does not show all possible kinds of assets, liabilities and equity, but it shows the most usual ones. Because it shows goodwill, it could be a consolidated balance sheet. Monetary values are not shown, summary (subtotal) rows are missing as well.

Under IFRS items are always shown based on liquidity from the least liquid assets at the top, usually land and buildings to the most liquid, i.e. cash. Then liabilities and equity continue from the most immediate liability to be paid (usual account payable) to the least i.e. long term debt such a mortgages and owner's equity at the very bottom.

Consolidated Statement of Finance Position of XYZ, Ltd.

As of 31 December 2025

Assets

Non-Current Assets (Fixed Assets)

Property, Plant and Equipment (PPE)

Less : Accumulated Depreciation

Goodwill

Intangible Assets (Patent, Copyright, Trademark, etc.)

Less : Accumulated Amortization

Investments in Financial assets due after one year

Investments in Associates and Joint Ventures

Other Non-Current Assets, e.g. Deferred Tax Assets, Lease Receivable and Receivables due after one year

Current Assets

Inventories

Prepaid Expenses

Investments in Financial assets due within one year

Non-Current and Current Assets Held for sale

Accounts Receivable (Debtors) due within one year

Less : Allowances for Doubtful debts

Cash and Cash Equivalents

Total Assets (this will Match/Balance the total for Liabilities and Equity below)

Liabilities and Equity

Current Liabilities (Creditors: amounts falling due within one year)

Accounts Payable

Current Income Tax Payable

Current portion of Loans Payable

Short-term Provisions

Other Current Liabilities, e.g. Deferred income, Security deposits

Non-Current Liabilities (Creditors: Amounts Falling due after more than One Year)

Loans Payable

Issued Debt Securities, e.g. Notes/Bonds Payable

Deferred Tax Liabilities

Provisions, e.g. Pension Obligations

Other Non-Current Liabilities, e.g. Lease Obligations

Equity

Paid-in Capital

Share Capital (Ordinary Shares, Preference Shares)

Share Premium

Less: Treasury Shares

Retained Earnings

Revaluation Reserve

Other Accumulated Reserves

Accumulated Other Comprehensive Income

Non-Controlling Interest

Total Liabilities and Equity (this will Match/Balance the Total for Assets Above)

Accounts Payable

Accounts payable (AP) is an accounting entry that represents a company's obligation to pay off a short-term debt to its creditors or suppliers. It appears on the balance sheet under the current liabilities. Another common usage of AP refers to a business department or division that is responsible for making payments owed by the company to suppliers and other creditors.

Accounts payable are debits that must be paid off within a given period to avoid default. For example, at the corporate level, AP refers to short-term debt payments to suppliers. The payable is essentially a short-term IOU from the business to another business or entity.

Record Accounts Payable

To record accounts payable, the accountant or bookkeeper credits the accounts payable account when they get the bill or invoice. Then, when they pay the bill, they debit accounts payable.

For example, imagine a business gets a $500 invoice for office supplies. When the AP department receives the invoice, it records a $500 debit in the accounts payable field and a $500 credit to office supply expense. As a result, if anyone looks at the balance in the accounts payable category, they will see the total amount the business owes all of its vendors and short-term lenders. The company then writes a check to pay the bill, so the accountant enters a $500 debit to the checking account and enters a credit for $500 in the accounts payable column.

Accounts Payable and Long-Term Debts

Accounts payable are a type of short-term debt. Other short-term business debts include expenses such as payroll costs, business income taxes, and short-term loans. In contrast, long-term debts include lease payments, retirement benefits, individual notes payable and a range of other debts repaid over a long term.

Accounts Payable vs. Trade Payables

While some people use the phrases accounts payable and trade payables interchangeably, the phrases refer to similar but slightly different things. Trade payables constitute the money a company owes the vendors for inventory-related goods, such as business supplies or materials that are part of the inventory. Accounts payable include all the short-term debts or obligations.

For example, if a restaurant owes money to a food or beverage company, those items are part of the inventory, and thus part of its trade payables. Meanwhile, obligations to other companies, such as the company that cleans the restaurant staff uniforms, falls into the accounts payable category. Some accounting methods roll both of these categories into the accounts payable category.

Internal Controls

A variety of checks against abuse are usually present to prevent embezzlement by accounts payable personnel. Segregation of duties is a common control. Nearly all companies have a junior employee process and print a cheque and a senior employee review and sign the cheque. Often, the accounting software will limit each employee to performing only the functions assigned to them, so that there is no way any one employee – even the controller – can singlehandedly make a payment.

Some companies also separate the functions of adding new vendors and entering vouchers. This makes it impossible for an employee to add himself as a vendor and then cut a cheque to himself without colluding with another employee. This file is referred to as the master vendor file. It is the repository of all significant information about the company's suppliers. It is the reference point for accounts payable when it comes to paying invoices.

In addition, most companies require a second signature on cheques whose amount exceeds a specified threshold.

Accounts payable personnel must watch for fraudulent invoices. In the absence of a purchase order system, the first line of defense is the approving manager. However, AP staff should become familiar with a few common problems, such as "Yellow Pages" ripoffs in which fraudulent operators offer to place an advertisement. The walking-fingers logo has never been trademarked, and there are many different Yellow Pages-style directories, most of which have a small distribution. According to an article in the Winter 2000 American Payroll Association's *Employer Practices*, "Vendors may send documents that look like invoices but in small print they state "this is not a bill." These may be charges for directory listings or advertisements. Recently, some companies have begun sending what appears to be a rebate or refund check; in reality, it is a registration for services that is activated when the document is returned with a signature."

In accounts payable, a simple mistake can cause a large overpayment. A common example involves duplicate invoices. An invoice may be temporarily misplaced or still in the approval status when the vendors calls to inquire into its payment status. After the AP staff member looks it up and finds it has not been paid, the vendor sends a duplicate invoice; meanwhile the original invoice shows up and gets paid. Then the duplicate invoice arrives and inadvertently gets paid as well, perhaps under a slightly different invoice.

Audits of accounts payable

Auditors often focus on the existence of approved invoices, expense reports, and other supporting documentation to support cheques that were cut. The presence of a confirmation or statement from the supplier is reasonable proof of the existence of the account. It is not uncommon for some of this documentation to be lost or misfiled by the time the audit rolls around. An auditor may decide to expand the sample size in such situations.

Auditors typically prepare an aging structure of accounts payable for a better understanding of outstanding debts over certain periods (30, 60, 90 days, etc.). Such structures are helpful in the correct presentation of the balance sheet as of fiscal year end.

Automation

Accounts payable automation or AP automation is a term used to describe the ongoing effort of many companies to streamline the business process of their accounts payable departments. The accounts payable department's main responsibility is to process and review transactions between the company and its suppliers. In other words, it is the accounts payable department's job to make sure all outstanding invoices from their suppliers are approved, processed, and paid. Processing an invoice includes recording important data from the invoice and inputting it into the company's financial, or bookkeeping, system. After this is accomplished, the invoices must go through the company's respective business process in order to be paid.

4 key points on accounts payable workflow essentials:

- Invoice entry and sequential categorization
- Invoice routing dispatch and appropriate approval
- Invoice data capture and validation step
- Invoice accurate matching and verification procedure

This process is straightforward but can become very cumbersome, especially if the company has a very large number of invoices. This problem is compounded when invoices that require processing are on paper. This can lead to lost invoices, human error during data entry, and invoice duplicates. These and other problems lead to a high cost per invoice metric. The goal of automating the accounts payable department is to streamline this invoicing process, eliminate potential human error, and lower the cost per invoice

Some of the most common AP automation solutions include E-invoicing, scanning and workflow, online tracking, reporting capabilities, electronic invoice user interfaces, supplier networks, payment services and spend analytics for all invoices.

Electronic Invoicing can be a very useful tool for the AP department. Electronic invoicing allows vendors to submit invoices over the internet and have those invoices automatically routed and processed. Because invoice arrival and presentation is almost immediate invoices are paid sooner; therefore, the amount of time and money it takes to process these invoices is greatly reduced. (Financial Operations Networks, 2008) These solutions usually involve a third party company that provides and supports an application which allows a supplier to submit an electronic invoice to their customer for immediate routing, approval, and payment. These applications are tied to databases which archive transaction information between trading partners. (US Bank, Scott Hesse, 2010) The invoices may be submitted in a number of ways, including EDI, CSV, or XML uploads. PDF files, or online invoice templates. Because E-invoicing includes so many different technologies and entry options, it is used as an umbrella term to describe any method by which an invoice is electronically presented to a customer for payment.

Accounts Receivable

Accounts receivable is the balance of money due to a firm for goods or services delivered or used but not yet paid for by customers. Said another way, account receivable are amounts of money owed by customers to another entity for goods or services delivered or used on credit but not yet paid for by clients.

Accounts receivable refers to the outstanding invoices a company has or the money clients owe the company. The phrase refers to accounts a business has a right to receive because it has delivered a product or service. Accounts receivable, or receivables represent a line of credit extended by a company and normally have terms that require payments due within a relatively short time period, ranging from a few days to a fiscal or calendar year.

Companies record accounts receivable as assets on their balance sheets since there is a legal obligation for the customer to pay the debt. Furthermore, accounts receivable are current assets, meaning the account balance is due from the debtor in one year or less. If a company has receivables, this means it has made a sale on credit but has yet to collect the money from the purchaser. Essentially, the company has accepted a short-term IOU from its client.

How Businesses have Accounts Receivable

Most companies operate by allowing a portion of their sales to be on credit. Sometimes, businesses offer this credit to frequent or special customers receive periodic invoices. The practice allows customers to avoid the hassle of physically making payments as each transaction occurs. In other cases, businesses routinely offer all of their clients the ability to pay after receiving the service. For example, electric companies typically bill their clients after the clients received the electricity. While the electricity company waits for its customers to pay their bills, the company considers unpaid invoices a part of its accounts receivable.

Importance of Accounts Receivable

Accounts receivable is an important aspect of a businesses' fundamental analysis. Accounts receivables are current assets so they are a measure of a company's liquidity or ability to cover short-term obligations without additional cash flows. Fundamental analysts often evaluate accounts receivable in the context of turnover, which they call accounts receivable turnover ratio, which measures the number of times a company has collected on its accounts receivable balance during an accounting period. Further analysis would include days sales outstanding analysis, which measures the average collection period for a firm's receivables balance over a specified period.

Payment Terms

An example of a common payment term is Net 30 days, which means that payment is due at the end of 30 days from the date of invoice. The debtor is free to pay before the due date; businesses can offer a discount for early payment. Other common payment terms include Net 45, Net 60 and 30 days end of month. The creditor may be able to charge late fees or interest if the amount is not paid by the due date.

Booking a receivable is accomplished by a simple accounting transaction; however, the process of maintaining and collecting payments on the accounts receivable subsidiary account balances can be a full-time proposition. Depending on the industry in practice, accounts receivable payments can be received up to 10 – 15 days after the due date has been reached. These types of payment practices are sometimes developed by industry standards, corporate policy, or because of the financial condition of the client.

Since not all customer debts will be collected, businesses typically estimate the amount of and then record an allowance for doubtful accounts which appears on the balance sheet as a contra account that offsets total accounts receivable. When accounts receivable are not paid, some companies turn them over to third party collection agencies or collection attorneys who will attempt to recover the debt via negotiating payment plans, settlement offers or pursuing other legal action.

Outstanding advances are part of accounts receivable if a company gets an order from its customers with payment terms agreed upon in advance. Since billing is done to claim the advances several times, this area of collectible is not reflected in accounts receivables. Ideally, since advance payment occurs within a mutually agreed-upon term, it is the responsibility of the accounts department to periodically take out the statement showing advance collectible and should be provided to sales & marketing for collection of advances. The payment of accounts receivable can be protected either by a letter of credit or by Trade Credit Insurance.

Accounts Receivable Age Analysis

An Accountants Receivable Age Analysis, also known as the Debtors Book is divided in categories for current, 30 days, 60 days, 90 days or longer. The analysis or report is commonly known as an Aged Trial Balance. Customers are typically listed in alphabetic order or by the amount outstanding, or according to the company chart of accounts. Zero balances are not usually shown.

Bookkeeping

On a company's balance sheet, accounts receivable are the money owed to that company by entities outside of the company. Account receivables are classified as current assets assuming that they are due within one calendar year or fiscal year. To record a journal entry for a sale on account, one must debit a receivable and credit a revenue account. When the customer pays off their accounts, one debits cash and credits the receivable in the journal entry. The ending balance on the trial balance sheet for accounts receivable is usually a debit.

Business organizations which have become too large to perform such tasks by hand (or small ones that could but prefer not to do them by hand) will generally use accounting software on a computer to perform this task.

Companies have two methods available to them for measuring the net value of accounts receivable, which is generally computed by subtracting the balance of an allowance account from the accounts receivable account.

The first method is the allowance method, which establishes a contra-asset account, *allowance for doubtful accounts*, or *bad debt provision*, that has the effect of reducing the balance for accounts receivable. The amount of the bad debt provision can be computed in two ways, either (1) by reviewing each individual debt and deciding whether it is doubtful (a specific provision); or (2) by providing for a fixed percentage (e.g. 2%) of total debtors (a general provision). The change in the bad debt provision from year to year is posted to the bad debt expense account in the income statement.

The second method is the *direct write-off method*. It is simpler than the allowance method in that it allows for one simple entry to reduce accounts receivable to its net realizable value. The entry would consist of debiting a bad debt expense account and crediting the respective accounts receivable in the sales ledger.

The two methods are not mutually exclusive, and some businesses will have a provision for doubtful debts, writing off specific debts that they know to be bad (for example, if the debtor has gone into liquidation).

Special uses

Companies can use their accounts receivable as collateral when obtaining a loan (asset-based lending). They may also sell them through factoring or on an exchange. Pools or portfolios of accounts receivable can be sold in capital markets through securitization.

For tax reporting purposes, a general provision for bad debts is not an allowable deduction from profit - a business can only get relief for specific debtors that have gone bad. However, for financial reporting purposes, companies may choose to have a general provision against bad debts consistent with their past experience of customer payments, in order to avoid over-stating debtors in the balance sheet.

Cost of Receivables

1. Cost of financing :

The credit sales delays the time of sales realization & therefore the time gap between incurring the cost & the sales realization is extended . This results in blocking of funds for a longer period. The firm on the other hand , has to arrange funds to meet its own obligations towards payment to the supplier, employees etc., These funds are to be procured at some explicit or implicit cost . This is known as cost of financing the receivables.

2. Administrative cost:

A firm will also required to incur various costs in order to maintain the record of credit customers both before the credit sales as well as after the credit sales

3. Delinquency Cost :

The firm have to incur additional costs known as delinquency costs, if there is delay in the payment by a customer. The firm may have to incur cost on reminders, phone calls, postages, legal notices etc. There is always an opportunity cost of the funds tied up in the receivables due to delay in payment.

4. Cost of default by the Customer:

If there is a default by the customer & the receivables becomes partly or wholly, unrealizable , then this amount is known as bad debt, also becomes cost to the firm. This cost does not appear in case of sales.

Benefits of Receivables

1. Increase in sales:

Most of the firms sell goods on credit, either because of trade customs or other conditions. The sales can be further increased by liberalizing the credit terms. This will attract more customers to the firm resulting in higher sales & growth of the firm.

2. Increase in profits:

Increase in sales help the firm in

a) to easily recover the fixed expenses & attaining the break-even level.

b) Increase the operating profit of the firm.

3. Extra profit:

Sometimes, the firm makes the credit sales higher than the usual cash selling price. This brings an opportunity to the firm to make extra profit over & above the normal profit.

Difference Between Accounts Receivables and Accounts Payable

When a company owes debts to its suppliers or other parties, these are accounts payable. Accounts payable are the opposite of accounts receivable. To illustrate, imagine Company A cleans Company B's carpets and sends a bill for the services. Company B owes the money, so it records the invoice in its accounts payable column. Company A is waiting to receive the money, so it records the bill in its accounts receivable column.

Income Statement

An income statement is a financial statement that reports a company's financial performance over a specific accounting period. Financial performance is assessed by giving a summary of how the business incurs its revenues and expenses through both operating and non-operating activities. It also shows the net profit or loss incurred over a specific accounting period.

Also known as the profit and loss statement or statement of revenue and expense, the income statement is one of three major financial statements in the annual report and 10-K. All public companies must submit these legal documents to the Securities and Exchange Commission (SEC) and investor public. The other two financial statements are the balance sheet and the statement of cash flows. All three provide investors with information about the state of the company's financial affairs, but the income statement is the only one that provides an overview of company sales and net income.

Income Statement

Unlike the balance sheet, which covers one moment in time, the income statement provides performance information about a time period. It begins with sales and works down to net income and earnings per share (EPS).

The income statement is divided into two parts: operating and non-operating. The operating portion of the income statement discloses information about revenues and expenses that are a direct result of regular business operations. For example, if a business creates sports equipment, it should make money through the sale and/or production of sports equipment. The non-operating section discloses revenue and expense information about activities that are not directly tied to a company's regular operations.

Continuing with the same example, if the sports company sells real estate and investment securities, the gain from the sale is listed in the non-operating items section.

Usefulness and Limitations of Income Statement

Income statements should help investors and creditors determine the past financial performance of the enterprise, predict future performance, and assess the capability of generating future cash flows through report of the income and expenses.

However, information of an income statement has several limitations:

- Items that might be relevant but cannot be reliably measured are not reported (*e.g.*, brand recognition and loyalty).
- Some numbers depend on accounting methods used (*e.g.*, using FIFO or LIFO accounting to measure inventory level).
- Some numbers depend on judgments and estimates (*e.g.*, depreciation expense depends on estimated useful life and salvage value).

-INCOME STATEMENT GREENHARBOR LLC -
For the year ended DECEMBER 31 2010

	€ Debit	€ Credit
Revenues		
GROSS REVENUES (including INTEREST income)		296,397

Expenses:		
ADVERTISING	6,300	
BANK & CREDIT CARD FEES	144	
BOOKKEEPING	2,350	
SUBCONTRACTORS	88,000	
ENTERTAINMENT	5,550	
INSURANCE	750	
LEGAL & PROFESSIONAL SERVICES	1,575	
LICENSES	632	
PRINTING, POSTAGE & STATIONERY	320	
RENT	13,000	
MATERIALS	74,400	

TELEPHONE	1,000	
UTILITIES	1,491	

TOTAL EXPENSES		(195,512)

NET INCOME		100,885

Guidelines for statements of comprehensive income and income statements of business entities are formulated by the International Accounting Standards Board and numerous country-specific organizations, for example the FASB in the U.S..

Names and usage of different accounts in the income statement depend on the type of organization, industry practices and the requirements of different jurisdictions.

If applicable to the business, summary values for the following items should be included in the income statement:

Operating Section

- Revenue - Cash inflows or other enhancements of assets (including accounts receivable) of an entity during a period from delivering or producing goods, rendering services, or other activities that constitute the entity's ongoing major operations. It is usually presented as sales minus sales discounts, returns, and allowances. Every time a business sells a product or performs a service, it obtains revenue. This often is referred to as gross revenue or sales revenue.
- Expenses - Cash outflows or other using-up of assets or incurrence of liabilities (including accounts payable) during a period from delivering or producing goods, rendering services, or carrying out other activities that constitute the entity's ongoing major operations.
    - Cost of Goods Sold (COGS) / Cost of Sales - represents the direct costs attributable to goods produced and sold by a business (manufacturing or merchandizing). It includes *material costs, direct labour*, and *overhead costs* (as in absorption costing), and excludes operating costs (period costs) such as selling, administrative, advertising or R&D, etc.
    - Selling, General and Administrative expenses (SG&A or SGA) - consist of the combined payroll costs. SGA is usually understood as a major portion of non-production related costs, in contrast to production costs such as direct labour.
        - Selling expenses - represent expenses needed to sell products (e.g., *salaries of sales people, commissions and travel expenses, advertising, freight, shipping, depreciation of sales store buildings and equipment*, etc.).

- ◇ General and Administrative (G&A) expenses - represent expenses to manage the business *(salaries of officers / executives, legal and professional fees, utilities, insurance, depreciation of office building and equipment, office rents, office supplies,* etc.).

- o Depreciation / Amortization - the charge with respect to fixed assets / intangible assets that have been capitalised on the balance sheet for a specific (accounting) period. It is a systematic and rational allocation of cost rather than the recognition of market value decrement.

- o Research & Development (R&D) expenses - represent expenses included in research and development.

Expenses recognised in the income statement should be analysed either by nature (raw materials, transport costs, staffing costs, depreciation, employee benefit etc.) or by function (cost of sales, selling, administrative, etc.). (IAS 1.99) If an entity categorises by function, then additional information on the nature of expenses, at least, – depreciation, amortisation and employee benefits expense – must be disclosed. (IAS 1.104) The major exclusive of costs of goods sold, are classified as operating expenses. These represent the resources expended, except for inventory purchases, in generating the revenue for the period. Expenses often are divided into two broad sub classicifications selling expenses and administrative expenses.

Non-Operating Section

- Other revenues or gains - revenues and gains from other than primary business activities (e.g., *rent, income from patents*, goodwill). It also includes unusual gains that are either unusual or infrequent, but not both (e.g., *gain from sale of securities or gain from disposal of fixed assets*).
- Other expenses or losses - expenses or losses not related to primary business operations, (e.g., *foreign exchange loss*).
- Finance costs - costs of borrowing from various creditors (e.g., *interest expenses, bank charges*).
- Income tax expense - sum of the amount of tax payable to tax authorities in the current reporting period (current tax liabilities/ tax payable) and the amount of deferred tax liabilities (or assets).

Irregular Items

They are reported separately because this way users can better predict future cash flows - irregular items most likely will not recur. These are reported *net of taxes*.

- Discontinued operations is the most common type of irregular items. Shifting business location(s), stopping production temporarily, or changes due to technological improvement do not qualify as discontinued operations. Discontinued operations *must* be shown separately.

Cumulative effect of changes in accounting policies (principles) is the difference between the book value of the affected assets (or liabilities) under the old policy (principle) and what the book value would have been if the new principle had been applied in the prior periods. For example, valuation of inventories using LIFO instead of weighted average method. The changes should be applied retrospectively and shown as adjustments to the *beginning* balance of affected components in Equity. All comparative financial statements should be restated. (IAS 8)

However, *changes in estimates* (e.g., estimated useful life of a fixed asset) only requires prospective changes. (IAS 8)

No items may be presented in the income statement as extraordinary items under IFRS regulations, but are permissible under US GAAP. (IAS 1.87) *Extraordinary* items are both unusual (abnormal) and infrequent, for example, unexpected natural disaster, expropriation, prohibitions under new regulations. [Note: natural disaster might not qualify depending on location (e.g., frost damage would not qualify in Canada but would in the tropics).]

Additional items may be needed to fairly present the entity's results of operations. (IAS 1.85)

Disclosures

Certain items must be disclosed separately in the notes (or the statement of comprehensive income), if material, including: (IAS 1.98)

- Write-downs of inventories to net realisable value or of property, plant and equipment to recoverable amount, as well as *reversals* of such write-downs
- Restructurings of the activities of an entity and *reversals* of any provisions for the costs of restructuring
- Disposals of items of property, plant and equipment
- Disposals of investments
- Discontinued operations
- Litigation settlements
- Other reversals of provisions

Earnings Per Share

Because of its importance, earnings per share (EPS) are required to be disclosed on the face of the income statement. A company which reports any of the irregular items must also report EPS for these items either in the statement or in the notes.

$$\text{Earnings per share} = \frac{\text{Net income- Preferred stock dividends}}{\text{Weighted average of common stock shares outstanding}}$$

There are two forms of EPS reported:

- Basic: in this case "weighted average of shares outstanding" includes only actual stocks outstanding.
- Diluted: in this case "weighted average of shares outstanding" is calculated as if all stock options, warrants, convertible bonds, and other securities that could be transformed into shares *are* transformed. This increases the number of shares and so EPS decreases. Diluted EPS is considered to be a more reliable way to measure EPS.

Sample Income Statement

The following income statement is a very brief example prepared in accordance with IFRS. It does not show all possible kinds of accounts, but it shows the most usual ones. Please note the difference between IFRS and US GAAP when interpreting the following sample income statements.

Fitness Equipment Limited

Income Statements
(in millions)

Year Ended March 31,	2009	2008	2007
Revenue	$14,580.2	$11,900.4	$8,290.3
Cost of sales	(6,740.2)	(5,650.1)	(4,524.2)
Gross profit	*7,840.0*	*6,250.3*	*3,766.1*
SGA expenses	(3,624.6)	(3,296.3)	(3,034.0)
Operating profit	*$ 4,215.4*	*$ 2,954.0*	*$ 732.1*
Gains from disposal of fixed assets	46.3	-	-
Interest expense	(119.7)	(124.1)	(142.8)
Profit *before* tax	4,142.0	2,829.9	589.3
Income tax expense	(1,656.8)	(1,132.0)	(235.7)
Profit (or loss) for the year	*$ 2,485.2*	*$ 1,697.9*	*$ 353.6*

Dexterity Inc. and Subsidiaries

Consolidated Statements of Operations
(In millions)

Year Ended December 31,	2009	2008	2007
Revenue	$36,525.9	$29,827.6	$21,186.8
Cost of sales	(18,545.8)	(15,858.8)	(11,745.5)
Gross profit	*17,980.1*	*13,968.8*	*9,441.3*
Operating expenses:			
Selling, general and administrative expenses	(4,142.1)	(3,732.3)	(3,498.6)
Depreciation	(602.4)	(584.5)	(562.3)
Amortization	(209.9)	(141.9)	(111.8)
Impairment loss	(17,997.1)	—	—
Total operating expenses	(22,951.5)	(4,458.7)	(4,172.7)
Operating profit (or loss)	*$ (4,971.4)*	*$ 9,510.1*	*$ 5,268.6*
Interest income	25.3	11.7	12.0
Interest expense	(718.9)	(742.9)	(799.1)
Profit (or loss) from continuing operations *before* tax, share of profit (or loss) from associates and non-controlling interest	$ (5,665.0)	$ 8,778.9	$ 4,481.5
Income tax expense	(1,678.6)	(3,510.5)	(1,789.9)
Profit (or loss) from associates, *net of tax*	(20.8)	0.1	(37.3)
Profit (or loss) from non-controlling interest, *net of tax*	(5.1)	(4.7)	(3.3)
Profit (or loss) from continuing operations	$ (3960.5)	$ 5,263.8	$ 2,651.0
Profit (or loss) from discontinued operations, *net of tax*	(1,090.3)	(802.4)	164.6
Profit (or loss) for the year	*$ (2,870.2)*	*$ 4,461.4*	*$ 2,486.4*

Bottom Line

"Bottom line" is the net income that is calculated after subtracting the expenses from revenue. Since this forms the last line of the income statement, it is informally called "bottom line." It is important to investors as it represents the profit for the year attributable to the shareholders.

After revision to IAS 1 in 2003, the Standard is now using profit or loss for the year rather than *net profit or loss or net income* as the descriptive term for the bottom line of the income statement.

Requirements of IFRS

On 6 September 2007, the International Accounting Standards Board issued a revised *IAS 1: Presentation of Financial Statements*, which is effective for annual periods beginning on or after 1 January 2009.

A business entity adopting IFRS must include:

- a statement of comprehensive income or
- *two* separate statements comprising:
    1. an income statement displaying components of profit or loss and
    2. a *statement of comprehensive income* that *begins* with profit or loss (bottom line of the income statement) and displays the items of other comprehensive income for the reporting period. (IAS1.81)

All non-owner changes in equity (i.e., *comprehensive income*) shall be presented in either in the statement of comprehensive income (or in a separate income statement and a statement of comprehensive income). Components of comprehensive income may not be presented in the statement of changes in equity.

Comprehensive income for a period includes profit or loss (net income) for that period and other comprehensive income recognised in that period.

All items of income and expense recognised in a period must be included in profit or loss unless a Standard or an Interpretation requires otherwise. (IAS 1.88) Some IFRSs require or permit that some components to be excluded from profit or loss and instead to be included in other comprehensive income. (IAS 1.89)

Items and Disclosures

The statement of comprehensive income should include: (IAS 1.82)

1. Revenue
2. Finance costs (including interest expenses)
3. Share of the profit or loss of associates and joint ventures accounted for using the equity method

4. Tax expense
5. A *single* amount comprising the total of (1) the *post-tax* profit or loss of *discontinued operations* and (2) the *post-tax* gain or loss recognised on the disposal of the assets or disposal group(s) constituting the *discontinued operation*
6. Profit or loss
7. Each component of other comprehensive income classified by nature
8. Share of the other comprehensive income of associates and joint ventures accounted for using the equity method
9. Total comprehensive income

The following items must also be disclosed in the statement of comprehensive income as allocations for the period: (IAS 1.83)

- Profit or loss for the period attributable to non-controlling interests and owners of the parent
- Total comprehensive income attributable to non-controlling interests and owners of the parent

No items may be presented in the statement of comprehensive income (or in the income statement, if separately presented) or in the notes as *extraordinary items.*

Trading Statement

A trading statement is similar to an income statement. It is a statement showing activity from a trading account, which is an account used to make trades in the stock market. A trading account is also called a profit-and-loss account and is used to find the net profit or net loss of stock trades. A trading statement takes into account all income or gains made and all expenses or losses incurred.

A trading statement is an announcement that has limited, but sometimes very important, disclosure. The essential part of a trading statement is some sort of update on a company's revenues: for example sales numbers and sales trends. In addition it is not uncommon for companies to reveal some other performance indicators, but, even then, it would not be usual to reveal any profit numbers: unless a surprise requires that the market be given a profit warning.

Trading statements allow analysts and investors to refine, and sometimes drastically revise, forecasts and valuations. Apart from total sales, other information, such as changes in the sales mix may change estimates of margins, and of growth prospects.

Trading statements are often issued as the last announcement to the market before the start of a close period. This allows the market to be reasonably up to date until the results announced at the end of the close period.

Ideally, trading statements should be generated monthly so that you can quickly identify and address any unusual trends. Trends towards a loss should be identified before the financial position becomes difficult.

Gross Profit

Gross profit is the difference between the total amount of money received — sales income — less the amount that was paid out to purchase those goods — cost of goods sold.

Gross profit objectives and mark-ups should be decided by the P&C. Base your decision on whether you want high profits or whether you want to provide an inexpensive service to students for items such as lunches and uniforms.

A low gross profit percentage indicates one or more of the following:

- prices are too low
- stock is being lost or wasted.
- Giveaways are too high
- Loss of money or stock due to theft

The Concept of Gross Profit

A key concept to understand is that gross profit (%) and the mark-up (%) on an item are different.

Gross profit is calculated from the sale price whereas the mark-up is calculated from the cost price.

If an item is marked up by 33 1/3 per cent, the gross profit is 25 per cent. This is demonstrated in the following example. Look at the worked example for details of this calculation.

Calculating gross and Net Profit for a Trading Activity

Look at the value of the gross profit for a period of sales.

Calculating gross and net profit for a trading activity				
Net sales income				$17 809.13
Less cost of goods sold				
	Opening stock	$5 000.00		
	Plus purchases	$9 300.00	$14 300.00	
	Less closing stock		$942.87	
		Cost of goods sold		$13 357.13
Gross profit				$4 452.00

This trading activity has generated a gross profit of 25 per cent. The calculated profit being:

($4 452.00 / $17 809.13) x 100 = 25 per cent

Cost of goods sold

The cost of goods sold needs to be calculated so that your gross profit can be determined. The cost of goods sold is calculated as follows:

Opening stock (saleable items on hand at start of period valued at cost)

plus Purchases (the total value of items purchased for resale during the period)

less Closing stock (saleable items on hand at end of period valued at cost)

The answer to this calculation equals cost of goods sold (the cost of saleable items sold during the period).

Net Profit

Your P&C will need to be aware of the net profit generated by a trading activity because this is the best indicator of whether an activity is worth continuing. If the net profit is small then your efforts may be better directed toward other activities. A small net profit can also highlight the need to increase profit margins or confirm that the service is very close to cost neutral.

You calculate net profit by deducting from gross profit the operating expenses such as cleaning, wages, paper bags and other items that do not affect the cost of goods sold.

The net profit generated by this trading activity is $1 597.86. This trading statement forms part of the annual financial statements.

Cash Flow Statement

The Statement of Cash Flows (also referred to as the cash flow statement) is one of the three key financial statements that reports the cash generated and spent during a specific period of time (i.e., a month, quarter, or year). The statement of cash flows acts as a bridge between the income statement and balance sheet by showing how money moved in and out of the business.

Three main sections of Statement of Cash Flows:

1. Operating Activities: The principal revenue-generating activities of an

organization and other activities that are not investing or financing; any cash flows from current assets and current liabilities.

2. Investing Activities: Any cash flows from the acquisition and disposal of long-term assets and other investments not included in cash equivalents.

3. Financing Activities: Any cash flows that result in changes in the size and composition of the contributed equity or borrowings of the entity (i.e., bonds, stock, cash dividends).

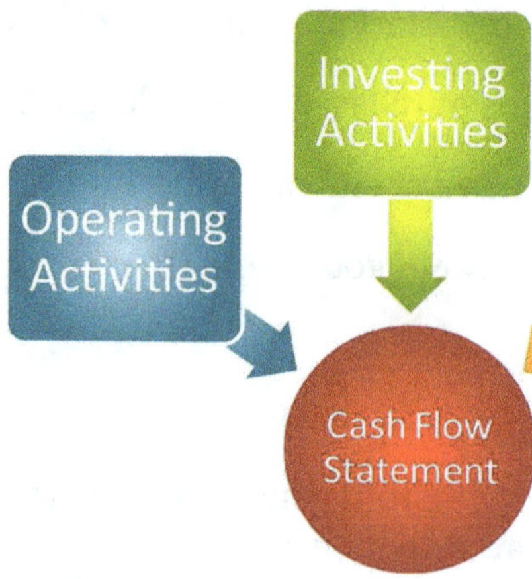

Cash Flow Definitions

Cash flows: Inflows and outflows of cash and cash equivalents.

Cash: Cash on hand and demand deposits (cash balance on the balance sheet).

Cash equivalents: Cash equivalents include cash held as bank deposits, short-term investments, and any very easily cash-convertible assets – includes overdrafts and cash equivalents with short-term maturities (less than three months).

Cash flow classification

1. Operating cash flow

Operating activities are the principal revenue-producing activities of the entity. Operating cash flows typically include the cash flows associated with sales, purchases, and other expenses.

The company's chief finance officer chooses between the direct and indirect presentation of operating cash flow:

- Direct presentation: Operating cash flows are presented as a list of cash flows; cash in from sales, cash out for purchases, etc. Simple but rarely used method, as the indirect presentation is more common.

- Indirect presentation: Operating cash flows are presented as a reconciliation from profit to cash flow:

Profit	P
Depreciation	D
Amortization	A
Impairment expense	I
Change in working capital	ΔWC
Change in provisions	ΔP
Interest Tax	(I)
Tax	(T)
Operating cash flow	OCF

The items in the cash flow statements are not cash flows but "reasons why cash flow is different from profit."

Depreciation expense reduces profit but does not impact cash flow. Hence, it is added back. Similarly, if the starting point profit is above interest and tax in the income statement, then interest and tax cash flows will need to be deducted if they are to be treated as operating cash flows.

There is no specific guidance on which the profit amount should be used in the reconciliation. Different companies use operating profit, profit before tax, profit after tax, or net income. Clearly, the exact starting point for the reconciliation will determine the exact adjustments made to get down to an operating cash flow number.

2. Investing cash flow

Investing activities are the acquisition and disposal of non-current assets and other investments not included in cash equivalents. Investing cash flows typically include the cash flows associated with buying or selling property, plant, and equiipment (PP&E), other non-current assets, and other financial assets.

Cash spent on purchasing PP&E is called capital expenditures (or CapEx for short).

3. Financing cash flow

Financing activities are activities that result in changes in the size and composition of the equity capital or borrowings of the entity. Financing cash flows typically include cash flows associated with borrowing and repaying bank loans, and issuing and buying back shares. The payment of a dividend is also treated as a financing cash flow.

Interest and Cash Flow

Under IFRS, there are two ways of presenting interest in the cash flow statement. Many companies present both the interest received and interest paid as operating cash flows. Others treat interest received as an investing cash flow and interest paid as a financing cash flow. The method used is the choice of the finance director.

Under U.S. GAAP, interest paid and received are always treated as operating cash flows.

Free Cash Flow

Bankers use different cash flow measures for different purposes. Free cash flow is a common measure used typically for DCF valuation. However, free cash flow has no definitive definition and can be calculated and used in different ways.

Ways to Prepare a Statement of Cash Flows

The operating section of the statement of cash flows can be shown through either the direct method or the indirect method. For either method, the investing and financing sections are identical; the only difference is in the operating section. The direct method is a method that shows the major classes of gross cash receipts and gross cash payments. The indirect method, on the other hand, starts with the net income and adjusts the profit/loss by the effects of the transactions. In the end, cash flows from the operating section will give the same result whether under the direct or indirect approach, however, the presentation will differ.

The International Accounting Standards Board (IASB) favors the direct method of reporting because it provides more useful information that the indirect method. However, it is believed that greater than 90% of companies use the indirect method.

Direct method vs Indirect method of presentation

There are two methods of producing a statement of cash flows, the direct method, and the indirect method.

In the direct method, all individual instances of cash being received or paid out are tallied up and the total is the resulting cash flow.

In the indirect method, the accounting line items such as net income, depreciation, etc. are used to arrive at cash flow. In financial modeling, the cash flow statement is always produced via the indirect method.

Below is a comparison of the direct method vs the indirect method.

Direct Method:

Operating Activities	
Cash received from customers	$800
Cash paid to suppliers	(150)
Employee compensations	(200)
Other operating expenses paid	(250)
Net cash from operating activities	200
Investing Activities	
Sale of land	200
Purchase of equipment	(300)
Net cash from investing activities	(100)
Financing Activities	
Common share dividends	(200)
Payment on long-term debt	(300)
Net cash from financing activities	(500)
Beginning Cash Balance	X
Ending Cash Balance	Y

Indirect Method:

Operating Activities		
Net Income		$50,000
Add: Depreciation expense	$10,000	
Decrease in AR	$2,000	
Increase in inventory	$3,000	
Decrease in prepaid expense	$4,000	
Increase in accounts payable	$5,000	
Net Cash provided by operating activities		$XXX
Investing Activities		
Sale of land	200	
Purchase of equipment	(300)	
Net cash from investing activities	(100)	
Financing Activities		
Common share dividends	(200)	
Payment on long-term debt	(300)	
Net cash from financing activities	(500)	
Beginning Cash Balance		X
Ending Cash Balance		Y

What can the Statement of Cash Flows Tell Us?

- Cash from operating activities can be compared to the company's net income to determine the quality of earnings. If cash from operating activities is higher than net income, earnings are said to be of "high quality."

- This statement is useful to investors because, under the notion that cash is king, it allows investors to get an overall sense of the company's cash inflows and outflows and obtain a general understanding of its overall performance.
- If a company is funding losses from operations or financing investments by raising money (debt or equity) it will quickly become clear on the statement of cash flows

Statement of Changes in Equity

The statement of changes in equity is a reconciliation of the beginning and ending balances in a company's equity during a reporting period. It is not considered an essential part of the monthly financial statements, and so is the most likely of all the financial statements not to be issued. However, it is a common part of the annual financial statements. The statement starts with the beginning equity balance, and then adds or subtracts such items as profits and dividend payments to arrive at the ending ending balance. The general calculation structure of the statement is:

Beginning equity + Net income – Dividends +/- Other changes

= Ending equity

The transactions most likely to appear on this statement are as follows:

- Net profit or loss
- Dividend payments
- Proceeds from the sale of stock
- Treasury stock purchases
- Gains and losses recognized directly in equity
- Effects of changes due to errors in prior periods
- Effects of changes in fair value for certain assets

The statement of changes in equity is most commonly presented as a separate statement, but can also be added to another financial statement.

It is also possible to provide a greatly expanded version of the statement that discloses the various elements of equity. For example, it could separately identify the par value of common stock, additional paid-in capital, retained earnings, and treasury stock, with all of these elements then rolling up into the ending equity total.

To prepare the statement, follow these steps:

1. Create separate accounts in the general ledger for each type of equity. Thus, there are different accounts for the par value of stock, additional paid-in capital, and retained earnings. Each of these accounts is represented by a separate column in the statement.
2. Transfer every transaction within each equity account to a spreadsheet, and identify it in the spreadsheet.
3. Aggregate the transactions within the spreadsheet into similar types, and transfer them to separate line items in the statement of changes in equity.
4. Complete the statement, and verify that the beginning and ending balances in it match the general ledger, and that the aggregated line items within it add up to the ending balances for all columns.

Example

Following is an illustrative example of a Statement of Changes in Equity prepared according to the format prescribed by IAS 1 *Presentation of Financial Statements*.

ABC Plc Statement of changes in equity for the year ended 31st December 2012

	Share Capital	**Retained Earnings**	**Revaluation Surplus**	**Total Equity**
	USD	USD	USD	USD
Balance at 1 January 2011	100,000	30,000	-	130,000
Changes in accounting policy	-	-	-	-
Correction of prior period error	-	-	-	-
Restated balance	100,000	30,000	-	130,000
Changes in equity for the year 2011				
Issue of share capital	-	-	-	-
Income for the year	-	25,000	-	25,000
Revaluation gain	-	-	10,000	10,000
Dividends	-	(15,000)	-	(15,000)
Balance at 31 December 2011	100,000	40,000	10,000	150,000

Changes in equity for the year 2012				
Issue of share capital	-	-	-	-
Income for the year	-	30,000	-	30,000
Revaluation gain	-	-	5,000	5,000
Dividends	-	(20,000)	-	(20,000)
Balance at 31 December 2012	100,000	50,000	15,000	165,000

Components

Following are the main elements of statement of changes in equity:

- Opening Balance

This represents the balance of shareholders' equity reserves at the start of the comparative reporting period as reflected in the prior period's statement of financial position. The opening balance is unadjusted in respect of the correction of prior period errors rectified in the current period and also the effect of changes in accounting policy implemented during the year as these are presented separately in the statement of changes in equity.

- Effect of Changes in Accounting Policies

Since changes in accounting policies are applied retrospectively, an adjustment is required in stockholders' reserves at the start of the comparative reporting period to restate the opening equity to the amount that would be arrived if the new accounting policy had always been applied.

- Effect of Correction of Prior Period Error

The effect of correction of prior period errors must be presented separately in the statement of changes in equity as an adjustment to opening reserves. The effect of the corrections may not be netted off against the opening balance of the equity reserves so that the amounts presented in current period statement might be easily reconciled and traced from prior period financial statements.

- Restated Balance

This represents the equity attributable to stockholders at the start of the comparative period after the adjustments in respect of changes in accounting policies and correction of prior period errors as explained above.

- Changes in Share Capital

Issue of further share capital during the period must be added in the statement of changes in equity whereas redemption of shares must be deducted therefrom. The effects of issue and redemption of shares must be presented separately for share capital reserve and share premium reserve.

- Dividends

Dividend payments issued or announced during the period must be deducted from shareholder equity as they represent distribution of wealth attributable to stockholders.

- Income/Loss for the period

This represents the profit or loss attributable to shareholders during the period as reported in the income statement.

- Changes in Revaluation Reserve

Revaluation gains and losses recognized during the period must be presented in the statement of changes in equity to the extent that they are recognized outside the income statement. Revaluation gains recognized in income statement due to reversal of previous impairment losses however shall not be presented separately in the statement of changes in equity as they would already be incorporated in the profit or loss for the period.

- Other Gains & Losses

Any other gains and losses not recognized in the income statement may be presented in the statement of changes in equity such as actuarial gains and losses arising from the application of IAS 19 *Employee Benefit*.

- Closing Balance

This represents the balance of shareholders' equity reserves at the end of the reporting period as reflected in the statement of financial position.

Purpose & Importance

Statement of changes in equity helps users of financial statement to identify the factors that cause a change in the owners' equity over the accounting periods. Whereas movement in shareholder reserves can be observed from the balance sheet, statement of changes in equity discloses significant information about equity reserves that is not presented separately elsewhere in the financial statements which may be useful in understanding the nature of change in equity reserves. Examples of such information include share capital issue and redemption during the period, the effects of changes in accounting policies and correction of prior period errors, gains and losses recognized outside income statement, dividends declared and bonus shares issued during the period.

References

- Williams, Jan R.; Susan F. Haka; Mark S. Bettner; Joseph V. Carcello (2008). Financial & Managerial Accounting. McGraw-Hill Irwin. p. 40. ISBN 978-0-07-299650-0

- "US Small Business Administration sample spreadsheet for a small business". Archived from the original on 2007-07-15. Retrieved 2003-08-10
- "Balance sheet comparing two year-end balance sheets". Archived from the original on 2007-10-19. Retrieved 2010-05-08
- Epstein, Barry J.; Eva K. Jermakowicz (2007). Interpretation and Application of International Financial Reporting Standards. John Wiley & Sons. p. 931. ISBN 978-0-471-79823-1
- tieto. (2009). The future of e-invoicing, Pg. 5. Retrieved from digitdoc: "Archived copy" (PDF). Archived from the original(PDF) on 2012-10-21. Retrieved 2013-06-17

4

Bookkeeping: Systematic Recording of Financial Transactions

Bookkeeping refers to the process of recording financial transactions in a business, such as purchases, sales and payments. This chapter closely examines the key concepts of bookkeeping to provide an extensive understanding of the recording of financial transactions such as accounting period, bank reconciliation, trial balance and adjusting entries as well as the ways to keep a general journal or a ledger.

Bookkeeping

Bookkeeping means the recording of financial transactions and other details on a day to day basis with the intention to prepare the financial statements from the books of accounts maintained.

Bookkeeping is the first step towards building books of accounts of any company. It involves recognition of transactions, operation and being a source of documents for other similar events.

There are several methods of bookkeeping, most popular being single entry bookkeeping system and double entry bookkeeping system.

Bookkeepers

Bookkeeping is done by bookkeepers, individuals who manage all the transactions for the companies. They are responsible for the accuracy and timeliness of the transactions. Without them, the transaction would not be entered in the books and the very start of building a book of accounts will not be initiated.

Reasons why Bookkeeping is Important

Bookkeeping is crucial for businesses of all sizes irrespective of the size, nature of the business, transactions, any specific industry. Bookkeeping quickly becomes more complex with the introduction of tax, assets, loans, and investments.

Accurate bookkeeping practices give companies a reliable source to measure the financial performance. It also provides information on general strategic decisions and a benchmark for its revenue and income goals.

The Task Involved

In bookkeeping below are the common transactions and task involved:

1. Billing for goods sold or services provided to clients
2. Recording receipts from customers
3. Verifying and recording invoices from suppliers
4. Paying suppliers
5. Processing employees' pay and the related governmental reports
6. Monitoring individual accounts receivable
7. Recording and monitoring asset depreciation and other adjusting entries
8. Generating and providing financial reports
9. Expense payments to suppliers
10. Loan payments

Bookkeeping although means recording and tracking the figures of transactions involved in the financials of the business in a systematic manner. It is essential for businesses but is also useful for individuals and non-profit organizations.

Example of Bookkeeping

Part of bookkeeping involves entering a transaction into a journal and then getting it posted to a ledger account. This first step shows a transaction of depreciation being recorded in a journal book in form of a journal entry.

Depreciation A/C	Debit
To Asset A/C	Credit

Once the above journal entry is posted in their respective ledger accounts it will show up as below.

Asset Account					
Date	Particulars	Amount	Date	Particulars	Amount
			Date	By Depreciation A/C	xxxx

Depreciation Account					
Date	Particulars	Amount	Date	Particulars	Amount
Date	To Asset A/C	xxxx			

Purpose of Bookkeeping

A business unit is involved in various financial transaction every day and over time it becomes difficult to keep track with these millions of transactions and use them for future reference.

Bookkeeping helps in organizing the data logically and chronologically for its further usability. Besides, bookkeeping is done also to:

- Understand the financial effect of each transaction
- Determine the factors responsible for profit or loss in a certain period
- Avoid errors in the process of accounting
- Determine tax-liability

Entry Systems

Two common bookkeeping systems used by businesses and other organizations are the single-entry bookkeeping system and the double-entry bookkeeping system. Single-entry bookkeeping uses only income and expense accounts, recorded primarily in a revenue and expense journal. Single-entry bookkeeping is adequate for many small businesses. In the double-entry accounting system, at least two accounting entries are required to record each financial transaction. These entries may occur in asset, liability, equity, expense, or revenue accounts.

Single-entry System

The primary bookkeeping record in single-entry bookkeeping is the *cash book*, which is similar to a checking account (UK: cheque account, current account) register, but allocates the income and expenses to various income and expense accounts. Separate account records are maintained for petty cash, accounts payable and receivable, and other relevant transactions such as inventory and travel expenses. These days, single-entry bookkeeping can be done with DIY bookkeeping software to speed up manual calculations.

Double-entry System

A *double-entry bookkeeping system* is a set of rules for recording financial information in a financial accounting system in which every transaction or event changes at least two different nominal ledger accounts.

Daybooks

A *daybook* is a descriptive and chronological (diary-like) record of day-to-day financial transactions also called a *book of original entry*. The daybook's details must be entered formally into journals to enable posting to ledgers. Daybooks include:

- Sales daybook, for recording all the sales invoices.
- Sales credits daybook, for recording all the sales credit notes.
- Purchases daybook, for recording all the purchase invoices.
- Purchases Debits daybook, for recording all the purchase Debit notes.
- Cash daybook, usually known as the cash book, for recording all money received as well as money paid out. It may be split into two daybooks: receipts daybook for money received in, and payments daybook for money paid out.
- General Journal daybook, for recording journals.

Petty Cash Book

A *petty cash* book is a record of small-value purchases before they are later transferred to the ledger and final accounts; it is maintained by a petty or junior cashier. This type of cash book usually uses the imprest system: a certain amount of money is provided to the petty cashier by the senior cashier. This money is to cater for minor expenditures (hospitality, minor stationery, casual postage, and so on) and is reimbursed periodically on satisfactory explanation of how it was spent.

Journals

Journals are recorded in the general journal daybook. A journal is a formal and chronological record of financial transactions before their values are accounted for in the general ledger as debits and credits. A company can maintain one journal for all transactions, or keep several journals based on similar activity (e.g., sales, cash receipts, revenue, etc.), making transactions easier to summarize and reference later. For every debit journal entry recorded, there must be an equivalent credit journal entry to maintain a balanced accounting equation.

Ledgers

A *ledger* is a record of accounts.The ledger is a permanent summary of all amounts entered in supporting Journals which list individual transactions by date. These accounts are recorded separately, showing their beginning/ending balance. A journal lists financial transactions in chronological order, without showing their balance but showing how much is going to be charged in each account. A ledger takes each financial transaction from the journal and records it into the corresponding account for every transaction listed. The ledger also sums up the total of every account, which is transferred into the balance sheet and the income statement. There are three different kinds of ledgers that deal with book-keeping:

- Sales ledger, which deals mostly with the accounts receivable account. This ledger consists of the records of the financial transactions made by customers to the business.
- Purchase ledger is the record of the purchasing transactions a company does; it goes hand in hand with the Accounts Payable account.

Chart of Accounts

A chart of accounts is a list of the accounts codes that can be identified with numeric, alphabetical, or alphanumeric codes allowing the account to be located in the general ledger. The equity section of the chart of accounts is based on the fact that the legal structure of the entity is of a particular legal type. Possibilities include *sole trader*, *partnership*, *trust*, and *company*.

Computerized Bookkeeping

Computerized bookkeeping removes many of the paper "books" that are used to record the financial transactions of an entity—instead, relational databases take their place, but they still typically enforce the double-entry bookkeeping system and methodology. CPAs design the internal controls for the computerized bookkeeping system, which serve to minimize errors in documenting the big number of activities that the entity engages in over the period.

Double-entry Bookkeeping System

The double entry system of accounting or bookkeeping means that every business transaction will involve two accounts (or more). For example, when a company borrows money from its bank, the company's Cash account will increase and its liability account Loans Payable will increase. If a company pays $200 for an advertisement, its Cash account will decrease and its account Advertising Expense will increase.

Double entry also allows for the accounting equation (assets = liabilities + owner's equity) to always be in balance. In our example involving Advertising Expense, the accounting equation remained in balance because expenses cause owner's equity to decrease. In that example, the asset Cash decreased and the owner's capital account within owner's equity also decreased.

A third aspect of double entry is that the amounts entered into the general ledger accounts as debits must be equal to the amounts entered as credits.

Types of Accounts

Bookkeeping and accounting are ways of measuring, recording, and communicating a firm's financial information. A business transaction is an economic event that is recorded for accounting/bookkeeping purposes; in general terms, it is a business interaction between economic entities, such as customers and businesses or vendors and businesses. Under the systematic process of accounting, these interactions are generally classified into accounts. There are seven different types of accounts that all business transactions can be classified: assets, liabilities, equities, revenue, expenses, gains, and losses. Bookkeeping and accounting track changes in each account as a company continues operations.

Debits and Credits

Debits and credits are essential to the double entry system. In accounting, debit refers to an entry on the left side of an account ledger, and credit refers to an entry on the right side of an account ledger. To be in balance, the total of debits and credits for a transaction must be equal. Debits do not always equate to increases and credits do not always equate to decreases. A debit may increase one account while decreasing another. For example, a debit increases asset accounts but decreases liability and equity accounts, which supports the general accounting equation of Assets = Liabilities + Equity. On the income statement, debits increase the balances in expense and loss accounts, while credits decrease their balances. Debits decrease revenue and gains account balances, while credits increase their balances.

	Debit	**Credit**
Asset	Increase	Decrease
Liability	Decrease	Increase
Income (revenue)	Decrease	Increase
Expense	Increase	Decrease
Capital	Decrease	Increase

The mnemonic DEADCLIC is used to help remember the effect of debit or credit transactions on the relevant accounts. DEAD: Debit to increase Expense, Asset and Drawing accounts and CLIC: Credit to increase Liability, Income and Capital accounts.

The account types are related as follows:

current equity = sum of equity changes across time (increases on the left side are debits, and increases on the right side are credits, and vice versa for decreases)
current equity = Assets - Liabilities

sum of equity changes across time = owner's investment (Capital above) + Revenues - Expenses

Accounting Entries

In the double-entry accounting system, at least two accounting entries are required to record each financial transaction. These entries may occur in asset, liability, equity, expense, or revenue accounts. Recording of a debit amount to one or more accounts and an equal credit amount to one or more accounts results in total debits being equal to total credits for all accounts in the general ledger. If the accounting entries are recorded without error, the aggregate balance of all accounts having *Debit* balances will be equal to the aggregate balance of all accounts having *Credit* balances. Accounting entries that debit and credit related accounts typically include the same date and identifying code in both accounts, so that in case of error, each debit and credit can be traced back to a journal and transaction source document, thus preserving an audit trail. The accounting entries are recorded in the "Books of Accounts". Regardless of which accounts and how many are impacted by a given transaction, the fundamental accounting equation of *assets equal liabilities plus capital* will hold.

Approaches

There are two different ways to memorize the effects of debits and credits on accounts in the double entry system of bookkeeping. They are the Traditional Approach and the Accounting Equation Approach. Irrespective of the approach used, the effect on the books of accounts remains the same, with two aspects (debit and credit) in each of the transactions.

- The British Approach

Following the British approach (also called the traditional approach) accounts are classified as real, personal, and nominal accounts. Real accounts are accounts relating to assets and liabilities including the capital account of the owners. Personal accounts are accounts relating to persons or organisations with whom the business has transactions and will mainly consist of accounts of debtors and creditors. Nominal accounts are revenue, expenses, gains, and losses. Transactions are entered in the books of accounts by applying the following golden rules of accounting:

1. Real account: Debit what comes in and credit what goes out

2. Personal account: Debit the receiver and credit the giver

3. Nominal account: Debit all expenses & losses and credit all incomes & gains

- Accounting Equation Approach

This approach is also called the American approach. Under this approach transactions are recorded based on the accounting equation, i.e., Assets = Liabilities + Capital. The accounting equation is a statement of equality between the debits and the credits. The rules of debit and credit depend on the nature of an account. For the purpose of the accounting equation approach, all the accounts are classified into the following five types: assets, liabilities, income/revenues, expenses, or capital gains/losses.

If there is an increase or decrease in a set of accounts, there will be equal decrease or increase in another set of accounts. Accordingly, the following rules of debit and credit hold for the various categories of accounts:

1. Assets Accounts: debit entry represents an increase in assets and a credit entry represents a decrease in assets
2. Capital Account: credit entry represents an increase in capital and a debit entry represents a decrease in capital
3. Liabilities Accounts: credit entry represents an increase in liabilities and a debit entry represents a decrease in liabilities
4. Revenues or Incomes Accounts: credit entry represents an increase in incomes and gains, and debit entry represents a decrease in incomes and gains
5. Expenses or Losses Accounts: debit entry represents an increase in expenses and losses, and credit entry represents a decrease in expenses and losses

These five rules help learning about accounting entries and also are comparable with traditional (British) accounting rules.

Books of Accounts

Each financial transaction is recorded in at least two different nominal ledger accounts within the financial accounting system, so that the total debits equals the total credits in the general ledger, i.e. the accounts balance. This is a partial check that each and every transaction has been correctly recorded. The transaction is recorded as a "debit entry" (Dr) in one account, and a "credit entry" (Cr) in a second account. The debit entry will be recorded on the debit side (left-hand side) of a general ledger account, and the credit entry will be recorded on the credit side (right-hand side) of a general ledger account. If the total of the entries on the debit side of one account is greater than the total on the credit side of the same nominal account, that account is said to have a debit balance.

Double entry is used only in nominal ledgers. It is not used in daybooks (journals), which normally do not form part of the nominal ledger system. The information from the daybooks will be used in the nominal ledger and it is the nominal ledgers that will ensure the integrity of the resulting financial information created from the daybooks (provided that the information recorded in the daybooks is correct).

The reason for this is to limit the number of entries in the nominal ledger: entries in the daybooks can be totalled before they are entered in the nominal ledger. If there are only a relatively small number of transactions it may be simpler instead to treat the daybooks as an integral part of the nominal ledger and thus of the double-entry system.

However, as can be seen from the examples of daybooks shown below, it is still necessary to check, within each daybook, that the postings from the daybook balance.

The double entry system uses nominal ledger accounts. From these nominal ledger accounts a trial balance can be created. The trial balance lists all the nominal ledger account balances. The list is split into two columns, with debit balances placed in the left hand column and credit balances placed in the right hand column. Another column will contain the name of the nominal ledger account describing what each value is for. The total of the debit column must equal the total of the credit column.

Debits and credits

Business transactions are events that have a monetary impact on the financial statements of an organization. When accounting for these transactions, we record numbers in two accounts, where the debit column is on the left and the credit column is on the right.

- A debit is an accounting entry that either increases an asset or expense account, or decreases a liability or equity account. It is positioned to the left in an accounting entry.
- A credit is an accounting entry that either increases a liability or equity account, or decreases an asset or expense account. It is positioned to the right in an accounting entry.

Debit and Credit Usage

Whenever an accounting transaction is created, at least two accounts are always impacted, with a debit entry being recorded against one account and a credit entry being recorded against the other account. There is no upper limit to the number of accounts involved in a transaction - but the minimum is no less than two accounts. The totals of the debits and credits for any transaction must always equal each other, so that an accounting transaction is always said to be "in balance." If a transaction were not in balance, then it would not be possible to create financial statements. Thus, the use of debits and credits in a two-column transaction recording format is the most essential of all controls over accounting accuracy.

There can be considerable confusion about the inherent meaning of a debit or a credit. For example, if you debit a cash account, then this means that the amount of cash on hand increases. However, if you debit an accounts payable account, this means that the amount of accounts payable liability decreases. These differences arise because debits and credits have different impacts across several broad types of accounts, which are:

- Asset accounts. A debit increases the balance and a credit decreases the balance.

- Liability accounts. A debit decreases the balance and a credit increases the balance.
- Equity accounts. A debit decreases the balance and a credit increases the balance.

The reason for this seeming reversal of the use of debits and credits is caused by the underlying accounting equation upon which the entire structure of accounting transactions are built, which is:

Assets = Liabilities + Equity

Thus, in a sense, you can only have assets if you have paid for them with liabilities or equity, so you must have one in order to have the other. Consequently, if you create a transaction with a debit and a credit, you are usually increasing an asset while also increasing a liability or equity account (or vice versa). There are some exceptions, such as increasing one asset account while decreasing another asset account.

If you are more concerned with accounts that appear on the income statement, then these additional rules apply:

- Revenue accounts. A debit decreases the balance and a credit increases the balance.
- Expense accounts. A debit increases the balance and a credit decreases the balance.
- Gain accounts. A debit decreases the balance and a credit increases the balance.
- Loss accounts. A debit increases the balance and a credit decreases the balance.

If you are really confused by these issues, then just remember that debits always go in the left column, and credits always go in the right column. There are no exceptions.

Debit and Credit Rules

The rules governing the use of debits and credits are as follows:

- All accounts that normally contain a debit balance will increase in amount when a debit (left column) is added to them, and reduced when a credit (right column) is added to them. The types of accounts to which this rule applies are expenses, assets, and dividends.
- All accounts that normally contain a credit balance will increase in amount when a credit (right column) is added to them, and reduced when a debit (left column) is added to them. The types of accounts to which this rule applies are liabilities, revenues, and equity.
- The total amount of debits must equal the total amount of credits in a transac-

tion. Otherwise, an accounting transaction is said to be unbalanced, and will not be accepted by the accounting software.

Debits and Credits in Common Accounting Transactions

The following bullet points note the use of debits and credits in the more common business transactions:

- Sale for cash: Debit the cash account | Credit the revenue account
- Sale on credit: Debit the accounts receivable account | Credit the revenue account
- Receive cash in payment of an account receivable: Debit the cash account | Credit the accounts receivable account
- Purchase supplies from supplier for cash: Debit the supplies expense account | Credit the cash account
- Purchase supplies from supplier on credit: Debit the supplies expense account | Credit the accounts payable account
- Purchase inventory from supplier for cash: Debit the inventory account | Credit the cash account
- Purchase inventory from supplier on credit: Debit the inventory account | Credit the accounts payable account
- Pay employees: Debit the wages expense and payroll tax accounts | Credit the cash account
- Take out a loan: Debit cash account | Credit loans payable account
- Repay a loan: Debit loans payable account | Credit cash account

Debit and Credit Examples

Arnold Corporation sells a product to a customer for $1,000 in cash. This results in revenue of $1,000 and cash of $1,000. Arnold must record an increase of the cash (asset) account with a debit, and an increase of the revenue account with a credit. The entry is:

	Debit	Credit
Cash	1,000	
Revenue		1,000

Arnold Corporation also buys a machine for $15,000 on credit. This results in an addition to the Machinery fixed assets account with a debit, and an increase in the accounts payable (liability) account with a credit.

The entry is:

	Debit	Credit
Machinery - Fixed Assets	15,000	
Accounts Payable		15,000

Other Debit and Credit Issues

A debit is commonly abbreviated as dr. in an accounting transaction, while a credit is abbreviated as cr. in an accounting transaction.

Debits and credits are not used in a single entry system. In this system, only a single notation is made of a transaction; it is usually an entry in a check book or cash journal, indicating the receipt or expenditure of cash. A single entry system is only designed to produce an income statement.

Aspects of Transactions

To determine whether one must debit or credit a specific account we use either the *accounting equation* approach which consists of five accounting rules or the *traditional approach* based on three rules (for Real accounts, Personal accounts, and Nominal accounts) to determine whether *to debit* or *to credit* an account.

- Real accounts are the assets of a firm, which may be *tangible* (machinery, buildings etc.) or *intangible* (goodwill, patents etc.)
- Personal accounts relate to individuals, companies, creditors, banks etc.
- Nominal accounts relate to expenses, losses, incomes or gains.

Whether a *debit* increases or decreases an account depends on what kind of account it is. For instance, an increase in an *asset* account is a debit. An increase in a *liability* or an *equity* account is a credit.

Kind of account	**Debit**	**Credit**
Asset	Increase	Decrease
Liability	Decrease	Increase
Income/Revenue	Decrease	Increase
Expense/Cost/Dividend	Increase	Decrease
Equity/Capital	Decrease	Increase

The complete system is very easy to remember if you focus on Assets, Expenses, Costs, Dividends. All those account types increase with debits or left side entries. Conversely, a decrease to any of those accounts is a credit or right side entry. On the other hand, increases in revenue, liability or equity accounts are credits or right side entries, and decreases are left side entries or debits.

Debits and credits occur simultaneously in every financial transaction in double-entry bookkeeping. In the accounting equation, Assets = Liabilities + Equity, so, if an asset account increases (a debit (left)), then either another asset account must decrease (a credit (right)), or a liability or equity account must increase (a credit (right)). Note also that in the extended equation, revenues increase equity and expenses, costs & dividends decrease equity, so their difference is the impact on the equation.

For example, if a company provides a service to a customer who does not pay immediately, the company records an increase in assets, Accounts Receivable with a debit entry, and an increase in Revenue, with a credit entry. When the company receives the cash from the customer, two accounts again change on the company side, the cash account is debited (increased) and the Accounts Receivable account is now decreased (credited). When the cash is deposited to the bank account, two things also change, on the bank side: the bank records an increase in its cash account (debit) and records an increase in its liability to the customer by recording a credit in the customer's account (which is not cash). Note that, technically, the deposit is not a decrease in the cash (asset) of the company and should not be recorded as such. It is just a transfer to a proper bank account of record in the company's books, not affecting the ledger.

To make it more clear, the bank views the transaction from a different perspective but follows the same rules: the bank's vault cash (asset) increases, which is a debit; the increase in the customer's account balance (liability from the bank's perspective) is a credit. A customer's periodic bank statement generally shows transactions from the bank's perspective, with cash deposits characterized as credits (liabilities) and withdrawals as debits (reductions in liabilities) in depositor's accounts. In the company's books the exact opposite entries should be recorded to account for the same cash. This concept is important since this is why so many people misunderstand what debit/credit really means.

In summary, debits are simply transaction entries on the left-hand side of ledger accounts, and credits are entries on the right-hand side.

Commercial Understanding

When dealing with one's own business, one must set up various accounts to record all transactions that may take place. When the owner of a business refers to their bank account, they are referring to the business's account, not to their personal account. In addition, all accounts referred to in bookkeeping belong to the business, *not* to other businesses, regardless of their title. For instance, if a business expects to receive money from another person or company and the account is labelled "Receivable A", this does not imply that the account in question belongs to "Receivable A". It is merely a recording of a current asset (a receivable) of one's own business. Therefore, when assessing any transaction, the transaction is from the point of view of one's own business or the business in question.

All accounts must first be classified as one of the five types of accounts (accounting elements). To determine how to classify an account into one of the five elements, the definitions of the five account types must be fully understood i.e. the definition of an asset according to IFRS is as follows, "An asset is a resource controlled by the entity as a result of past events from which future economic benefits are expected to flow to the entity". To understand this definition we can break it down into its constituent parts with an example:

> Example: Classify what type of account the business "Bank account" is.
>
> The bank account of a business is "a resource controlled by the entity" as it belongs to the business. "As a result of past events" such as the opening of the business. "From which future economic benefits are expected to flow to the entity" – a business such as a grocers can expect to make money due to the sale of their goods. This basic analogy can be applied to any asset account.
>
> All of the five accounting elements have their own definitions that must be fully understood in order to classify an account correctly.

A business will most often have more than one asset account. An essential asset account in any business is the business's *bank account*. The same applies to liability accounts i.e. if I have borrowed money from two sources (called creditors or payables), then I must open two accounts to represent this present liability, called 'Creditor/Payable A' and 'Creditor/Payable B'. In this manner I may have multiple, different accounts. However all these accounts are all classified as one of the five types of accounts, therefore my entire business can be described in terms of its assets, expenses, liabilities, income and equity/capital. This is the extent of "my" business in relation to accounts, regardless of the business' practices (the business may be a retail franchise, furniture shop, restaurant, etc.). With respect to my business, each of the five accounting elements will have a monetary value, and this can be used to assess the financial position of my business at any time.

Traditionally, transactions are recorded in two separate columns of numbers (known as a ledger or "T-account"): debit transactions in the left hand column and credit transactions in the right hand column. Keeping the debits and credits in separate columns allows each column to be recorded and totaled *independently*. Accounts within the *general ledger* are known colloquially as "T-accounts" due to the "T" shape that the table resembles. Each column of a ledger account lists transactions affecting that account.

The Five Accounting Elements

There are five fundamental elements within accounting. These elements are as follows: Assets, Liabilities, Equity (or Capital), Income (or Revenue) and Expenses. The five accounting elements are all affected in either a positive or negative way. A credit transaction does not always dictate a positive value or increase in a transaction and similarly, a debit does not always indicate a negative value or decrease in a transaction. An asset account is often referred to as a "debit account" due to the account's standard *increasing* attribute on the debit side. When an asset (e.g. an espresso machine) has been acquired in a business, the transaction will affect the debit side of that asset account illustrated below:

Asset

Debits (Dr)	Credits (Cr)
X	

The "X" in the debit column denotes the increasing effect of a transaction on the asset *account balance* (total debits less total credits), because a debit to an asset account is an increase. The asset account above has been *added to* by a debit value X, i.e. the balance has increased by £X or $X. Likewise, in the liability account below, the X in the credit column denotes the increasing effect on the liability account balance (total credits less total debits), because a credit to a liability account is an increase.

All "mini-ledgers" in this section show standard increasing attributes for the five elements of accounting.

Liability

Debits (Dr)	Credits (Cr)
	X

Income

Debits (Dr)	Credits (Cr)
	X

Expenses

Debits (Dr)	Credits (Cr)
X	

Equity

Debits (Dr)	Credits (Cr)
	X

Summary table of standard increasing and decreasing attributes for the five accounting elements:

Account Type	Debit	Credit
Asset	+	–
Liability	–	+
Income	–	+
Expense	+	–
Equity	–	+

Principle

Each transaction that takes place within the business will consist of at least one debit to a specific account and at least one credit to another specific account. A debit to one account can be balanced by more than one credit to other accounts, and vice versa. For all transactions, the total debits must be equal to the total credits and therefore *balance*.

The *general* accounting equation is as follows:

Assets = Equity + Liabilities,

A = E + L.

The equation thus becomes A – L – E = 0 (zero). When the total debts equals the total credits for each account, then the equation balances.

The *extended* accounting equation is as follows:

Assets + Expenses = Equity/Capital + Liabilities + Income,

A + Ex = E + L + I.

In this form, increases to the amount of accounts on the left-hand side of the equation are recorded as debits, and decreases as credits. Conversely for accounts on the right-hand side, increases to the amount of accounts are recorded as credits to the account, and decreases as debits.

This can also be rewritten in the equivalent form:

Assets = Liabilities + Equity/Capital + (Income – Expenses),

A = L + E + (I – Ex),

where the relationship of the Income and Expenses accounts to Equity and profit is a bit clearer. Here Income and Expenses are regarded as temporary or nominal accounts which pertain only to the current accounting period whereas Asset, Liabilities and Equity accounts are permanent or real accounts pertaining to the lifetime of the business. The temporary accounts are closed to the Equity account at the end of the accounting period to record profit/loss for the period. Both sides of these equations must be equal (balance).

Each transaction is recorded in a ledger or "T" account, e.g. a ledger account named "Bank" that can be changed with either a debit or credit transaction.

In accounting it is acceptable to draw-up a ledger account in the following manner for representation purposes:

Bank

Debits (Dr)	**Credits (Cr)**

Accounts Pertaining to the Five Accounting Elements

Accounts are created/opened when the need arises for whatever purpose or situation the entity may have. For example, if your business is an airline company they will have to purchase airplanes, therefore even if an account is not listed below, a bookkeeper or accountant can create an account for a specific item, such as an asset account for airplanes. In order to understand how to classify an account into one of the five elements, a good understanding of the *definitions* of these accounts is required. Below are examples of some of the more common accounts that pertain to the five accounting elements:

- Asset Accounts

Asset accounts are economic resources which benefit the business/entity and will continue to do so. They are Cash, bank, accounts receivable, inventory, land, buildings/plant, machinery, furniture, equipment, supplies, vehicles, trademarks and patents, goodwill, prepaid expenses, prepaid insurance, debtors (people who owe us money, due within one year), VAT input etc.

Two types of basic asset classification:

- o Current assets: Assets which operate in a financial year or assets that can be used up, or converted within one year or less is called current assets. For example, Cash, bank, accounts receivable, inventory (people who owe us money, due within one year), prepaid expenses, prepaid insurance, VAT input and many more.
- o Non-current assets: Assets that are not recorded in transactions or hold for more than one year or in an accounting period is called Non-current assets. For example, land, buildings/plant, machinery, furniture, equipment, vehicles, trademarks and patents, goodwill etc.

- Liability Accounts

Liability accounts record debts or future obligations the business/entity owes to others. When an institution borrows from an institution for a period of time, in the ledger of the institution that borrows calls the argument as liability accounts.

Basic classification of liability accounts are:

- o Current Liability: A person or an organization owe for the accounting period or periodical this is called current liability; such as Accounts payable, salaries and wages payable, income taxes, bank overdrafts, accrued expenses, sales taxes, advance payments (unearned revenue), debt and accrued interest on debt, customer deposits, VAT output etc.
- o Long-term liability: When an organization or person may owe money for more than one year is called long-term liability. long-term liability is trust accounts, debenture, mortgage loan and many more.

- Equity Accounts

Equity accounts record the claims of the owners of the business/entity to the assets of that business/entity. Capital, retained earnings, drawings, common stock, accumulated funds, etc.

- Income/Revenue Accounts

Income accounts record all increases in Equity other than that contributed by the owner/s of the business/entity. Services rendered, sales, interest income, membership fees, rent income, interest from investment, recurring receivables,donation etc.

- Expense Accounts

Expense accounts record all decreases in the owners' equity which occur from using the assets or increasing liabilities in delivering goods or services to a customer - the costs of doing business. Telephone, water, electricity, repairs, salaries, wages, depreciation, bad debts, stationery, entertainment, honorarium, rent, fuel, utility, interest etc.

Example

Quick Services business purchases a computer for £500, on credit, from ABC Computers. Recognize the following transaction for Quick Services in a ledger account (T-account):

Quick Services has acquired a new computer which is classified as an asset within the business. According to the accrual basis of accounting, even though the computer has been purchased on credit, the computer is already the property of Quick Services and must be recognised as such. Therefore, the equipment account of Quick Services increases and is debited:

Equipment (Asset)

(Dr)	(Cr)
500	

As the transaction for the new computer is made *on credit*, the payable "ABC Computers" has not yet been paid. As a result, a liability is created within the entity's records. Therefore, to balance the accounting equation the corresponding liability account is credited:

Payable ABC Computers (Liability)

(Dr)	(Cr)
	500

The above example can be written in journal form:

	Dr	Cr
Equipment	500	
ABC Computers (Payable)		500

The journal entry "ABC Computers" is indented to indicate that this is the credit transaction. It is accepted accounting practice to indent credit transactions recorded within a journal.

In the accounting equation form:

A = E + L,

500 = 0 + 500 (the accounting equation is therefore balanced).

Further Examples

1. A business pays rent with cash: You increase rent (expense) by recording a debit transaction, and decrease cash (asset) by recording a credit transaction.
2. A business receives cash for a sale: You increase cash (asset) by recording a debit transaction, and increase sales (income) by recording a credit transaction.
3. A business buys equipment with cash: You increase equipment (asset) by recording a debit transaction, and decrease cash (asset) by recording a credit transaction.
4. A business borrows with a cash loan: You increase cash (asset) by recording a debit transaction, and increase loan (liability) by recording a credit transaction.
5. A business pays salaries with cash: You increase salary (expenses) by recording a debit transaction, and decrease cash (asset) by recording a credit transaction.
6. The totals show the net effect on the accounting equation and the double-entry principle, where the transactions are balanced.

	Account	Debit (Dr)	Credit (Cr)
1.	Rent	100	
	Bank		100
2.	Bank	50	
	Sales		50
3.	Equipment	5200	
	Bank		5200
4.	Bank	11000	
	Loan		11000
5.	Salary	5000	
	Bank		5000
6.	Total (Dr)	$21350	
	Total (Cr)		$21350

T-accounts

The process of using debits and credits creates a ledger format that resembles the letter "T". The term "T-account" is accounting jargon for a "ledger account" and is often used when discussing bookkeeping. The reason that a ledger account is often referred to as a T-account is due to the way the account is physically drawn on paper (representing a "T"). The left side (column) of the "T" for Debit (Dr) transactions and the right side (column) of the "T" for Credit (Cr) transactions.

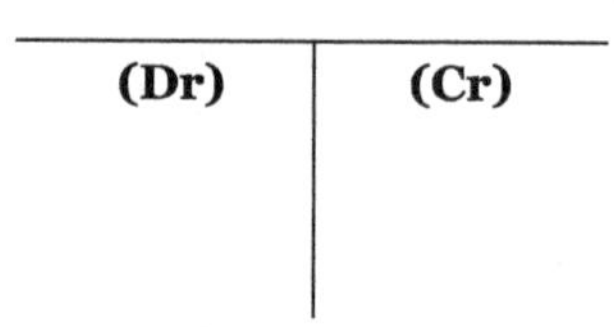

Contra Account

All accounts have corresponding contra accounts depending on what transaction has taken place e.g., when a vehicle is purchased using cash, the asset account "Vehicles" is *debited* as the vehicle account increases, and simultaneously the asset account "Bank" is *credited* due to the payment for the vehicle using cash. Some balance sheet items have corresponding contra accounts, with negative balances, that offset them. Examples are accumulated depreciation against equipment, and allowance for bad debts (also known as allowance for doubtful accounts) against accounts receivable. United States GAAP utilizes the term *contra* for specific accounts only and doesn't recognize the second half of a transaction as a contra, thus the term is restricted to accounts that are related. For example, sales returns and allowance and sales discounts are contra revenues with respect to sales, as the balance of each contra (a debit) is the opposite of sales (a credit). To understand the actual value of sales, one must net the contras against sales, which gives rise to the term net sales (meaning net of the contras).

A more specific definition in common use is an account with a balance that is the opposite of the normal balance (Dr/Cr) for that section of the general ledger. An example is an office coffee fund: Expense "Coffee" (Dr) may be immediately followed by "Coffee - employee contributions" (Cr). Such an account is used for clarity rather than being a necessary part of GAAP (generally accepted accounting principles).

Real, Personal, and Nominal Accounts

Real accounts are assets. Personal accounts are liabilities and owners' equity and represent people and entities that have invested in the business. Nominal accounts are revenue, expenses, gains, and losses. Accountants close nominal accounts at the end of each accounting period. This method is used in the United Kingdom, where it is simply known as the Traditional approach.

Transactions are recorded by a debit to one account and a credit to another account using these three "golden rules of accounting":

1. Real account: Debit what comes in and credit what goes out
2. Personal account: Debit who receives and Credit who gives.
3. Nominal account: Debit all expenses & losses and Credit all incomes & gains

	Debit	**Credit**
Real (assets)	Increase	Decrease
Personal (liability)	Decrease	Increase
Personal (owner's equity)	Decrease	Increase
Nominal (revenue)	Decrease	Increase
Nominal (expenses)	Increase	Decrease
Nominal (gain)	Decrease	Increase
Nominal (loss)	Increase	Decrease

Accounting Equation

The accounting equation is used in double-entry accounting. It shows the relationship between your business's assets, liabilities, and equity. By using the accounting equation, you can see if your assets are financed by debt or business funds. The accounting equation is also called the balance sheet equation.

Balance Sheet Equation Parts

Use your business's balance sheet to calculate the accounting equation. The balance sheet is a financial statement that tracks your company's progress. The balance sheet has three parts: assets, liabilities, and equity.

Assets are items of value that your business owns. For example, your business bank account, company vehicles, and equipment are assets.

Liabilities are debts that you owe to others. For example, your payables are liabilities.

Business equity shows your ownership in the business. If you are a sole proprietor, you hold all the ownership. If there is more than one owner, you split the equity. Calculate equity by subtracting your assets from liabilities.

The Basic Accounting Equation

The accounting equation requires liabilities and equity to equal assets. The following is the accounting calculation:

Assets = Liabilities + Equity

Each side of the accounting equation has to equal the other because you must purchase things with either debt or capital.

Equity has an equal effect on both sides of the equation. If you know any two parts of the accounting equation, you can calculate the third.

You can write the accounting equation with the liabilities by itself:

Liabilities = Assets – Equity

Or, you can write the accounting equation with equity by itself:

Equity = Assets – Liabilities

Accounting Equation Examples

The following examples are connected to the same business. Take a look at how different transactions affect the accounting equation.

Example 1

You're starting a business selling printed T-shirts. You save for a year before opening and contribute $10,000 to the new company. By doing this, you increase your business's assets and owner's equity by the same amount:

$10,000 Assets = Liabilities + $10,000 Equity

Example 2

Let's say that after you form your company, you need to buy equipment to print the T-shirts. You purchase $2,000 of the equipment on credit. In this situation, you gain a liability (debt) and an asset. Your assets and liabilities increase by $2,000, so the equation looks like:

$2,000 Assets = $2,000 Liabilities + Equity

Example 3

As your T-shirt company grows, you get an order for 50 shirts from a customer. The customer pays $10 per shirt, or $500 total. You gain an asset and equity from the transaction:

$500 Assets = Liabilities + $500 Equity

Example Balance Sheet

You will record each of the above transactions on the balance sheet. The assets should equal the liabilities plus equity. Here is what the balance sheet looks like:

Asset Account	Sub Account Type	Balance
Checking	Bank Account	$10,500.00
Savings	Bank Account	$0.00
Petty Cash	Cash	$0.00
Equipment		$2,000.00
Total Assets		**$12,500.00**

Liability Account	Sub Account Type	Balance
Sales Tax Collected	Sales Tax Payable	$0.00
Net Income		$500.00
Total Equity		**$10,500.00**

Assets		Liabilities and Equity
$12,500.00	=	$12,500.00

Here is the full accounting equation for this example:

$12,500 Assets = $2,000 Liabilities + $10,500 Equity

Expanded Accounting Equation

The expanded accounting equation shows the relationship between your income statement and balance sheet. You can see how equity is created from its two main sources: revenue and owner contributions.

This the expanded accounting equation:

Assets = Liabilities + Owner's Equity + Revenue – Expenses – Draws

Revenues are what your business earns through regular operations. Expenses are what it costs to provide your products and services.

Certain patterns occur as figures in the expanded accounting equation change:

- Revenue increases owner's equity
- Expenses decrease owner's equity
- Owner's draw decreases owner's equity

The two sides of the equation must equal each other. If the expanded accounting equation is not balanced, your financial reports are inaccurate.

Reasons why the Accounting Equation is Important

The accounting equation can give you a clear picture your business's financial situation. You must calculate the accounting equation to read your balance sheet. The accounting equation helps you understand the relationship between your financial statements. In a Fundera article, Heather D. Satterley, founder of Satterley Training & Consulting, LLC, explains:

> "The purpose of the balance sheet is to show the financial position of the business on any given day. The balance sheet can tell you how much money the business has in the bank and how likely it is that the business will be able to meet all of its financial obligations. It can also tell you how much profit (or loss) the business has retained since it started."

By using the accounting equation, you can see if you can fund the purchase of an asset with your business's existing assets. And, the equation will reveal if you should pay off debts with assets (like cash) or by taking on more liabilities.

Accounting Period

An accounting period is the span of time covered by a set of financial statements. This period defines the time range over which business transactions are accumulated into financial statements, and is needed by investors so that they can compare the results of successive time periods. For internal financial reporting, an accounting period is generally considered to be one month. A few firms compile financial information in four-week increments, so that they have 13 accounting periods per year.

A publicly-held company must report to the Securities and Exchange Commission on a quarterly basis, so the accounting period for its financial reports to the SEC span three months. If a set of financial statements cover the results of an entire year, then the accounting period is one year. If the accounting period is for a twelve month period ending on a date other than December 31, then the accounting period is called a fiscal year, as opposed to a calendar year. For example, a fiscal year ended June 30 spans the period from July 1 of the preceding year to June 30 of the current year. Ideally, the fiscal year should end on a date when business activity is at a low point, so that there are fewer assets and liabilities to audit.

Yet another variation on the accounting period is when a business has just been started, so that its first accounting period may only span a few days. For example, if a business begins on January 17, its first monthly accounting period will only cover the period from January 17 to January 31. The same concept applies to a business that has been terminated. For example, if a business were to be shut down on January 10, its final monthly accounting period would only cover the period from January 1 to January 10.

Technically, an accounting period only applies to the income statement and statement of cash flows, since the balance sheet reports information as of a specific date. Thus, if an entity reports on its results for January, the header of the income statement says "for the month ended January 31," while the header of the balance sheet states "as of January 31."

52–53-week Fiscal Year

The 52–53-week fiscal year (or 4–4–5 calendar) is used by companies that desire that their fiscal year always end on the same day of the week. Any day of the week may be used, and Saturday and Sunday are common because the business may more easily be closed for counting inventory and other end-of-year accounting activities. There are two methods in use:

Last Saturday of the Month at Fiscal Year End

Under this method the company's fiscal year is defined as the final Saturday (or other day selected) in the fiscal year end month. For example, if the fiscal year end month is August, the company's year end could fall on any date from August 25 to August 31. Currently it would end on the following days:

2006-08-26 2006 August 26

2007-08-25 2007 August 25

2008-08-30 2008 August 30 (leap year)

2009-08-29 2009 August 29

2010-08-28 2010 August 28

2011-08-27 2011 August 27

2012-08-25 2012 August 25 (leap year)

2013-08-31 2013 August 31

2014-08-30 2014 August 30

2015-08-29 2015 August 29

2016-08-27 2016 August 27 (leap year)

2017-08-26 2017 August 26

2018-08-25 2018 August 25

2019-08-31 2019 August 31

The end of the fiscal year would move one day earlier on the calendar each year (two days in leap years) until it would otherwise reach the date seven days before the end of the month (August 24 in this case). At that point it resets to the end of the month (August 31) and the fiscal year has 53 weeks instead of 52. In this example the fiscal years ending in 2008, 2013, and 2019 have 53 weeks.

Saturday Nearest the End Of Month

Under this method the company's fiscal year is defined as the Saturday (or other day selected) that falls closest to the last day of the fiscal year end month. For example, if the fiscal year end month is August, the company's year end could fall on any date from August 28 to September 3. Currently it would end on the following days:

2006-09-02 2006 September 2

2007-09-01 2007 September 1

2008-08-30 2008 August 30 (leap year)

2009-08-29 2009 August 29

2010-08-28 2010 August 28

2011-09-03 2011 September 3

2012-09-01 2012 September 1 (leap year)

2013-08-31 2013 August 31

2014-08-30 2014 August 30

2015-08-29	2015 August 29	
2016-09-03	2016 September 3	(leap year)
2017-09-02	2017 September 2	
2018-09-01	2018 September 1	
2019-08-31	2019 August 31	

The end of the fiscal year would move one day earlier on the calendar each year (two days in leap years) until it would otherwise reach the date four days before the end of the month (August 27 in this case). At that point the first Saturday in the following month (September 3 in this case) becomes the date closest to the end of August and it resets to that date and the fiscal year has 53 weeks instead of 52. In this example the fiscal years ending in 2011 and 2016 have 53 weeks.

The 52–53 week method is permitted by generally accepted accounting principles in the United States, by US Internal Revenue Code Regulation 1.441-2.

Bank Reconciliation

A bank reconciliation is the process of matching the balances in an entity's accounting records for a cash account to the corresponding information on a bank statement. The goal of this process is to ascertain the differences between the two, and to book changes to the accounting records as appropriate. The information on the bank statement is the bank's record of all transactions impacting the entity's bank account during the past month.

A bank reconciliation should be completed at regular intervals for all bank accounts, to ensure that a company's cash records are correct. Otherwise, it may find that cash balances are much lower than expected, resulting in bounced checks or overdraft fees. A bank reconciliation will also detect some types of fraud after the fact; this information can be used to design better controls over the receipt and payment of cash.

If there is so little activity in a bank account that there really is no need for a periodic bank reconciliation, you should question why the account even exists. It may be better to terminate the account and roll any residual funds into a more active account. By doing so, it may be easier to invest the residual funds, as well as to monitor the status of the investment.

At a minimum, conduct a bank reconciliation shortly after the end of each month, when the bank sends the company a bank statement containing the bank's beginning cash balance, transactions during the month, and ending cash balance. It is even better to conduct a bank reconciliation every day, based on the bank's month-to-date information, which should be accessible on the bank's web site. By completing a bank reconciliation every day, you can spot and correct problems immediately. In particular, a daily reconciliation will highlight any ACH debits from the account that you did not authorize; you can then install a debit block on the account to prevent these ACH debits from being used to withdraw funds from the account without your permission.

It is extremely unlikely that a company's ending cash balance and the bank's ending cash balance will be identical, since there are probably multiple payments and deposits in transit at all times, as well as bank service fees (for accepting checks, recording deposits, and so forth), penalties (usually for overdrafts), and not sufficient funds deposits that the company has not yet recorded.

The essential process flow for a bank reconciliation is to start with the bank's ending cash balance, add to it any deposits in transit from the company to the bank, subtract any checks that have not yet cleared the bank, and either add or deduct any other items. Then, go to the company's ending cash balance and deduct from it any bank service fees, NSF checks and penalties, and add to it any interest earned. At the end of this process, the adjusted bank balance should equal the company's ending adjusted cash balance.

Bank Reconciliation Terminology

The key terms to be aware of when dealing with a bank reconciliation are:

- Deposit in transit. Cash and/or checks that have been received and recorded by an entity, but which have not yet been recorded in the records of the bank where the entity deposits the funds. If this occurs at month-end, the deposit will not appear in the bank statement, and so becomes a reconciling item in the bank reconciliation. A deposit in transit occurs when a deposit arrives at the bank too late for it to be recorded that day, or if the entity mails the deposit to the bank (in which case a mail float of several days can cause a delay), or the entity has not yet sent the deposit to the bank at all.
- Outstanding check. A check payment that has been recorded by the issuing entity, but which has not yet cleared its bank account as a deduction from cash. If it has not yet cleared the bank by the end of the month, it does not appear on the month-end bank statement, and so is a reconciling item in the month-end bank reconciliation.
- NSF check. A check that was not honored by the bank of the entity issuing the check, on the grounds that the entity's bank account does not contain sufficient funds. NSF is an acronym for "not sufficient funds." The entity attempting to cash an NSF check may be charged a processing fee by its bank. The entity issuing an NSF check will certainly be charged a fee by its bank.

Bank Reconciliation Procedure

The following bank reconciliation procedure assumes that you are creating the bank reconciliation in an accounting software package, which makes the reconciliation process easier:

1. Enter the bank reconciliation software module. A listing of uncleared checks and uncleared deposits will appear.
2. Check off in the bank reconciliation module all checks that are listed on the bank statement as having cleared the bank.
3. Check off in the bank reconciliation module all deposits that are listed on the bank statement as having cleared the bank.
4. Enter as expenses all bank charges appearing on the bank statement, and which have not already been recorded in the company's records.
5. Enter the ending balance on the bank statement. If the book and bank balances match, then post all changes recorded in the bank reconciliation and close the module. If the balances do not match, then continue reviewing the bank reconciliation for additional reconciling items. Look for the following items:
    - *Checks recorded in the bank records at a different amount from what is recorded in the company's records.*
    - *Deposits recorded in the bank records at a different amount from what is recorded in the company's records.*
    - *Checks recorded in the bank records that are not recorded at all in the company's records.*
    - *Deposits recorded in the bank records that are not recorded at all in the company's records.*
    - *Inbound wire transfers from which a lifting fee has been extracted.*

Bank Reconciliation Problems

There are several problems that continually arise as part of the bank reconciliation, and which you should be aware of. They are:

- *Uncleared* checks that continue to not be presented. There will be a residual number of checks that either are not presented to the bank for payment for a long time, or which are never presented for payment. In the short term, you should treat them in the same manner as any other uncleared checks - just keep them in the uncleared checks listing in your accounting software, so they will be an ongoing reconciling item. In the long term, you should contact the payee to see if they ever received the check; you will likely need to void the old check and issue them a new one.

- *Checks clear the bank after having been voided.* As noted in the preceding special issue, if a check remains uncleared for a long time, you will probably void the old check and issue a replacement check. But what if the payee then cashes the original check? If you voided it with the bank, the bank should reject the check when it is presented. If you did not void it with the bank, then you must record the check with a credit to the cash account and a debit to indicate the reason for the payment (such as an expense account, or an increase in a cash account or decrease in a liability account). If the payee has not yet cashed the replacement check, you should void it with the bank at once to avoid a double payment. Otherwise, you will need to pursue repayment of the second check with the payee.
- *Deposited checks are returned.* There are cases where the bank will refuse to deposit a check, usually because it is drawn on a bank account located in another country. In this case, you must reverse the original entry related to that deposit, which will be a credit to the cash account to reduce the cash balance, with a corresponding debit (increase) in the accounts receivable account.

Another possibility that may be causing problems is that the dates covered by the bank statement have changed, so that some items are included or excluded. This situation should only arise if someone at the company requested the bank to alter the closing date for the company's bank account.

Bank Reconciliation Example

ABC International is closing its books for the month ended April 30. ABC's controller must prepare a bank reconciliation based on the following issues:

1. The bank statement contains an ending bank balance of $320,000.
2. The bank statement contains a $200 check printing charge for new checks that the company ordered.
3. The bank statement contains a $150 service charge for operating the bank account.
4. The bank statement rejects a deposit of $500 due to not sufficient funds, and charges the company a $10 fee associated with the rejection.
5. The bank statement contains interest income of $30.
6. ABC issued $80,000 of checks that have not yet cleared the bank.

7. ABC deposited $25,000 of checks at month-end that were not deposited in time to appear on the bank statement.

The controller creates the following reconciliation:

		Item #	Adjustment to Books
Bank balance	$320,000	1	
- Check printing charge	-200	2	Debit expense, credit cash
- Service charge	-150	3	Debit expense, credit cash
- NSF fee	-10	4	Debit expense, credit cash
- NSF deposit rejected	- 500	4	Debit receivable, credit cash
+ Interest income	+ 30	5	Debit cash, credit interest income
- Uncleared checks	- 80,000	6	None
+ Deposits in transit	+ 25,000	7	None
Book balance	$264,170		

Bank Reconciliation Statement

When the bank reconciliation process is complete, you should be able to print a report through your accounting software that shows the bank and book balances, the identified differences between the two (mostly uncleared checks), and any remaining unreconciled difference. Retain a copy of this report for each month. The auditors will want to see it as part of their year-end audit. The format of the report will vary by software package; a simplistic layout is:

Bank Reconciliation Statement For Month Ended March 31, 20X3	
Bank balance	$850,000
Less: Checks outstanding	-225,000
Add: Deposits in transit	+100,000
+/- Other adjustments	0
Book balance	$725,000
Unreconciled difference	$0

Bank Reconciliation Record Keeping

If you complete the bank reconciliation at month-end, then print the bank reconciliation report and file it in the monthly journal entries binder. This gives the auditors ready access to the information if they want to examine the reconciliations at a later date.

General Journal

The general journal is part of the accounting record keeping system. When an event occurs that must be recorded, it is called a transaction, and may be recorded in a specialty journal or in the general journal. There are four specialty journals, which are so named because specific types of routine transactions are recorded in them. These journals are:

- Sales journal
- Cash receipts journal
- Purchases journal
- Cash disbursements journal

There could be more specialty journals, but the four accounting areas represented by these journals contain the bulk of all accounting transactions, so there is usually no need for additional journals. Instead, by default, all remaining transactions are recorded in the general journal.

General Journal Entries

Examples of transactions recorded in the general journal are:

- Asset sales
- Depreciation
- Interest income and expense
- Stock sales

Once entered, the general journal provides a chronological record of all non-specialized entries that would otherwise have been recorded in one of the specialty journals.

Journal Entry Format

Transactions are recorded in all of the various journals in a debit and credit format, and are recorded in order by date, with the earliest entries being recorded first. These entries are called journal entries (since they are entries into journals). Each journal entry includes the date, the amount of the debit and credit, the titles of the accounts being debited and credited (with the title of the credited account being indented), and also a short narration of why the journal entry is being recorded.

General Journal Accounting Example

An example of a journal entry that would be recorded in the general journal is:

Date	Account	Debit	Credit
June 30	Depreciation expense	10,000	
	Accumulated depreciation		10,000
	To record depreciation for the month of June		

Journal Process Flow

After the transactions are recorded in these journals, a summary of all the transactions is posted in each journal to the general ledger, which contains all of a company's accounts. An account is a separate, detailed record associated with a specific asset, liability, equity, revenue, or expense item. Examples of accounts are:

- Accounts Receivable (an asset account)
- Accounts Payable (a liability account)
- Retained Earnings (an equity account)
- Product Sales (a revenue account)
- Cost of Goods Sold (an expense account)

In summary, an accounting transaction is recorded into a journal, and then the information in the journal is posted into the accounts which are stored in the general ledger. The general journal is the repository for transactions that are not recorded in a specialty journal. Thus, the general journal can be considered an intermediate repository of information for some types of information, on the way to its final recordation in the general ledger.

Other Issues

The general journal was more visible in the days of manual record keeping. With nearly everyone now using accounting software to record their accounting transactions, it is not so readily apparent. Instead, the software makes it appear as though all transactions center around the general ledger, with no specialty journals in use at all.

Ledger

It is also known as the principal book of accounts as well as the book of final entry. It is a book in which all ledger accounts and related monetary transactions are maintained in a summarized and classified form. All accounts combined together make a ledger and form a permanent record of all transactions.

It is the most important book of accounting as it helps in the creation of trial balance which then acts as a base for the preparation of financial statements.

Example: An account can be either an Asset, Liability, Capital, Revenue or an Expense account. Few examples of each are Furniture, Cash, Creditors, Bank Loan, Capital, Drawings, Sales, Rent, etc.

Sample Format of a Ledger Account

Date	Particular	Folio	Amounts	Date	Particular	Folio	Amount

- It is shown in "T" format and divided into 2 columns: the left-hand side represents the debit side and the right-hand side represents the credit side.
- The process of transferring a transaction from journal to a ledger account is called Posting. It is an essential task as it summarizes all transactions related to that account at one place.
- Posting is made to accounts from journal entries and various subsidiary books.

Account Types and their Ledger Balances

Type of Account	Normal Balance
Assets	Debit
Liabilities	Credit
Capital	Credit
Revenue	Credit
Expenses	Debit
Drawings	Debit

Types on the Basis of Purpose

The three types of ledgers are the general, debtors, and creditors. The general ledger accumulates information from journals. Each month all journals are totaled and posted to the General Ledger. The purpose of the General Ledger is therefore to organize and summarize the individual transactions listed in all the journals. The Debtor Ledger accumulates information from the sales journal. The purpose of the Debtors Ledger is to provide knowledge about which customers owe money to the business, and how much. The Creditors Ledger accumulates information from the purchases journal. The purpose of the Creditors Ledger is to provide knowledge about which suppliers the business owes money to, and how much.

Types on the Basis of Format

A ledger can have the following two formats.

- Physical Ledger

  This type of ledger is made up of paper. It can be physically touched. It was very common in the early years for business transactions as the digital ledgers were not fully developed.

- Digital Ledger

  This type of ledger is based on digital medium.

General Ledger

A general ledger is the master set of accounts that summarize all transactions occurring within an entity. There may be a subsidiary set of ledgers that summarize into the general ledger. The general ledger, in turn, is used to aggregate information into the financial statements of a business; this can be done automatically with accounting software, or by manually compiling financial statements from the information in a trial balance report (which is a summarization of the ending balances in the general ledger).

The general ledger contains a debit and credit entry for every transaction recorded within it, so that the total of all debit balances in the general ledger should always match the total of all credit balances. If they do not match, the general ledger is said to be out of balance, and must be corrected before reliable financial statements can be compiled from it.

The general ledger is comprised of all the individual accounts needed to record the assets, liabilities, equity, revenue, expense, gain, and loss transactions of a business. In most cases, detailed transactions are recorded directly in these general ledger accounts. In some cases where the volume of transactions would overwhelm the record keeping in the general ledger, transactions are shunted off to a subsidiary ledger, from which just the account totals are recorded in a control account in the general ledger. In the latter case, a person researching an issue in the financial statements must refer back to the subsidiary ledger to find information about the original transaction. The general ledger is usually printed and stored in an organization's year-end book, which serves as the annual archive of its business transactions.

General ledger accounts are assigned unique identifying account numbers. These numbers may range from a simple three-digit code to a more complex version that identifies individual departments and subsidiaries.

Purchase Ledger

The purchase ledger is a subledger in which purchases are recorded. The purchase ledger is part of the accounting department's database; it is not maintained by the purchasing department. The ledger is useful for segregating into one location a record of the amounts a company spends with its suppliers. The purchase ledger shows which purchases have been paid for and which purchases remain outstanding. A typical transaction entered into the purchase ledger will record an account payable, followed at a later date by a payment transaction that eliminates the account payable. Thus, there is likely to be an outstanding account payable balance in the ledger at any time.

If the purchasing volume is relatively low, then there is no need for a purchase ledger. Instead, this information is recorded directly within the general ledger.

If you were to maintain a manual record of the purchase ledger, it could contain substantially more information than was just indicated. The data fields in a manually-prepared purchase ledger might include the following information for each transaction:

- Purchase date
- Supplier code (or name)
- Supplier invoice number
- Purchase order number (if used)
- Identifying code for item purchased (could be item master code or the supplier's reference number)
- Amount paid
- Sales tax paid
- Payment flag (states whether paid or not)

The primary document recorded in the purchase ledger is the supplier invoice. Also, if suppliers grant a credit back to the business for such items as returned goods or items damaged in transit, then you also record credit memos issued by suppliers in the purchase ledger. A credit memo may also be issued for a volume discount, though this credit may apply to a number of purchases in aggregate, and so cannot be traced back to an individual purchase transaction.

The information in the purchase ledger is aggregated periodically and posted to an account in the general ledger, which is known as a control account. The purchase ledger control account is used to keep from cluttering up the general ledger with the massive amount of information that is typically stored in the purchase ledger. Immediately after posting, the balance in the control account should match the balance in the purchase ledger. Since no detailed transactions are stored in the control account, anyone wanting to research purchase transactions will have to drill down from the control account to the purchase ledger to find them.

Before closing the books and generating financial statements at the end of an accounting period, you must complete all entries in the purchase ledger, close the ledger for that period, and post the totals from the purchase ledger to the general ledger.

Distributed Ledger

Distributed ledger technology (DLT) is a digital system for recording the transaction of assets in which the transactions and their details are recorded in multiple places at the same time. Unlike traditional databases, distributed ledgers have no central data store or administration functionality

In a distributed ledger, each node processes and verifies every item, thereby generating a record of each item and creating a consensus on each item's veracity. A distributed ledger can be used to record static data, such as a registry, and dynamic data, i.e., transactions.

This computer architecture represents a significant revolution in record-keeping by changing how information is gathered and communicated.

Distributed Ledger Implementations

Blockchain, which bundles transactions into blocks that are chained together, and then broadcasts them to the nodes in the network, is probably the best-known type of distributed ledger technology. It powers bitcoin, the digital currency created in 2009. Bitcoin is also known as being a peer-to-peer network.

A representation of how blockchain, a distributed ledger technology, works.

Other entities using blockchain include Overstock.com, the online retailer based in Salt Lake City that delivered a first when it traded stock on a blockchain-based platform in December 2016.

Reasons why they're Important

Distributed ledger technologies have the potential to speed transactions because they remove the need for a central authority or middleman. Similarly, distributed ledgers have the potential to reduce costs of transactions.

Experts also believe that a distributed ledger technology is much more secure because each node of the network holds records, thereby creating a system that's more difficult to manipulate or successfully attack.

Many also consider a distributed ledger a much more transparent way of handling records because the information is shared, and thereby witnessed across a network, which also makes a successful cyberattack much more unlikely.

Distributed Ledger Benefits

Much of the early interest in distributed ledger technology has been around its application in financial transactions. That's understandable, considering that the cryptocurrency bitcoin gained worldwide use, while also simultaneously proving that DLT can, indeed, work. Banks and other finance-related institutions became early innovators in this space, as well.

However, DLT proponents say digital ledgers can be used in multiple areas, including government and business dealings, in addition to financial transactions. Experts believe digital ledgers can be used in tax collection, property deed transfers, social benefits distribution and even voting procedures. They also say DLT can be used to process and execute legal documents and other similar exchanges.

Some believe that individuals can use this technology to hold and better control personal information, and then selectively share pieces of those records when needed; use cases here include individual medical records and corporate supply chains.

Additionally, proponents say digital ledgers can help better track intellectual property rights and ownership for art, commodities, music, film and more.

The Future of Distributed Ledger Technology

Whether distributed ledger technologies, such as blockchain, will revolutionize how governments, institutions and industries work is an open question. Articles in the academic and financial press have questioned whether distributed ledger technologies as they exist now are sufficiently reliable to put into wide-scale use. Issues include the paucity of regulations for this new form of exchange and security concerns.

Trial Balance

Trial Balance is a list of closing balances of ledger accounts on a certain date and is the first step towards the preparation of financial statements. It is usually prepared at the end of an accounting period to assist in the drafting of financial statements. Ledger balances are segregated into debit balances and credit balances. Asset and expense accounts appear on the debit side of the trial balance whereas liabilities, capital and income accounts appear on the credit side. If all accounting entries are recorded correctly and all the ledger balances are accurately extracted, the total of all debit balances appearing in the trial balance must equal to the sum of all credit balances.

Purpose of a Trial Balance

- Trial Balance acts as the first step in the preparation of financial statements. It is a working paper that accountants use as a basis while preparing financial statements.
- Trial balance ensures that for every debit entry recorded, a corresponding credit entry has been recorded in the books in accordance with the double entry concept of accounting. If the totals of the trial balance do not agree, the differences may be investigated and resolved before financial statements are prepared. Rectifying basic accounting errors can be a much lengthy task after the financial statements have been prepared because of the changes that would be required to correct the financial statements.

- Trial balance ensures that the account balances are accurately extracted from accounting ledgers.
- Trail balance assists in the identification and rectification of errors.

Example

Following is an example of what a simple Trial Balance looks like:

ABC LTD Trial Balance as at 31 December 2011		
Account Title	Debit	Credit
	$	$
Share Capital		15,000
Furniture & Fixture	5,000	
Building	10,000	
Creditor		5,000
Debtors	3,000	
Cash	2,000	
Sales		10,000
Cost of sales	8,000	
General and Administration Expense	2,000	
Total	30,000	30,000

- Title provided at the top shows the name of the entity and accounting period end for which the trial balance has been prepared.
- Account Title shows the name of the accounting ledgers from which the balances have been extracted.
- Balances relating to assets and expenses are presented in the left column (debit side) whereas those relating to liabilities, income and equity are shown on the right column (credit side).
- The sum of all debit and credit balances are shown at the bottom of their respective columns.

Limitations

A trial balance only checks the sum of debits against the sum of credits. That is why it does not guarantee that there are no errors. The following are the main classes of errors that are not detected by the trial balance.

- An error of original entry is when both sides of a transaction include the wrong amount. For example, if a purchase invoice for £21 is entered as £12, this will result in an incorrect debit entry (to purchases), and an incorrect credit entry (to the relevant creditor account), both for £9 less, so the total of both columns will be £9 less, and will thus balance.
- An error of omission is when a transaction is completely omitted from the accounting records. As the debits and credits for the transaction would balance, omitting it would still leave the totals balanced. A variation of this error is omitting one of the ledger account totals from the trial balance (but in this case the trial balance will not balance).
- An error of reversal is when entries are made to the correct amount, but with debits instead of credits, and vice versa. For example, if a cash sale for £100 is debited to the Sales account, and credited to the Cash account. Such an error will not affect the totals.
- An error of commission is when the entries are made at the correct amount, and the appropriate side (debit or credit), but one or more entries are made to the wrong account of the correct type. For example, if fuel costs are incorrectly debited to the postage account (both expense accounts). This will not affect the totals.
- An error of principle is when the entries are made to the correct amount, and the appropriate side (debit or credit), as with an error of commission, but the *wrong* type of account is used. For example, if fuel costs (an expense account), are debited to stock (an asset account). This will not affect the totals.
- Compensating errors are multiple unrelated errors that would individually lead to an imbalance, but together cancel each other out.

Adjusting Entries

Adjusting entries are journal entries recorded at the end of an accounting period to alter the ending balances in various general ledger accounts. These adjustments are made to more closely align the reported results and financial position of a business with the requirements of an accounting framework, such as GAAP or IFRS. This generally involves the matching of revenues to expenses under the matching principle, and so impacts reported revenue and expense levels.

The use of adjusting journal entries is a key part of the period closing processing, as noted in the accounting cycle, where a preliminary trial balance is converted into a final trial balance. It is usually not possible to create financial statements that are fully in compliance with accounting standards without the use of adjusting entries.

An adjusting entry can used for any type of accounting transaction; here are some of the more common ones:

- To record depreciation and amortization for the period
- To record an allowance for doubtful accounts
- To record a reserve for obsolete inventory
- To record a reserve for sales returns
- To record the impairment of an asset
- To record an asset retirement obligation
- To record a warranty reserve
- To record any accrued revenue
- To record previously billed but unearned revenue as a liability
- To record any accrued expenses
- To record any previously paid but unused expenditures as prepaid expenses
- To adjust cash balances for any reconciling items noted in the bank reconciliation

As shown in the preceding list, adjusting entries are most commonly of three types, which are:

- Accruals. To record a revenue or expense that has not yet been recorded through a standard accounting transaction.
- Deferrals. To defer a revenue or expense that has been recorded, but which has not yet been earned or used.
- Estimates. To estimate the amount of a reserve, such as the allowance for doubtful accounts or the inventory obsolescence reserve.

When you record an accrual, deferral, or estimate journal entry, it usually impacts an asset or liability account. For example, if you accrue an expense, this also increases a liability account. Or, if you defer revenue recognition to a later period, this also increases a liability account. Thus, adjusting entries impact the balance sheet, not just the income statement.

Since adjusting entries so frequently involve accruals and deferrals, it is customary to set up these entries as reversing entries. This means that the computer system automatically creates an exactly opposite journal entry at the beginning of the next accounting period. By doing so, the effect of an adjusting entry is eliminated when viewed over two accounting periods.

A company usually has a standard set of potential adjusting entries, for which it should evaluate the need at the end of every accounting period. These entries should be listed in the standard closing checklist. Also, consider constructing a journal entry template for each adjusting entry in the accounting software, so there is no need to reconstruct them every month. The standard adjusting entries used should be re-evaluated from time to time, in case adjustments are needed to reflect changes in the underlying business.

Adjusting Entry Examples

Depreciation: Arnold Corporation records the $12,000 of depreciation associated with its fixed assets during the month. The entry is:

	Debit	Credit
Depreciation expense	12,000	
Accumulated depreciation		12,000

Allowance for bad debts: Arnold Corporation adds $5,000 to its allowance for doubtful accounts. The entry is:

	Debit	Credit
Bad debts expense	5,000	
Allowance for doubtful accounts		5,000

Accrued revenue: Arnold Corporation accrues $50,000 of earned but unbilled revenue. The entry is:

	Debit	Credit
Accounts receivable - accrued	50,000	
Sales		50,000

Billed but unearned revenue: Arnold Corporation bills a customer for $10,000, but has not yet earned the revenue, so it creates an adjusting entry to record the billed amount as a liability. The entry is:

	Debit	Credit
Sales	10,000	
Unearned sales (liability)		10,000

Accrued expenses: A supplier is late in sending Arnold Corporation a materials-related invoice for $22,000, so the company accrues the expense. The entry is:

	Debit	Credit
Cost of goods sold (expense)	22,000	
Accrued expenses (liability)		22,000

Prepaid assets: Arnold Corporation pays $30,000 toward the next month's rent. The company records this as a prepaid expense. The entry is:

	Debit	Credit
Prepaid expenses (asset)	30,000	
Rent expense		30,000

References

- Jack Sands (2003). Accounting for Business: What the Numbers Mean and how to Use Them. Arena Books Inc. pp. 42–. ISBN 978-0-9702461-2-7
- "Pittsburgh Waste Book and Fort Pitt Trading Post Papers". Guides to Archives and Manuscript Collections at the University of Pittsburgh Library System. Retrieved 2015-09-04
- Lee, Geoffrey A. (1977). "The Coming of Age of Double Entry: The Giovanni Farolfi Ledger of 1299-1300". Accounting Historians Journal. 4 (2): 79–95. JSTOR 40697544
- MEDIEVAL TRADERS AS INTERNATIONAL CHANGE AGENTS: A COMMENT, Michael Scorgie, The Accounting Historians Journal, Vol. 21, No. 1 (June 1994), pp. 137-143
- Accountancy: Higher Secondary First Year (PDF) (First ed.). Tamil Nadu Textbooks Corporation. 2004. pp. 28–34. Retrieved 12 July 2011
- Michael Chatfield; Richard Vangermeersch (5 February 2014). The History of Accounting (RLE Accounting): An International Encyclopedia. Routledge. pp. 587–. ISBN 978-1-134-67545-6
- Parker, L. M., "Medieval Traders as International Change Agents: A Comparison With Twentieth Century International Accounting Firms," The Accounting Historians Journal, 16(2) (1989): 107-118

5

Understanding Auditing

An audit refers to a systematic examination and evaluation of an organization's financial statements and non-financial disclosures to fairly judge whether the records represent an accurate picture of the claims that they make. All the diverse aspects of auditing, such as audit management, internal audit, cost auditing, continuous auditing, auditor's report and internal audit, have been carefully analyzed in this chapter.

Financial auditing is the process of examining an organization's (or individual's) financial records to determine if they are accurate and in accordance with any applicable rules (including accepted accounting standards), regulations, and laws.

External auditors come in from outside the organization to examine accounting and financial records and provide an independent opinion on these records. Law requires that all public companies have their financial statements externally audited.

Internal auditors work for the organization as internal employees to examine records and help improve internal processes such as operations, internal controls, risk management, and governance.

Auditing Standards

The Public Company Accounting Oversight Board (PCAOB) maintains external auditing standards for public companies (issuers) registered with the Securities and Exchange Commission (SEC).

As of 2012, PCAOB has 15 permanent standards approved by the SEC and a number of interim standards that reflect generally accepted auditing standards, as described in standards issued by the Auditing Standards Board (ASB), which is part of the American Institute of CPAs (AICPA).

The ASB also issues Statements on Auditing Standards (SASs) that apply to preparing and releasing audit reports for nonissuers (companies not required to register with the SEC). AICPA members who audit a nonissuer are required by the AICPA Code of Professional Conduct to comply with these standards. As of 2012, there are more than 60 active standards.

For internal auditing, the Institute of Internal Auditors provides a conceptual framework called the International Professional Practices Framework (IPPF) that provides guidance for internal audits. Some of the guidance is mandatory, while others are considered strongly recommended, but not required by law.

Audit Planning

Audit planning includes deciding on the overall audit strategy and developing an audit plan.

Auditing Standard No. 9 from the PCAOB describes an external auditor's responsibility and the requirements for planning an audit. According to standard No. 9, an audit plan is expected to describe the planned nature, extent, and timing of the procedures for risk assessment and the tests to be done on the controls and substantive procedures, along with a description of other audit procedures planned to ensure the audit meets PCAOB standards.

For internal auditing, the Institute of Internal Auditors provides guidance for audit planning. Planning starts with determining the scope and objectives of the audit.

Internal auditors need to understand the business, operations, and unique characteristics of the department/unit being audited and to develop an audit plan that defines the procedures needed to do an efficient and effective audit.

Information Technology Audit

An information technology audit, or information systems audit, is an examination of the management controls within an Information technology (IT) infrastructure. The evaluation of obtained evidence determines if the information systems are safeguarding assets, maintaining data integrity, and operating effectively to achieve the organization's goals or objectives. These reviews may be performed in conjunction with a financial statement audit, internal audit, or other form of attestation engagement.

Accounting

Due to strong incentives (including taxation, misselling and other forms of fraud) to misstate financial information, auditing has become a legal requirement for many entities who have the power to exploit financial information for personal gain. Traditionally, audits were mainly associated with gaining information about financial systems and the financial records of a company or a business.

Financial audits are performed to ascertain the validity and reliability of information, as well as to provide an assessment of a system's internal control. As a result of this, a third party can express an opinion of the person/organisation/system (etc.) in question. The opinion given on financial statements will depend on the audit evidence obtained.

Due to constraints, an audit seeks to provide only reasonable assurance that the statements are free from material error. Hence, statistical sampling is often adopted in audits. In the case of financial audits, a set of financial statements are said to be true and fair when they are free of material misstatements – a concept influenced by both quantitative (numerical) and qualitative factors. But recently, the argument that auditing should go beyond just true and fair is gaining momentum. And the US Public Company Accounting Oversight Board has come out with a concept release on the same.

Cost accounting is a process for verifying the cost of manufacturing or producing of any article, on the basis of accounts measuring the use of material, labor or other items of cost. In simple words, the term, *cost audit* means a systematic and accurate verification of the cost accounts and records, and checking for adherence to the cost accounting objectives. According to the Institute of Cost and Management Accountants, cost audit is "an examination of cost accounting records and verification of facts to ascertain that the cost of the product has been arrived at, in accordance with principles of cost accounting."

In most nations, an audit must adhere to generally accepted standards established by governing bodies. These standards assure third parties or external users that they can rely upon the auditor's opinion on the fairness of financial statements or other subjects on which the auditor expresses an opinion. The audit must therefore be precise and accurate, containing no additional misstatements or errors.

Integrated Audits

In the US, audits of publicly traded companies are governed by rules laid down by the Public Company Accounting Oversight Board (PCAOB), which was established by Section 404 of the Sarbanes–Oxley Act of 2002. Such an audit is called an integrated audit, where auditors, in addition to an opinion on the financial statements, must also express an opinion on the *effectiveness* of a company's *internal control* over financial reporting, in accordance with PCAOB Auditing Standard No. 5.

There are also new types of integrated auditing becoming available that use unified compliance material. Due to the increasing number of regulations and need for operational transparency, organizations are adopting risk-based audits that can cover multiple regulations and standards from a single audit event. This is a very new but necessary approach in some sectors to ensure that all the necessary governance requirements can be met without duplicating effort from both audit and audit hosting resources.

Assessments

The purpose of an assessment is to measure something or calculate a value for it. Although the process of producing an assessment may involve an audit by an independent professional, its purpose is to provide a measurement rather than to express an opinion about the fairness of statements or quality of performance.

Auditors

Auditors of financial statements & non-financial information (including compliance audit) can be classified into three categories:

- External auditor/Statutory auditor is an independent firm engaged by the client subject to the audit to express an opinion on whether the company's financial statements are free of material misstatements, whether due to fraud or error. For publicly traded companies, external auditors may also be required to express an opinion on the effectiveness of internal controls over financial reporting. External auditors may also be engaged to perform other agreed-upon procedures, related or unrelated to financial statements. Most importantly, external auditors, though engaged and paid by the company being audited, should be regarded as independent.
- Cost auditor/Statutory cost auditor is an independent firm engaged by the client subject to the cost audit to express an opinion on whether the company's cost statements and cost sheet are free of material misstatements, whether due to fraud or error. For publicly traded companies, external auditors may also be required to express an opinion on the effectiveness of internal controls over cost reporting. These are Specialised Persons called Cost Accountants in India & CMA globally either Cost & Management Accountants or Certified Management Accountants.

  Government Auditors review the finances and practices of federal agencies. These auditors report their finds to congress, which uses them to create and manage policies and budgets. Government auditors work for the U.S. Government Accountability Office, and most state governments have similar departments to audit state and municipal agencies.
- Secretarial auditor/Statutory secretarial auditor is an independent firm engaged by the client subject to the audit of secretarial and applicable laws/ compliances of other applicable laws to express an opinion on whether the company's secretarial records and compliance of applicable laws are free of material misstatements, whether due to fraud or error and inviting heavy fines or penalties. For bigger public companies, external secretarial auditors may also be required to express an opinion on the effectiveness of internal controls over compliances system management of the company. These are Specialized

Persons called Company Secretaries in India who are the members of Institute of Company Secretaries of India and holding Certificate of Practice.

The most commonly used external audit standards are the US GAAS of the American Institute of Certified Public Accountants and the International Standards on Auditing (ISA) developed by the International Auditing and Assurance Standard.

- Internal auditors are employed by the organisations they audit. They work for government agencies (federal, state and local); for publicly traded companies; and for non-profit companies across all industries. The internationally recognised standard setting body for the profession is the Institute of Internal Auditors - IIA. The IIA has defined internal auditing as follows: "Internal auditing is an independent, objective assurance and consulting activity designed to add value and improve an organisation's operations. It helps an organisation accomplish its objectives by bringing a systematic, disciplined approach to evaluate and improve the effectiveness of risk management, control, and governance processes". Thus professional internal auditors provide independent and objective audit and consulting services focused on evaluating whether the board of directors, shareholders, stakeholders, and corporate executives have reasonable assurance that the organization's governance, risk management, and control processes are designed adequately and function effectively. Internal audit professionals (Certified Internal Auditors - CIAs) are governed by the international professional standards and code of conduct of the Institute of Internal Auditors. While internal auditors are not independent of the companies that employ them, independence and objectivity are a cornerstone of the IIA professional standards; and are discussed at length in the standards and the supporting practice guides and practice advisories. Professional internal auditors are mandated by the IIA standards to be independent of the business activities they audit. This independence and objectivity are achieved through the organizational placement and reporting lines of the internal audit department. Internal auditors of publicly traded companies in the United States are required to report functionally to the board of directors directly, or a sub-committee of the board of directors (typically the audit committee), and not to management except for administrative purposes. As described often in the professional literature for the practice of internal auditing (such as Internal Auditor, the journal of the IIA) -, or other similar and generally recognized frameworks for management control when evaluating an entity's governance and control practices; and apply COSO's "Enterprise Risk Management-Integrated Framework" or other similar and generally recognized frameworks for entity-wide risk management when evaluating an organization's entity-wide risk management practices. Professional internal auditors also use control self-assessment (CSA) as an effective process for performing their work.
- Consultant auditors are external personnel contracted by the firm to perform

an audit following the firm's auditing standards. This differs from the external auditor, who follows their own auditing standards. The level of independence is therefore somewhere between the internal auditor and the external auditor. The consultant auditor may work independently, or as part of the audit team that includes internal auditors. Consultant auditors are used when the firm lacks sufficient expertise to audit certain areas, or simply for staff augmentation when staff are not available.

Performance Audits

Performance audit refers to an independent examination of a program, function, operation or the management systems and procedures of a governmental or non-profit entity to assess whether the entity is achieving economy, efficiency and effectiveness in the employment of available resources. Safety, security, information systems performance, and environmental concerns are increasingly the subject of audits. There are now audit professionals who specialize in security audits and information systems audits. With nonprofit organisations and government agencies, there has been an increasing need for performance audits, examining their success in satisfying mission objectives.

Quality Audits

Quality audits are performed to verify conformance to standards through review of objective evidence. A system of quality audits may verify the effectiveness of a quality management system. This is part of certifications such as ISO 9001. Quality audits are essential to verify the existence of objective evidence showing conformance to required processes, to assess how successfully processes have been implemented, and to judge the effectiveness of achieving any defined target levels. Quality audits are also necessary to provide evidence concerning reduction and elimination of problem areas, and they are a hands-on management tool for achieving continual improvement in an organization.

To benefit the organisation, quality auditing should not only report non-conformance and corrective actions but also highlight areas of good practice and provide evidence of conformance. In this way, other departments may share information and amend their working practices as a result, also enhancing continual improvement.

Project Management

A project audit provides an opportunity to uncover issues, concerns and challenges encountered during the project lifecycle. Conducted midway through the project, an audit affords the project manager, project sponsor and project team an interim view of what has gone well, as well as what needs to be improved to successfully complete the project. If done at the close of a project, the audit can be used to develop success criteria for future projects by providing a forensic review. This review identifies which elements of the project were successfully managed and which ones presented challenges. As a result, the review will help the organisation identify what it needs to do to avoid repeating the same mistakes on future projects.

Projects can undergo 2 types of Project audits:

- Regular Health Check Audits: The aim of a regular health check audit is to understand the current state of a project in order to increase project success.
- Regulatory Audits: The aim of a regulatory audit is to verify that a project is compliant with regulations and standards. Best practices of NEMEA Compliance Centre describe that, the regulatory audit must be accurate, objective, and independent while providing oversight and assurance to the organisation.

Other forms of Project audits:

Formal: Applies when the project is in trouble, sponsor agrees that the audit is needed, sensitivities are high, and need to be able prove conclusions via sustainable evidence.

Informal: Apply when a new project manager is provided, there is no indication the projects in trouble and there is a need to report whether the project is as opposed to where its supposed to Informal audits can apply the same criteria as formal audit but there is no need for such a in depth report or formal report.

Energy audits

An energy audit is an inspection, survey and analysis of energy flows for energy conservation in a building, process or system to reduce the amount of energy input into the system without negatively affecting the output(s).

Operations audit

An operations audit is an examination of the operations of the client's business. In this audit the auditor thoroughly examines the efficiency, effectiveness and economy of the operations with which the management of the entity (client) is achieving its objective. The operational audit goes beyond the internal controls issues since management does not achieve its objectives merely by compliance of satisfactory system of internal controls. Operational audits cover any matters which may be commercially unsound. The objective of operational audit is to examine Three E's, namely: Effectiveness – doing the right things with least wastage of resources. Efficiency – performing work in least possible time. Economy – balance between benefits and costs to run the operations.

A control self-assessment is a commonly used tool for completing an operations audit.

Forensic Audits

Also refer to forensic accountancy, forensic accountant or forensic accounting. It refers to an investigative audit in which accountants with specialised on both accounting and investigation seek to uncover frauds, missing money and negligences.

Audit Management

Audit management can be defined as a set of tools; techniques and planning that enable an organized examination of whether an object meets the predefined requirements. To put it more simply, audit management helps in the better organization of the workflow and collaborative process of audit reporting. It is an eclectic management of auditing involving the preparation of a detailed question list and evaluating the results and documents. Auditing management broadly involves the process of recruiting, training and overseeing the audit staff (internal and external) and running the auditing program.

Some of the important elements that make audit management successful are proactive and strong leadership, cohesion within the team, intricate planning, controls and a well-defined methodology. The process of managing an audit comprises of three dimensions, namely internal auditing, external auditing and third-party auditing.

Internal audit management: It refers to a set of auditing processes which the organization sets up in order to protect it from fraudulent activities and ensure that the organization's management and control are running at their optimum. The role of internal auditors is to be objective, neutral and report any issues only to the highest executive in the organization.

External audit management: It is the organization of auditing processes in order to determine whether the documentations filed are accurate and meet the required standards set by the organization or meets the government laid rules and regulations. The external auditor is independent of the firm is able to provide a more objective report and use the discretion in reporting to the concerned authorities in case of a breach.

Third party auditing: The question of third-party auditing arises only when the company intends to run a *quality management* system to meet or qualify for the desired certification.

Internal Audit

Internal audit is a function setup within the organisation to reduce the risk of fraud in the organisation and runs according to the management commands. This is the main difference between internal and external audit where external auditors are independent of management and hence external auditors give an opinion on the financial statements as presented by the management of the organisation. This is performed by the companies internal auditing team, this can help companies improve because strengths and weaknesses are identified. Senior internal audit managers need to manage the responsibilities of what different people want.

Like all supervisor that are part of the business there is a need to:

- Understand what a person with an interest or concern in the business and customers want
- Agree aim and priorities
- Plan activities
- Establish resources and processes
- Record performance, making changes to keep things on track if required.

External Audit

The objectives of an external audit or audits being conducted by someone not part of the business, is when one business audits a different business to determine if the accounting records are complete and correctly prepared according to GAAP (GAAP is the highest U.S. power on accounting standards and they must be followed by jurisprudence when preparing financial information for businesses) provisions. The organisations have a formal agreement for the supply of goods and services. External audits make good business exercise.

Smaller businesses benefit from external audit because it can act as a education for small business owners, as many small business owners don't have an in-depth understanding of accounting. Businesses can use external auditor to spot mistakes that might have occurred and went noticed. Errors that occur in accounting statements can lead to businesses making bad decisions. For larger corporation audit provide confidence to the shareholder and investors that the figures shown in the books is reliable. Audit management for external auditors might be surpass than the businesses they work with because they are likely to be investing in the best software possible and are a specialist for that particular area.

Companies have to appoint an auditor to do an annual external audit on your accounts if your business is:

- an authorised professional firm
- a BIPRU investment firm
- an insurance intermediary
- an investment management firm

- a mortgage administrator
- a mortgage intermediary
- a mortgage lender
- a personal investment firm
- a securities and futures firm
- a service company

Third Party Audit

A third party audit gives feedback to important documents and processes including quality manuals or performance development plan, records including instructing, organisational charts, and examination of the processes within the extent of the audit. A third party audit is conducted by an audit organisation that doesn't have the traditional customer-supplier relationship and does not carry any conflict of interest. Institutions such as registrars (certification bodies) or legislature are usually the types of organisations that perform these types of audit.

Managing an Audit

To manage an audit team in a manner to achieve good results, it is important that audit managers have strong leadership skills, workers want to work for someone that has moved up the ranks which shows that the manager they work with has experience doing the job team members are doing. It is important that the teams works efficiently, carrying out audit can be time consuming so being organised and managing different information helps with the productiveness. Auditing involves planning, method, facts, procedures, controls, risk, and management. Communication skills is key to many successful auditors, as you develop through your career getting you message across in your unique way clearly helps project your professionalism. Auditors from different countries may work with each other to help the same client, it is common for auditors to work directly at their client company in their offices.

Audit Directive and Regulation

It is important that the United Kingdom economy has organised and effective capital markets and there is self-assurance in the business framework through greater transparency. Offering reliable and informative reporting supplies to this pledge. It includes the application of global accounting principles and global principles on auditing and requires an ongoing conversation with UK stakeholders and EU or international law makers on measures to encourage market firmness. Companies that are publicly traded may be required to submit an audit.

Financial Audit

Financial auditing refers to an accounting process applied in business. The process involves using an individual body for evaluating the financial transactions and statements of a business. The ultimate purpose of financial audit is presenting an accurate amount of the business transactions of a company. Besides, it ensures that the accounts presented to the public and shareholders are accurate and justified.

This examination by a knowledgeable outsider is needed to provide credibility to an organization's financial statements. If an auditor does not find any issues, then he or she issues an audit opinion, which accompanies the certified financial statements when they are issued. Lenders, creditors, and investors want to see an audit opinion, as proof that the financial statements are correct.

An auditor will conduct a variety of tests to verify that the financial records are complete, and fairly represent the financial results and condition of an organization. These tests may include tests of controls, tests of transactions, analytical procedures, and tests of balances. Financial audits are most commonly conducted for the financial statements of a firm, but may be targeted at more specific areas, such as tax records.

Financial audits dig deep into a company's financial situation, probing accounting records, internal controls policies, cash holdings and other sensitive financial areas. Publicly-traded corporations are subject to external financial audits on a regular basis, and even privately owned small businesses can be subjected to an external financial audit by the IRS or other government authority. Knowing how to perform a financial audit on your own books can help you to prepare for a possible external audit, keep your accounting system in order and discourage internal fraud and theft.

The Big Four

Greenwood et al. (1990) defined the audit firm as professional partnership which has a decentralized organization relationship between the national head office and local offices. Local offices can make most decision except for the drawing up professional standard and maintaining it.

The Big Four are the four largest international professional services networks, offering audit, assurance, tax, consulting, advisory, actuarial, corporate finance, and legal services. They handle the vast majority of audits for publicly traded companies as well as many private companies, creating an oligopoly in auditing large companies. It is reported that the Big Four audit 99% of the companies in the FTSE 100, and 96% of the companies in the FTSE 250 Index, an index of the leading mid-cap listing companies. The Big Four firms are shown below, with their latest publicly available data. None of the Big Four firms is a single firm; rather, they are professional services networks. Each is a network of firms, owned and managed independently, which have entered into agreements with other member firms in the network to share a common name, brand and quality standards. Each network has established an entity to co-ordinate the activities of the network. In one case (KPMG), the co-ordinating entity is Swiss, and in three cases (Deloitte Touche Tohmatsu, PricewaterhouseCoopers and Ernst & Young) the co-ordinating entity is a UK limited company. Those entities do not themselves perform external professional services, and do not own or control the member firms. They are similar to law firm networks found in the legal profession. In many cases each member firm practises in a single country, and is structured to comply with the regulatory environment in that country. In 2007 KPMG announced a merger of four member firms (in the United Kingdom, Germany, Switzerland and Liechtenstein) to form a single firm. Ernst & Young also includes separate legal entities which manage three of its four areas: Americas, EMEIA (Europe, The Middle East, India and Africa), and Asia-Pacific. (Note: the Japan area does not have a separate area management entity). These firms coordinate services performed by local firms within their respective areas but do not perform services or hold ownership in the local entities. This group was once known as the "Big Eight", and was reduced to the "Big Six" and then "Big Five" by a series of mergers. The Big Five became the Big Four after the demise of Arthur Andersen in 2002, following its involvement in the Enron scandal.

Costs

Costs of audit services can vary greatly dependent upon the nature of the entity, its transactions, industry, the condition of the financial records and financial statements, and the fee rates of the CPA firm. A commercial decision such as the setting of audit fees is handled by companies and their auditors. Directors are responsible for setting the overall fee as well as the audit committee. The fees are set at a level that could not lead to audit quality being compromised. The scarcity of staffs and the lower audit fee lead to very low billing realization rates. As a result, accounting firms, such as KPMG, PricewaterhouseCoopers and Deloitte who used to have very low technical inefficiency, have started to use AI tools.

Governance and Oversight

Seal of the United States Government Accountability Office

In the United States, the SEC has generally deferred to the accounting industry (acting through various organisations throughout the years) as to the accounting standards for financial reporting, and the U.S. Congress has deferred to the SEC.

This is also typically the case in other developed economies. In the UK, auditing guidelines are set by the institutes (including ACCA, ICAEW, ICAS and ICAI) of which auditing firms and individual auditors are members. While in Australia, the rules and professional code of ethics are set by The Institute of Chartered Accountants Australia (ICAA), CPA Australia (CPA) and The National Institute of Accountants (NIA).

Accordingly, financial auditing standards and methods have tended to change significantly only after auditing failures. The most recent and familiar case is that of Enron. The company succeeded in hiding some important facts, such as off-book liabilities, from banks and shareholders. Eventually, Enron filed for bankruptcy, and (as of 2006) is in the process of being dissolved. One result of this scandal was that Arthur Andersen, then one of the five largest accountancy firms worldwide, lost their ability to audit public companies, essentially killing off the firm.

A recent trend in audits (spurred on by such accounting scandals as Enron and Worldcom) has been an increased focus on internal control procedures, which aim to ensure the completeness, accuracy and validity of items in the accounts, and restricted access to financial systems. This emphasis on the internal control environment is now a mandatory part of the audit of SEC-listed companies, under the auditing standards of the Public Company Accounting Oversight Board (PCAOB) set up by the Sarbanes-Oxley Act.

Many countries have government sponsored or mandated organizations who develop and maintain auditing standards, commonly referred to generally accepted auditing standards or GAAS. These standards prescribe different aspects of auditing such as the opinion, stages of an audit, and controls over work product (*i.e.*, working papers).

Some oversight organisations require auditors and audit firms to undergo a third-party quality review periodically to ensure the applicable GAAS is followed.

Stages of an Audit

The following are the stages of a typical audit:

Phase I: plan and Design an Audit Approach

- Accept Client and Perform Initial Planning.
- Understand the Client's Business and Industry.
    - What should auditors understand?
        - The relevant industry, regulatory, and other external factors including the applicable financial reporting framework

- ◇ The nature of the entity
- ◇ The entity's selection and application of accounting policies
- ◇ The entity's objectives and strategies, and the related business risks that may result in material misstatement of the financial statements
- ◇ The measurement and review of the entity's financial performance
- ◇ Internal control relevant to the audit

- Assess Client's Business Risk
- Set Materiality and Assess Accepted Audit Risk (AAR) and Inherent Risk (IR).
- Understand Internal Control and Assess Control Risk (CR).
- Develop Overall Audit Plan and Audit Program.

Phase II: Perform test of Controls and Substantive Test of Transactions

- Test of Control: if the auditor plans to reduce the determined control risk, then the auditor should perform the test of control, to assess the operating effectiveness of internal controls (e.g. authorisation of transactions, account reconciliations, segregation of duties) including IT General Controls. If internal controls are assessed as effective, this will reduce (but not entirely eliminate) the amount of 'substantive' work the auditor needs to do.
- Substantive test of transactions: evaluate the client's recording of transactions by verifying the monetary amounts of transactions, a process called substantive tests of transactions. For example, the auditor might use computer software to compare the unit selling price on duplicate sales invoices with an electronic file of approved prices as a test of the accuracy objective for sales transactions. Like the test of control in the preceding paragraph, this test satisfies the accuracy transaction-related audit objective for sales. For the sake of efficiency, auditors often perform tests of controls and substantive tests of transactions at the same time.
- Assess Likelihood of Misstatement in Financial Statement.

Notes:

- At this stage, if the auditor accept the CR that has been set at the phase I and does not want to reduce the controls risk, then the auditor may not perform test of control. If so, then the auditor perform substantive test of transactions.
- This test determines the amount of work to be performed i.e. substantive testing or test of details.

Phase III: Perform Analytical Procedures And Tests of Details Of Balances

- Where internal controls are strong, auditors typically rely more on Substantive Analytical Procedures (the comparison of sets of financial information, and financial with non-financial information, to see if the numbers 'make sense' and that unexpected movements can be explained)
- Where internal controls are weak, auditors typically rely more on Substantive Tests of Detail of Balance (selecting a sample of items from the major account balances, and finding hard evidence (e.g. invoices, bank statements) for those items)

Notes:

- Some audits involve a 'hard close' or 'fast close' whereby certain substantive procedures can be performed before year-end. For example, if the year-end is 31 December, the hard close may provide the auditors with figures as at 30 November. The auditors would audit income/expense movements between 1 January and 30 November, so that after year end, it is only necessary for them to audit the December income/expense movements and 31 December balance sheet. In some countries and accountancy firms these are known as 'rollforward' procedures.

Phase IV: Complete the Audit and Issue an Audit Report

After the auditor has completed all procedures for each audit objective and for each financial statement account and related disclosures, it is necessary to combine the information obtained to reach an overall conclusion as to whether the financial statements are fairly presented. This highly subjective process relies heavily on the auditor's professional judgment. When the audit is completed, the CPA must issue an audit report to accompany the client's published financial statements.

Responsibilities of an Auditor

Corporations Act 2001 requires the auditor to:

- Gives a true and fair view about whether the financial report complies with the accounting standards
- Conduct their audit in accordance with auditing standards
- Give the directors and auditor's independence declaration and meet independence requirements
- Report certain suspected contraventions to ASIC

Commercial Relationships Versus Objectivity

One of the major issues faced by private auditing firms is the need to provide independent auditing services while maintaining a business relationship with the audited company.

The auditing firm's responsibility to check and confirm the reliability of financial statements may be limited by pressure from the audited company, who pays the auditing firm for the service. The auditing firm's need to maintain a viable business through auditing revenue may be weighed against its duty to examine and verify the accuracy, relevancy, and completeness of the company's financial statements. This is done by auditor.

Numerous proposals are made to revise the current system to provide better economic incentives to auditors to perform the auditing function without having their commercial interests compromised by client relationships. Examples are more direct incentive compensation awards and financial statement insurance approaches. See, respectively, Incentive Systems to Promote Capital Market Gatekeeper Effectiveness and Financial Statement Insurance.

Auditors and Technology

Currently, many entities being audited are using information systems, which generate information electronically. For the audit evidences, auditors get dynamic information generated from the information systems in real time. There are less paper documents and pre-numbered audit evidences available, which leads a revolution to audit mythology.

Internal Audit

An internal audit (IA) is an organizational initiative to monitor and analyze its own business operations in order to determine how well it conforms to a set of specific criteria.

In the enterprise, an internal audit can focus on enterprise risk management functions, security processes or maintaining regulatory compliance, as well as many other business departments and activities. As part of the internal audit plan, auditors try to find discrepancies between operational processes and what those processes are designed to do. If internal auditors do find discrepancies, these issues are included in the final report issued to company leadership so the processes can be improved.

Internal audit plans are often designed as a pre-emptive maneuver to maintain operational efficiency and financial reliability, as well as to safeguard assets.

Reasons why Internal Audits Matter

Regular internal audits assess a company's controls and help uncover evidence of fraud, waste or abuse. The frequency of internal audits will depend on the department or process being examined. Some types of manufacturing may require daily audits for quality control, while a department such as human resources may require only an annual audit of records.

Unlike an external auditor that primarily considers financial risk, the internal auditor examines issues relating to wide-ranging risks to the organization's reputation and growth. For example, an internal audit can uncover threats to the organization's reputation if it finds employee safety violations or instances where employees are treated unfairly. One of the internal auditor's primary goals is to assess the management of risk and to ensure that risk management processes are efficient, effective, secure and compliant.

Once the internal audits are completed, auditors issue a final audit report outlining how well the systems and processes are working. This report is often provided first to the most senior levels of executive management, as well as to its internal audit committee. When required, internal auditors offer consulting help to improve areas in which systems and processes are lacking and conduct a follow-up audit to determine how well the improvements are working.

Information provided by internal auditors can help the company thrive in a competitive business environment and inform new initiatives to help it continue to prosper.

Organizational Independence

While internal auditors are not independent of the companies that employ them, independence and objectivity are a cornerstone of the IIA professional standards; and are discussed at length in the standards and the supporting practice guides and practice advisories. Professional internal auditors are mandated by the IIA standards to be independent of the business activities they audit. This independence and objectivity are achieved through the organizational placement and reporting lines of the internal audit department. Internal auditors of publicly traded companies in the United States are required to report functionally to the board of directors directly, or a sub-committee of the board of directors (typically the audit committee), and not to management except for administrative purposes.

The required organizational independence from management enables unrestricted evaluation of management activities and personnel and allows internal auditors to perform their role effectively. Although internal auditors are part of company management and paid by the company, the primary customer of internal audit activity is the entity charged with oversight of management's activities. This is typically the Audit Committee, a sub-committee of the Board of Directors. Organizational independence is effectively achieved when the chief audit executive reports functionally to the board. Examples of functional reporting to the board involve the board: Approving the internal audit charter; Approving the risk based internal audit plan; Approving the internal audit budget and resource plan; Receiving communications from the chief audit executive on the internal audit activity's performance relative to its plan and other matters; Approving decisions regarding the appointment and removal of the chief audit executive; Approving the remuneration of the chief audit executive; and Making appropriate inquiries of management and the chief audit executive to determine whether there are inappropriate scope or resource limitations.

Role in Internal Control

Internal auditing activity is primarily directed at evaluating internal control. Under the COSO Framework, internal control is broadly defined as a process, effected by an entity's board of directors, management, and other personnel, designed to provide reasonable assurance regarding the achievement of the following core objectives for which all businesses strive:

- Effectiveness and efficiency of operations.
- Reliability of financial and management reporting.
- Compliance with laws and regulations.
- Safeguarding of Assets

Management is responsible for internal control, which comprises five critical components: the control environment; risk assessment; risk focused control activities; information and communication; and monitoring activities. Managers establish policies, processes, and practices in these five components of management control to help the organization achieve the four specific objectives listed above. Internal auditors perform audits to evaluate whether the five components of management control are present and operating effectively, and if not, provide recommendations for improvement.

In the United States, internal auditors may assist management with compliance with the Sarbanes-Oxley Act (SOX).

Role in Risk Management

Internal auditing professional standards require the function to evaluate the effectiveness of the organization's Risk management activities. Risk management is the process by which an organization identifies, analyzes, responds, gathers information about, and monitors strategic risks that could actually or potentially impact the organization's ability to achieve its mission and objectives.

Under the COSO enterprise risk management (ERM) Framework, an organization's strategy, operations, reporting, and compliance objectives all have associated strategic business risks - the negative outcomes resulting from internal and external events that inhibit the organization's ability to achieve its objectives. Management assesses risk as part of the ordinary course of business activities such as strategic planning, marketing planning, capital planning, budgeting, hedging, incentive payout structure, credit/lending practices, mergers and acquisitions, strategic partnerships, legislative changes, conducting business abroad, etc. Sarbanes-Oxley regulations require extensive risk assessment of financial reporting processes. Corporate legal counsel often prepares comprehensive assessments of the current and potential litigation a company faces. Internal auditors may evaluate each of these activities, or focus on the overarching process used to manage risks entity-wide. For example, internal auditors can advise management regarding the reporting of forward-looking operating measures to the Board, to help identify emerging risks; or internal auditors can evaluate and report on whether the board and other stakeholders can have reasonable assurance the organization's management team has implemented an effective enterprise risk management program.

In larger organizations, major strategic initiatives are implemented to achieve objectives and drive changes. As a member of senior management, the Chief Audit Executive (CAE) may participate in status updates on these major initiatives. This places the CAE in the position to report on many of the major risks the organization faces to the Audit Committee, or ensure management's reporting is effective for that purpose.

The internal audit function may help the organization address its risk of fraud via a fraud risk assessment, using principles of fraud deterrence. Internal auditors may help companies establish and maintain Enterprise Risk Management processes. This process is highly valued by many businesses for establishing and implementing effective management systems and ensuring quality is maintained & professional standards are met Internal auditors also play an important role in helping companies execute a SOX 404 top-down risk assessment. In these latter two areas, internal auditors typically are part of the risk assessment team in an advisory role.

Role in Corporate Governance

Internal auditing activity as it relates to corporate governance has in the past been generally informal, accomplished primarily through participation in meetings and discussions with members of the Board of Directors. According to COSO's ERM framework, governance is the policies, processes and structures used by the organization's leadership to direct activities, achieve objectives, and protect the interests of diverse stakeholder groups in a manner consistent with ethical standards. The internal auditor is often considered one of the "four pillars" of corporate governance, the other pillars being the Board of Directors, management, and the external auditor.

A primary focus area of internal auditing as it relates to corporate governance is helping the Audit Committee of the Board of Directors (or equivalent) perform its responsibilities effectively. This may include reporting critical management control issues, suggesting questions or topics for the Audit Committee's meeting agendas, and coordinating with the external auditor and management to ensure the Committee receives effective information. In recent years, the IIA has advocated more formal evaluation of Corporate governance, particularly in the areas of board oversight of enterprise risk, corporate ethics, and fraud.

Audit Project Selection or "Annual Audit Plan"

Based on the risk assessment of the organization, internal auditors, management and oversight boards determine where to focus internal auditing efforts. This focus or prioritization is part of the annual/ multi-year Annual Audit Plan. The Audit Plan is typically proposed by the CAE (sometimes with several options or alternatives) for the review and approval of the Audit Committee or the Board of Directors. Internal Auditing activity is generally conducted as one or more discrete assignments.

Internal Audit Execution

A typical Internal Audit Assignment involves the following steps:

1. Establishing and communicating the scope and objectives of the Audit to appropriate members of management.
2. Developing an understanding of the business area under review - this includes objectives, measurements & key transaction types and involves interviews and a review of documents - flowcharts and narratives may be created, if necessary.
3. Describing the key risks facing the business activities within the scope of the Audit.
4. Identifying management practices in the five components of control used to ensure that each key risk is properly controlled and monitored. Internal Audit Checklist can be a helpful tool to identify common risks and desired controls in the specific process or specific industry being audited.
5. Developing and executing a risk-based sampling and testing approach to determine whether the most important management controls are operating as intended.
6. Reporting issues and challenges identified and negotiating action plans with the management to address these problems.
7. Following-up on reported findings at appropriate intervals. Internal Audit Departments maintain a follow-up database for this purpose.

Audit Assignment length varies based on the complexity of the activity being audited and Internal Audit resources available. Many of the above steps are iterative and may not all occur in the sequence indicated.

In addition to assessing business processes, specialists called Information Technology (IT) Auditors review Information technology controls.

Internal Audit Reports

Internal auditors typically issue reports at the end of each audit that summarize their findings, recommendations, and any responses or action plans from management. An audit report may have an executive summary–a body that includes the specific issues or findings identified and related recommendations or action plans, and appendix information such as detailed graphs and charts or process information. Each audit finding within the body of the report may contain five elements, sometimes called the "5 C's":

1. Condition: What is the particular problem identified?
2. Criteria: What is the standard that was not met? The standard may be a company policy or other benchmark.
3. Cause: Why did the problem occur?
4. Consequence: What is the risk/negative outcome (or opportunity foregone) because of the finding?
5. Corrective action: What should management do about the finding? What have they agreed to do and by when?

The recommendations in an internal audit report are designed to help the organization achieve effective and efficient governance, risk and control processes associated with operations objectives, financial and management reporting objectives; and legal/regulatory compliance objectives.

Audit findings and recommendations may also relate to particular assertions about transactions, such as whether the transactions audited were valid or authorized, completely processed, accurately valued, processed in the correct time period, and properly disclosed in financial or operational reporting, among other elements.

Under the IIA standards, a critical component of the audit process is the preparation of a balanced report that provides executives and the board with the opportunity to evaluate and weigh the issues being reported in the proper context and perspective. In providing perspective, analysis and workable recommendations for business improvements in critical areas, auditors help the organization meet its objectives.

Quality of Internal Audit Report

- Objectivity - The comments and opinions expressed in the Report should be objective and unbiased.
- Clarity - The language used should be simple and straightforward.
- Accuracy - The information contained in the report should be accurate.
- Brevity - The report should be concise.
- Timeliness - The report should be released promptly immediately after the audit is concluded, within a month.

Strategy

Internal audit functions may also develop functional strategies described in multi-year strategic plans. Professional guidance on building an Internal Audit strategic plan was issued by the *Institute of Internal Auditors* in July 2012 via a Practice Guide called *Developing the Internal Audit Strategic Plan*. A key aspect of developing IA strategy is understanding the expectations of stakeholders, such as the Audit Committee and top management. This helps guide the IA function in its mission of helping the organization address the risks it faces. Specific topics considered in IA strategic planning include:

- Scope and emphasis: An IA function may be involved in addressing risks related to financial reporting, operations, legal and regulatory compliance, and the company strategy. There may also be special topics of interest to stakeholders that change considerably year-to-year.
- Portfolio of services: IA functions may provide traditional audit assurance across the risk spectrum as well as consulting project support in a variety of areas such as project management, data analysis, and monitoring of major company initiatives. Larger audit functions may establish specialty areas to handle their service portfolio.
- Competency development: The stakeholder expectations around scope and service portfolio determine what competencies the function needs, which drives decisions regarding hiring of specific skills and training programs. The internal audit function is often used as a "management training ground" to provide employees with a deeper knowledge of the company's operations before they are rotated into a management position.
- Technology: IA functions use a variety of technology tools/software to support audit process workflow, statistical analysis, and obtaining data from systems.

Building the IA strategy may involve a variety of strategic management concepts and frameworks, such as strategic planning, strategic thinking, and SWOT analysis.

Measuring the Internal Audit Function

The measurement of the internal audit function can involve a balanced scorecard approach. Internal audit functions are primarily evaluated based on the quality of counsel and information provided to the Audit Committee and top management. However, this is primarily qualitative and therefore difficult to measure. "Customer surveys" sent to key managers after each audit engagement or report can be used to measure performance, with an annual survey to the Audit Committee. Scoring on dimensions such as professionalism, quality of counsel, timeliness of work product, utility of meetings, and quality of status updates are typical with such surveys. Understanding the expectations of senior management and the audit committee represent important steps in developing a performance measurement process, as well as how such measures help align the audit function with organizational priorities. Independent peer reviews are part of the quality assurance process for many internal audit groups as they are often required by standards. The resulting peer review report is made available to the Audit Committee.

Reporting of Critical Findings

The Chief Audit Executive (CAE) typically reports the most critical issues to the Audit Committee quarterly, along with management's progress towards resolving them. Critical issues typically have a reasonable likelihood of causing substantial financial or reputational damage to the company. For particularly complex issues, the responsible manager may participate in the discussion. Such reporting is critical to ensure the function is respected, that the proper "tone at the top" exists in the organization, and to expedite resolution of such issues. It is a matter of considerable judgment to select appropriate issues for the Audit Committee's attention and to describe them in the proper context.

Operational Auditing

Operational auditing is a comprehensive and constructive review of organisational structure or components thereof, i.e. method of operation and use of physical facilities'. Operational Auditing is essentially a frame of mind, a method of approach; one can approach any area from a financial or accounting point of view or from operating or management point of view.

A control system via appraisal system to keep the management informed of 'opportunities gained' and 'opportunities lost' is Operation Audit or Operational Auditing. Federal Financial Officers' Institute in Canada defines Operational Audit as a systematic independent appraisal activity within an organisation for a review of the entire departmental operations as a service to management.

The overall objective of operational auditing is to assist all levels of management in the effective discharge of their responsibilities by furnishing them with objective analyses, appraisals, recommendations and pertinent comments concerning the activities reviewed.

This definition does not specifically mention about financial and accounting areas of the operation but a careful review of the use of the words 'entire departmental operations' in the definition characterizes the inclusion of both financial and operational areas.

Thus operational audit may be conceived of as a body of knowledge which seeks to:

(a) Determine effectiveness of performance in each delegated functional area, and

(b) Establish potential impact of successes and failures (especially, failures) in the specialised functional areas of operation.

Objectives of Operation Audit:

The objectives of any company are:

Productivity, profitability, market expansion, innovation, efficient managerial performance, upgrading the employees attitude and work performance and discharging social responsibilities. The operational audit may serve the business in discharging these objectives.

The objectives of the operational auditing may, therefore, be stated as below:

i. Appraisal of company's objectives,

ii. Evaluation of company's policies,

iii. Evaluation of company's plans,

iv. Evaluation of the structure of organisation,

v. Evaluation of controls,

vi. Appraisal of performance, which involves examination of work flow, determination of work force, performance of work load, measurement of productivity, measurement of profitability, performance of job, and appraisal of costs,

vii. Evaluation of company's social responsibilities, e.g. extent of benefits passed on to the consumers, creation of employment opportunities, etc.

Advantages and Disadvantages

Going through the operational audit process provides a company with objective opinions. Those opinions often generate quicker production or sales turnaround, better allocation of costs, improved control systems, the location of areas of delay and an overall streamlined workflow. However, similar to any audit, operational audits cost money to perform. Those involved in the audit cannot be engaged in other operational processes when they are meeting with the auditor or gathering data for the auditor to use. Additionally, operational audits take considerable time to complete, and it can be harder to determine exactly what is causing problems the more complex operations are. Additionally, even though overhauling operations based on audit results may save the business money in the long run, doing so can rattle employees, cause initial confusion and necessitate increased training or significant staffing alterations.

Cost Auditing

Cost Audit is a critical review undertaken to verify the correctness of Cost Accounts and to check that cost accounting principles and planning have been efficiently followed. It is noteworthy that India is the only country which has introduced statutory cost audit to regulate about 45 vital industries of the country. Cost Audit has been defined by the Chartered Institute of Management Accountants (CIMA) of Landon as "the verification of cost accounts and a check on the adherence to the cost accounting plan."

This implies the following:

(i) The objects of cost accounting with reference to which the cost accounting plan must have been drawn up have to be kept in mind to see whether or not the plan itself and the figures collected will lead to the achievement of the goal or objective set. For instance, if the objective is to achieve maximum efficiency, the plan and the analysis of data will be different from the case where the only objective is to fix prices.

(ii) It has to be examined whether the methods laid down for ascertaining costs and other relevant decisions are being implemented. Treatment and determination of abnormal losses of gains or treatment of certain expenses as direct or indirect are cases in point.

(iii) The correctness of the figures has to be vouched.

The concept of cost audit has been elaborated by ICWA as 'an audit of efficiency of minute details of expenditure, while the work is in progress and not a post mortem examination. Financial audit is a 'fait accompli', cost audit is mainly a preventive measure, a guide for management policy and decision in addition, to being a barometer of performance'.

Cost Audit can be called efficiency audit. It is evidenced by amendment in section 209 which reads. 'The object of the amendment of the section is to ensure specified company proper records relating to utilisation of material labour are available which would make efficiency audit (cost- audit) possible'.

Advantages of Cost Audit

(i) A close check will be maintained on all wastages—materials in store, labour, etc.—and they will be promptly located and reported.

(ii) Inefficiencies in production (or efficiencies) will be located and converted into monetary terms.

(iii) Through fixation of individual responsibility, management by exception will be possible.

(iv) The system of budgetary control and standard costing will be greatly facilitated with cost audit at the hands of a qualified cost accountant.

(v) Records will be up-to-date and information for various purposes will be available.

(vi) Cost audit may unearth a number of errors and frauds which may not be revealed otherwise. This is because a cost auditor examines expenditure minutely and compares it with standards and ascertains exact reasons for discrepancy.

Cost audit offers many advantages to management, cost accountant, shareholders, statutory auditor, consumers and the government.

Advantages to Management:

(i) Errors in following costing principles and techniques are detected. Inconsistencies and frauds can also be detected. This keeps everyone alert and promotes efficiency.

(ii) Cost audit can serve to measure performance of managers and better performance can be rewarded.

(iii) It helps to prepare accurate cost reports and this business planning can be more accurate.

(iv) Inter-firm comparisons can be made with ease and this might be a very useful proposition if industrial intelligence is good.

(v) Cost audit can give an idea about the comparative operational efficiency of each department of division; and may thus pin-point deficiencies and also encourage to operate in a competitive spirit.

Advantages to Management/Cost Accountant:

Important advantages are:

(i) His task is facilitated since errors, deficiencies, etc., are pointed out. Costing plans can be prepared to take care of these things.

(ii) Cost audit may help in easier reconciliation of cost and financial accounts.

(iii) If the cost auditor is an outsider and is an expert, he can certainly give some practical and sound advice to streamline costing systems and organisation.

(iv) Cost audit helps to focus attention of management on the problems faced by the cost accountant. This helps him to realize his goals and objectives with ease.

Advantages to Statutory Auditor:

(i) Audited cost data helps him to determine the value of stocks, remuneration of managerial personnel, etc., with ease and accuracy.

(ii) Data and statements of cost audit help him to prepare his audit programme and plan so that he concentrates more on those aspects which have not been adequately covered by cost audit.

Advantages to Consumers:

(i) The direct benefit accrues where a statutory cost audit has been done to fix a reasonable price for the consumers.

(ii) Since cost audit aims at ensuring efficiency in the organisation, this may also get reflected in reduced prices to the consumers.

Advantages to Labour:

(i) If cost audit is done thoroughly labour also stands to gain through increased profitability in the shape of bonus and other benefits.

(ii) Also it brings into focus the role of labour in improving efficiency in term of increased productivity.

Advantages to Shareholders:

(i) There is correct valuation of all kinds of inventories. This may project a true picture of the organisation before shareholders and other investors and help them to assess its performance.

(ii) External cost audit highlights efficiency or inefficiency, utilisation of manpower and other resources, adequacy of return, etc.

Advantages to Government and Economy:

(i) It helps the government to settle accounts where cost-plus contracts have been made.

(ii) The government can intervene to protect the interests of the consumers, labour, shareholders and investors from exploit-age or inefficient managements.

(iii) At the national level, cost audit promotes cost consciousness and overall efficiency. This means that every rupee invested produces the maximum quantity of goods and services.

Types of Cost Audit:

(i) Cost Audit as an Aid to Management:

The aim is to see that all information placed before management is relevant, reliable and prompt so that management can discharge its duties well. It must also be seen that no relevant or pertinent information is suppressed.

(ii) Cost Audit on Behalf of a Customer:

Often contracts are placed on "Cost Plus" basis. In other words, the customer will determine the final price to be paid on the basis of exact cost plus an agreed margin of profit. The customer, in such a case, usually gets cost accounts of the product concerned audited to establish correct cost and, therefore, price.

(iii) Cost Audit on Behalf of Government:

Sometimes the Government is approached with request for financial help or protection. Before taking a decision on the request, the Government may choose to get cost accounts of the applicant audited to establish whether the need for help is genuine or is a result of mere inefficiency.

(iv) Cost Audit under Statute:

The Amendment Act of 1965 has inserted a new section, 233B, in the Companies Act, 1956 whereby the Central Government may order that certain classes of companies will get their cost accounts audited by a member of the Institute of Cost and Works Accounts of India. Only such companies as are required to maintain proper records regarding materials consumed, labour and other expenses under Section 209 (as amended to date) and may be required to get their cost accounts audited.

The powers and duties and manner of appointment of the cost auditor are the same as that of external financial auditor and the same disqualifications will apply. The cost auditor will submit his report to the Company Law Board with a copy to the company. The right to investigate all aspects of cost accounts is presumably granted to the cost auditor.

The aim of cost audit under statute seems to be that the Government wishes to know, as an instrument of control, the costs of various goods. Government has the power to prescribe the forms in which cost audit reports are to be made out. These are designed not only to verify information, but also to convey good deal of information to Government.

(v) Cost Audit on Behalf of the Trade Association:

Sometimes trade associations seek to maintain prices at a certain level. For this purpose, the accuracy of costing information submitted by various concerns has to be checked. The trade associations may seek to have full information about production capacity and the relative efficiency of productive processes.

Objectives of Cost Auditor

1. Prospective Objective: Under which cost audit aims to identify the undue wastage or losses and ensure that costing system determines the correct and realistic cost of production.
2. Constructive Objectives: Cost audit provides useful information to the management regarding regulating production, economical method of operation, reducing cost of operation and reformulating Cost accounting plans

Continuous Auditing

Continuous auditing has been defined as a methodology or framework that enables auditors to present written results on the subject matter by means of one or a series of reports issued at the same time. The ability to report on events in a concurrent environment can provide important benefits to the users of audit reports. Continuous auditing is consequently designed to enable auditors to report on subject matter in a much shorter timeframe than under the conventional model. In theory, in some environments it should be probable to reduce the reporting timeframe to provide auditing on almost an instantaneous basis. The article focuses on the reliability of continuous auditing, applicability of continuous auditing to organizations and relevance of continuous auditing to auditors.

Reliability of Continuous Auditing

While there has been noteworthy academic research on continuous auditing, as well as numerous efforts by professional standard setting bodies the world over, there has been little, if any, reporting on a constant basis. This is a consequence of a number of factors, which are inclusive of such things as demand, cost vs. benefit and technological issues. While the notion of continuous auditing has been around for many years the real practice and demand for this service has been low. At least from the external audit viewpoint, this is a consequence of the perceived cost outweighing the perceived benefit in continuous auditing. This perspective is a straight result of focusing on continuous auditing only from the financial reporting perspective.

Indisputably, the price of issuing an audit report on a complete set of financial statements each week, month or quarter would be significant and would exceed its value. Nevertheless, if the audit report only addressed definite types of related data in the financial or non-financial category, performance measures or some other information that was of significance to users and could be audited at a rational cost, then the benefits of this type of reporting may be in excess of its cost. If continuous auditing is needed to be established, organizations and auditors must start small. They should start with effortlessly auditable data that has important value to users, such as investors and the equity markets, and structure an obligation to permit an auditor to report within a timeframe that provides value to users of the data.

Applicability of Continuous Auditing to Organizations

Many organizations are not ready for continuous auditing from either a maturity level or a technological level. This is a factor concerning the maturity of their processes, systems and controls. The cost and time required to execute a continuous auditing exercise increases as the strength of an organization's processes and controls decreases. It is observed that organizations with strong processes and controls and mature systems are better suited to a continuous auditing engagement since the auditor can place greater reliance on the processes, controls and systems to lessen the degree, nature and timing of testing to provide support to a continuous auditing opinion. For example, if an organization wanted to make public audited monthly sales and production information two days after month end, the auditor must execute all audit procedures within two days to meet the reporting deadline. On the contrary, the auditor could place dependence on the processes and controls over the systems that process monthly sales and production data and test those processes.

Relevance of Continuous Auditing to Auditors

The special skills and knowledge that auditors have are necessary for the assessment of these controls and for the performance of these engagements related to continuous auditing. This means that auditors are the solution to the issuance of any continuous auditing report; in spite its subject matter. Organizations with superior internal control environments and well-controlled information systems were well-matched for the process of continuous auditing. This conclusion was founded on the assumption that, to make continuous auditing achievable and gainful, important dependence on controls was required. The study noted that auditors would have a vital involvement in continuous auditing engagements as it was projected that many of the controls would be IT controls.

Components

Continuous auditing is made up of three main parts: continuous data assurance (CDA), continuous controls monitoring (CCM), and continuous risk monitoring and assessment (CRMA).

Continuous Data Assurance

Continuous data assurance verifies the integrity of data flowing through the information systems. Continuous data assurance uses software to extract data from IT systems for analysis at the transactional level to provide more detailed assurance. CDA systems provide the ability to design expectation models for analytical procedures at the business-process level, as opposed to the current practice of relying on ratio or trend analysis at higher levels of data aggregation. CDA software can continuously and automatically monitor transactions, comparing their generic characteristics with predetermined benchmarks, thereby identifying anomalous situations. When significant discrepancies occur, alarms are triggered and routed to appropriate stakeholders and auditors.

Continuous Controls Monitoring

Continuous controls monitoring consists of a set of procedures used for monitoring the functionality of internal controls. CCM relies on automatic procedures, presuming that both the controls themselves and the monitoring procedures are formal or able to be formalized. CCM can be used for monitoring access control and authorizations, system configurations, and business process settings. CDA and CCM are complementary processes. Neither process is self-sufficient or comprehensive. Even if no data faults are found it cannot be concluded that controls are fail-safe. Further, even if controls are being implemented, data integrity cannot be assumed. When combined, however, these monitoring approaches present a more complete reliance picture.

Continuous Risk Monitoring and Assessment

Continuous risk monitoring and assessment is used to dynamically measure risk and provide input for audit planning. CRMA is a real-time integrated risk assessment approach, aggregating data across different functional tasks in organizations to assess risk exposures and provide reasonable assurance on the firms' risk assessments.

Black Box Logging

In addition to the aforementioned three components, the black box audit log file is also an important part of continuous auditing. This file can be viewed as an extension of the existing practice of documenting audit activities in manual or automated work papers. A black box log file is a read-only, third-party controlled record of the actions of auditors. The objective of black box logging is to protect a continuous auditing system against auditor and management manipulations.

Continuous Reporting

Continuous reporting is the release of financial and non-financial information on a real-time or near real-time basis. The purpose of continuous reporting is to allow external parties access to information as underlying events take place, rather than waiting for end-of-period reports. The adoption of XBRL by companies makes the release of continuous reporting information more feasible. Continuous reporting also benefits users under Regulation Fair Disclosure. Continuous reporting is a point of constant debate. Some parties, including analysts and investors, are interested in knowing how a company is doing at a given point in time. They argue that near real-time information would provide them with the ability to take advantage of important business moves as they happen. However, opponents are skeptical of how the raw information can be useful and fear information overload, or that there would be too much irrelevant information out there. Additionally, some companies are fearful that continuously reported financial information would give away important strategic moves and undermine competitive advantage.

Implementation

Generally, the implementation of continuous auditing consists of six procedural steps, which are usually administered by a continuous audit manager. Knowing about these steps will enable auditors to better monitor the continuous audit process and provide recommendations for its improvement, if needed. These steps include:

- Establishing priority areas.

This entails choosing which organizational areas to audit. When performing the actions listed above, auditors need to consider the key objectives from each audit procedure. Objectives can be classified as one of four types: detective, deterrent (also known as preventive), financial, and compliance. A particular audit priority area may satisfy any one of these four objectives.

- Identifying monitoring and continuous audit rules.

The second step consists of determining the rules or analytics that will guide the continuous audit activity, which need to be programmed, repeated frequently, and reconfigured when needed. In addition, monitoring and audit rules must take into consideration legal and environmental issues, as well as the objectives of the particular process.

- Determining the process' frequency.

Continuous auditing need not be literally continuous. Auditors need to consider the natural rhythm of the process being audited, including the timing of computer and business processes as well as the timing and availability of auditors trained or with experience in continuous auditing.

- Configuring continuous audit parameters.

Rules used in each audit area need to be configured before the continuous audit procedure (CAP) is implemented. In addition, the frequency of each parameter might need to be changed after its initial setup based on changes stemming from the activity being audited. When defining a CAP, auditors should consider the costs and benefits of error detection as well as audit and management follow-up activities.

- Following up.

Another type of parameter relates to the treatment of alarms and detected errors. Questions such as who will receive the alarm (e.g., line managers, internal auditors, or both – usually the alarm is sent to the process manager, the manager's immediate supervisor, or the auditor in charge of that CAP) and when the follow-up activity must be completed, need to be addressed when establishing the continuous audit process.

- Communicating results.

A final item to be considered is how to communicate with auditees. When informing auditees of continuous audit activity results, it is important for the exchange to be independent and consistent.

Demand

Demand for continuous auditing has come from a variety of sources, primarily user-driven requirements. External disclosure, internal drivers, laws and regulation, and technology all play important roles in pushing up demand.

External Disclosure

More frequent disclosure will drive the nature of the audit process. This increase improves the quality of earnings while reducing manager aggressiveness and decreasing stock market volatility.

Internal Drivers

As companies have become more integrated within their own departments and with other companies, such as suppliers and retailers, a desire for data integrity throughout the electronic data exchange process is also driving demand for continuous auditing.

Laws and Regulation

Laws and regulation require activities and ways a company followed in order to achieve a specific goal to be monitored. Under such laws and regulation company commenced for continuous auditing.

Technology

XBRL

XBRL facilitates the development of continuous auditing modules by providing a way for systems to understand the meaning of tagged data. Proper use of XBRL assures that relevant data gathered from multiple sources is easily comparable and analyzable. XBRL is a derivative of the XML file format, which tags data with contextual and hierarchical information. It is expected that many enterprise resource planning systems will provide data in the XBRL-GL format to facilitate machine readability.

Security

Because of the nature of the information passing through continuous auditing systems, security and privacy issues are also being addressed. Data assurance techniques, as well as access control mechanisms and policies are being implemented into CA systems to prevent unauthorized access and manipulation, and CCM can help test these controls.

Challenges

For many organizations, there are a number of challenges to implementing a continuous auditing approach. The following are some common challenges with associated recommendations.

- Accessing Complex, Diverse System Environment

Few organizations have a completely homogenous, seamless system environment. There is typically a mix of ERPs or multiple instances of one ERP, mainframe systems, off-the-shelf applications, and legacy systems—all of which may contain valuable data. Technology is available to access all of this data to gain a complete picture.

- Reluctance to Expand the use of Technology

Technology may be viewed as a threat to those who perceive that automation might replace jobs. A benefit of continuous auditing is that it performs routine, repetitive tasks and provides the opportunity for the more interesting exploratory work that adds far more value to the organization.

- Overwhelming Results

When not properly implemented, continuous auditing can result in hundreds—even thousands—of false positives and wasted effort. Many companies that have experienced success with continuous auditing recommend that you start small. Select which area of the company poses the greatest risk and where its transactions and control systems are most important to the company for your initial foray into continuous auditing. Automate a small number of key initial tests, such as comparing your accounts payable vendor master file with the employee address file, to uncover potential policy violations or fraud. Moving forward, increase the tests and gradually expand into other business processes in stages.

- Training

Training is essential for optimum results. A number of institutions, including ACL Services Ltd., offer training on computer-aided audit techniques including continuous auditing through automation. Training can be conducted either on-site or remotely, depending on the need of companies.

Comparison to Computer-aided Auditing

Continuous auditing is often confused with computer-aided auditing. The purpose and scope of the two techniques, however, are quite different. Computer-aided auditing employs end user technology including spreadsheet software, such as Microsoft Excel, to allow traditional auditors to run audit-specific analyses as they conduct the periodic audit. Continuous auditing, on the other hand, involves advanced analytical tools that automate a majority of the auditing plan. Where auditors manually extract data and run their own analyses in computer-aided auditing during the course of their traditional audit, high-powered servers automatically extract and analyze data at specified intervals as a part of continuous auditing.

Auditor's Report

An auditor's report provides an opinion on the validity and reliability of a company's financial statements

When financial statements are finalised, they usually must contain an evaluation – an auditor's report - from a licensed accountant or auditor. This report provides an overview of the evaluation of the validity and reliability of a company or organization's financial statements.

The goal of an auditor's report is to document reasonable assurance that a company's financial statements are free from error.

Along with balance sheets, profit & loss statements, and directors reports, auditor's reports make up part of a company's statutory accounts.

Preparation of the Report

An audit of a company's financial statements should result in a report wherein the accountant or auditor is free to share their opinion about the validity and reliability of a company's financial statements.

In this report, the auditor should provide an accurate picture of the company and their financial statements. The auditor should also state whether they are externally or internally connected to the company.

Within the report, the auditor can share any reservations about the condition of the company's finances or relevant additional information. Reservations could arise if the auditor disagrees with something found in the financial statements, e.g. if the auditor disagrees with management about the valuation of an asset because they believe that this has a more significant impact on the financial statements.

In the Report

There are rules concerning what an auditor's report should include and the order in which various items should be reported.

Auditor's reports must adhere to accepted standards established by governing bodies. Standards such as those set by the UK Generally Accepted Accounting Practice (UK GAAP) help to assure external users that the auditor's opinion on the fairness of financial statements is based on a commonly accepted framework.

A typical auditor's report will state:

1. The company that has been audited and what their accounting method is
2. The responsibility of the auditor and their report
3. Reservations (if any)
4. Conclusion
5. Any additional information
6. A management report
7. The date and auditor's signature

Types of Auditor's Report

There are four common types of auditor's reports, each one presenting a different situation encountered during the auditor's work. The four reports are as follows:

Unqualified Opinion

An opinion is said to be unqualified when he or she does not have any significant reservation in respect of matters contained in the Financial Statements. The most frequent type of report is referred to as the "Unqualified Opinion", and is regarded by many as the equivalent of a "clean bill of health" to a patient, which has led many to call it the "Clean Opinion", but in reality it is not a clean bill of health, because the Auditor can only provide reasonable assurance regarding the Financial Statements, not the health of the company itself, or the integrity of company records not part of the foundation of the Financial Statements. This type of report is issued by an auditor when the financial statements are free of material misstatements and are presented fairly in accordance with the Generally Accepted Accounting Principles (GAAP), which in other words means that the company's financial condition, position, and operations are fairly presented in the financial statements. It is the best type of report an auditee may receive from an external auditor.

An Unqualified Opinion indicates the following –

(1) The Financial Statements have been prepared using the Generally Accepted Accounting Principles which have been consistently applied;

(2) The Financial Statements comply with relevant statutory requirements and regulations;

(3) There is adequate disclosure of all material matters relevant to the proper presentation of the financial information subject to statutory requirements, where applicable;

(4) Any changes in the accounting principles or in the method of their application and the effects thereof have been properly determined and disclosed in the Financial Statements.

The report consists of a title and header, a main body, the auditor's signature and address, and the report's issuance date. US auditing standards require that the title includes "independent" to convey to the user that the report was unbiased in all respects. Traditionally, the main body of the unqualified report consists of three main paragraphs, each with distinct standard wording and individual purpose. Nonetheless, certain auditors have since modified the arrangement of the main body (but not the wording) in order to differentiate themselves from other audit firms, even though such modification is contrary to the clarified US AICPA standards on auditing.

The first paragraph (commonly referred to as the introductory paragraph) states the audit work performed and identifies the responsibilities of the auditor and the auditee in relation to the financial statements. The second paragraph (commonly referred to as the scope paragraph) details the scope of audit work, provides a general description of the nature of the work, examples of procedures performed, and any limitations the audit faced based on the nature of the work. This paragraph also states that the audit was performed in accordance with the country's prevailing generally accepted auditing standards and regulations. The third paragraph (commonly referred to as the opinion paragraph) simply states the auditor's opinion on the financial statements and whether they are in accordance with generally accepted accounting principles.

Qualified Opinion report

Qualified report is given by the auditor in either of these two cases:

1. When the financial statements are materially misstated due to misstatement in

one particular account balance, class of transaction or disclosure that does not have pervasive effect on the financial statements.

2. When the auditor is unable to obtain audit evidence regarding particular account balance, class of transaction or disclosure that does not have pervasive effect on the financial statements.

The report is mostly like a Clear Opinion Report and only includes a paragraph viz. Basis for Qualification after Scope paragraph and before Opinion paragraph. Opinion paragraph in addition to its standard wording includes "except for the matter described in Basis for Qualification paragraph the financial statements give true and fair view."

Detailed below:

A Qualified Opinion report is issued when the auditor encountered one of the two types of situations which do not comply with generally accepted accounting principles, however the rest of the financial statements are fairly presented. This type of opinion is very similar to an unqualified or "clean opinion", but the report states that the financial statements are fairly presented with a certain exception which is otherwise misstated. The two types of situations which would cause an auditor to issue this opinion over the Unqualified opinion are:

- Single deviation from GAAP – this type of qualification occurs when one or more areas of the financial statements do not conform with GAAP (e.g. are misstated), but do not affect the rest of the financial statements from being fairly presented when taken as a whole. Examples of this include a company dedicated to a retail business that did not correctly calculate the depreciation expense of its building. Even if this expense is considered material, since the rest of the financial statements do conform with gaap, then the auditor qualifies the opinion by describing the depreciation misstatement in the report and continues to issue a clean opinion on the rest of the financial statements.
- Limitation of scope – this type of qualification occurs when the auditor could not audit one or more areas of the financial statements, and although they could not be verified, the rest of the financial statements were audited and they conform to GAAP. Examples of this include an auditor not being able to observe and test a company's inventory of goods. If the auditor audited the rest of the financial statements and is reasonably sure that they conform with GAAP, then the auditor simply states that the financial statements are fairly presented, with the exception of the inventory which could not be audited.

The wording of the qualified report is very similar to the Unqualified opinion, but an explanatory paragraph is added to explain the reasons for the qualification after the scope paragraph but before the opinion paragraph. The introductory paragraph is left exactly the same as in the unqualified opinion, while the scope and the opinion paragraphs receive a slight modification in line with the qualification in the explanatory paragraph.

The scope paragraph is edited to include the following phrase in the first sentence, so that the user may be immediately aware of the qualification. This placement also informs the user that, except for the qualification, the rest of the audit was performed without qualifications:

> "*Except as discussed in the following paragraph,* we conducted our audit..."

The opinion paragraph is also edited to include an additional phrase in the first sentence, so that the user is reminded that the auditor's opinion explicitly excludes the qualification expressed. Depending on the type of qualification, the phrase is edited to either state the qualification and the adjustments needed to correct it, or state the scope limitation and that adjustments could have but not necessarily been required in order to correct it.

For a qualification arising from a deviation from GAAP, the following phrase is added to the opinion paragraph:

> "In our opinion, *except for the effects of the Company's incorrect determination of depreciation expense,* the financial statement referred to in the first paragraph presents fairly, in all material respects, the financial position of..."

For a qualification arising from a scope of limitation, the following phrase is added to the opinion paragraph:

> "In our opinion, *except for the effects of such adjustments, if any, as might have been determined to be necessary had we been able to perform proper tests and procedures on the Company's inventory,* the financial statement referred to in the first paragraph presents fairly, in all material respects, the financial position of."

Adverse Opinion Report

An Adverse Opinion Report is issued on the financial statements of a company when the financial statements are materially misstated and such misstatements have pervasive effect on the financial statements.

In Audit Report after Scope paragraph but before Opinion paragraph, Basis for Adverse Opinion paragraph is added. In Opinion paragraph the wording changes to, "Because of situations mentioned in Basis for Adverse Opinion paragraph, in our opinion the financial statements of XYZ Co. Ltd. as mentioned in first paragraph does not give true and fair view/are not free from material misstatements."

An Adverse Opinion is issued when the auditor determines that the financial statements of an auditee are materially misstated and, when considered as a whole, do not conform with GAAP. It is considered the opposite of an unqualified or clean opinion, essentially stating that the information contained is materially incorrect, unreliable, and inaccurate in order to assess the auditee's financial position and results of operations. Investors, lending institutions, and governments very rarely accept an auditee's financial statements if the auditor issued an adverse opinion, and usually request the auditee to correct the financial statements and obtain another audit report.

Generally, an adverse opinion is only given if the financial statements pervasively differ from GAAP. An example of such a situation would be failure of a company to consolidate a material subsidiary.

The wording of the adverse report is similar to the qualified report. The scope paragraph is modified accordingly and an explanatory paragraph is added to explain the reason for the adverse opinion after the scope paragraph but before the opinion paragraph. However, the most significant change in the adverse report from the qualified report is in the opinion paragraph, where the auditor clearly states that the financial statements are not in accordance with GAAP, which means that they, as a whole, are unreliable, inaccurate, and do not present a fair view of the auditee's position and operations.

> "In our opinion, *because of the situations mentioned above* (in the explanatory paragraph), the financial statements referred to in the first paragraph *do not* present fairly, in all material respects, the financial position of."

Disclaimer of Opinion Report

A Disclaimer of Opinion is issued in either of the following cases:

- When the auditor is not independent or when there is conflict of interest.
- When the limitation on scope is imposed by client, as a result the auditor is unable to obtain sufficient appropriate audit evidence.
- When there are significant uncertainties in the business of client.

The audit report changes significantly when there is Disclaimer of opinion. An additional paragraph "Basis for Disclaimer" is added in audit report which is placed after Scope paragraph and before Opinion paragraph. In Scope paragraph the wording changes to "We were engaged to audit the financial statements of XYZ Co. Ltd." from "We have audited the financial statements of XYZ Co. Ltd." In Opinion paragraph wording changes to "We do not express an opinion on the financial statements of XYZ Co. Ltd. due to situations explained in Basis for Disclaimer paragraph"

A Disclaimer of Opinion, commonly referred to simply as a Disclaimer, is issued when the auditor could not form and consequently refuses to present an opinion on the financial statements. This type of report is issued when the auditor tried to audit an entity but could not complete the work due to various reasons and does not issue an opinion. The disclaimer of opinion report can be traced back to 1949, when the Statement on Auditing Procedure No. 23: *Recommendation Made To Clarify Accountant's Representations When Opinion Is Not Expressed* was published in order to provide guidance to auditors in presenting a disclaimer.

Statements on Auditing Standards (SAS) provide certain situations where a disclaimer of opinion may be appropriate:

- A lack of independence, or material conflict(s) of interest, exist between the auditor and the auditee (SAS No. 26)
- There are significant scope limitations, whether intentional or not, which hinder the auditor's work in obtaining evidence and performing procedures (SAS No. 58);
- There is a substantial doubt about the auditee's ability to continue as a going concern or, in other words, continue operating (SAS No. 59)
- There are significant uncertainties within the auditee (SAS No. 79).

Although this type of opinion is rarely used, the most common examples where disclaimers are issued include audits where the auditee willfully hides or refuses to provide evidence and information to the auditor in significant areas of the financial statements, where the auditee is facing significant legal and litigation issues in which the outcome is uncertain (usually government investigations), and where the auditee has going concern issues (the auditee may not continue operating in the near future). Investors, lending institutions, and governments typically reject an auditee's financial statements if the auditor disclaimed an opinion, and will request the auditee to correct the situations the auditor mentioned and obtain another audit report.

A disclaimer of opinion differs substantially from the rest of the auditor's reports because it provides very little information regarding the audit itself, and includes an explanatory paragraph stating the reasons for the disclaimer. Although the report still contains the letterhead, the auditee's name and address, the auditor's signature and address, and the report's issuance date, every other paragraph is modified extensively, and the scope paragraph is entirely omitted since the auditor is basically stating that an audit could not be realized.

In the introductory paragraph, the first phrase changes from "We have audited" to "We were engaged to audit" in order to let the user know that the auditee commissioned an audit, but does not mention that the auditor necessarily completed the audit. Additionally, since the audit was not completely and/or adequately performed, the auditor refuses to accept any responsibility by omitting the last sentence of the paragraph. The scope paragraph is omitted in its entirety since, effectively, no audit was performed.

Similar to the qualified and the adverse opinions, the auditor must briefly discuss the situations for the disclaimer in an explanatory paragraph.

Auditor's Report on Internal Controls of Public Companies

Following the enactment of the Sarbanes-Oxley Act of 2002, the Public Company Accounting Oversight Board (PCAOB) was established in order to monitor, regulate, inspect, and discipline audit and public accounting firms of public companies. The PCAOB Auditing Standards No. 2 now requires auditors of public companies to include an additional disclosure in the opinion report regarding the auditee's internal controls, and to opine about the company's and auditor's assessment on the company's internal controls over financial reporting. These new requirements are commonly referred to as the COSO Opinion.

The auditor's report is modified to include all necessary disclosures by either presenting the report subsequent to the report on the financial statements, or combining both reports into one auditor's report.

Going Concern

Going concern is a term which means that an entity will continue to operate in the near future which is generally more than next 12 months, so long as it generates or obtains enough resources to operate. If the auditee is not a going concern, it means that the entity might not be able to sustain itself within the next twelve months. Auditors are required to consider the going concern of an auditee before issuing a report. If the auditee is a going concern, the auditor does not modify his/her report in any way. However, if the auditor considers that the auditee is not a going concern, or will not be a going concern in the near future, then the auditor is required to include an explanatory paragraph before the opinion paragraph or following the opinion papragraph, in the audit report explaining the situation, which is commonly referred to as the going concern disclosure. Such an opinion is called an "unqualified modified opinion".

Unfortunately, many auditors are increasingly reluctant to include this disclosure in their opinions, since it is considered a "self-fulfilling prophecy" by some. This is because a disclosure for a lack of going concern is viewed negatively by investors, lending institutions, and credit agencies, and therefore reduces the chance that the auditee may obtain the capital or borrowing it needs to survive once the disclosure is made. If this situation occurs, the auditee is more likely to stop being a going concern while the auditor loses potential future audit engagements, and so the auditor may be pressured to avoid including a going concern disclosure. In a study performed on 2001 bankruptcies, nearly half (48%) of selected public companies who faced bankruptcy in 2001 did not have a "going concern disclosure" in the previous auditor's reports. Additionally, 12 of the 20 largest bankruptcies in U.S. history occurred between 2001 and 2002 and none of them had a "going concern disclosure" in their previous auditor's report.

As for the actual wording of the auditor's report, when a lack of going concern is determined by the auditor, the disclosure paragraph should state the situation, state the auditor's determination, and state the auditee's plan to correct the situation. The disclosure paragraph should immediately follow the opinion paragraph.

Other Explanatory Information and Paragraphs

Although the auditor reports are the standard reports for financial statement audits, the auditor may add additional information to the report if it is deemed necessary without changing the overall opinion of the report. Usually, this additional information is included after the opinion paragraph, although some situations require that the additional information be included in paragraphs before the opinion paragraph. The most frequent paragraphs include:

- Limiting distribution of the report – In some occasions, the audit report is restricted to a specified user and the auditor includes this restriction in the report, such as a report for financial statements made in cash basis which are prepared for tax purposes only, financial statements for a wholly owned subsidiary whose sole user of its financial statements is its parent company, etc.
- Additional or supplemental information – Certain auditees include additional and/or supplemental information with their financial statements which is not directly related to the financial statements. Examples due to size, time, location, and/or technical constraints. When the main auditor has to rely on another auditor's work, the main auditor may either accept responsibility for the component's information and not modify the audit report, or may chose to disclaim the audit on the specific component, stating that the main auditor did not audit the component, that another auditor audited the component, that the component's audited information is therefore the responsibility of another auditor, and that the main auditor is simply including it in the original auditee's information. If used, this disclaimer is usually included in the introductory paragraph.

Auditor's Reports on Financial Statements in Different Countries

The auditor's report usually does not vary from country to country, although some countries do require either additional or less wording. In the United States, auditors are required to include in the scope paragraphs a phrase stating that they conducted their audit "in accordance with generally accepted auditing standards in the United States of America", and, in the opinion paragraph, state whether the financial statements are presented "in conformity with generally accepted accounting principles in the United States of America". Some countries, such as the Philippines, use similar reports to those issued in the United States, with the exception that second paragraph would state that the audit was conducted in accordance with Philippine Standards on Auditing, and that the financial statements are in accordance with Philippine Financial Reporting Standards.

Opinion Shopping

Opinion shopping is a term used by external auditors and, after the Enron and Arthur Andersen accounting scandals, the media and general public refer to auditees who contract or reject auditors based on the type of opinion report they will issue on the auditee. The underlying principles of this concept are that auditees determine the compensation to auditors for their work (called "audit fees") as well as awarding future audit engagements; that such fees are the auditor's main source of income; that certain auditees may try to contract auditors that will issue audit opinions based on the auditees' needs; and that certain auditors are willing to comply with such demands so long as they are assured future audit engagements.

The most common example is an auditee that knows that the current auditor is going to issue a qualified, adverse, or disclaimer of opinion report, who then rescinds the audit engagement before the opinion is issued, and subsequently "shops" for another auditor who is willing to issue an "unqualified" opinion, regardless of any qualifying situations mentioned in the previous sections. However, opinion shopping is not limited to auditees contracting auditors based on issuing opinions. It also includes auditors who are over-pleasing to auditees by issuing unqualified reports without properly auditing, or by simply overlooking material issues affecting the audit. These auditors' objective is to appear much more attractive and easy-going than other auditors in order to secure future audit engagements and fees.

Although the great majority of auditors are not willing to jeopardize their profession and reputation for guaranteed audit fees, there are some that will issue opinions solely based on obtaining or maintaining audit engagements. This includes auditors who knowingly emit unmodified unqualified opinions for auditees who are engaged in illegal activities, auditees who have caused a material limitation of scope, auditees that have a lack of going concern, or auditees who present fraudulent financial statements (e.g. Enron and Arthur Andersen). This situation is a clear conflict of interest which should hinder an auditor's independence and the ability to audit (AICPA Code of Ethics), but some auditors willingly ignore this statute.

Recent laws and industry standards have been implemented in order to correct this situation, which include the Sarbanes-Oxley Act and the AICPA's practice-monitoring program and Peer Review Program, which are in some cases voluntary, and in other cases, required.

Other Engagements and Reports

There are various other audits and evaluations which an external auditor performs in addition to the engagements mentioned in the previous sections, each with their respective standard report(s):

- Certification audit reports (for example, an ISO 9000 audit report)
- Compilations (not an audit, but requires a report)
- Due Diligence
- Environmental audit report
- Financial forecasts
- Filing of a public company's Form 10-Q and Form 10-K
- Agreed Upon Procedures
- Internal audit reports
- Regulatory inspection reports
- Review of financial statements (an overview with very limited auditing procedures)
- Fraud & Materiality Memo
- Second opinion
- XBRL assurance
- Information security audit information technology audit or information technology security audit

Internal Control

Internal control is an interlocking set of activities that are layered onto the normal operating procedures of an organization, with the intent of safeguarding assets, minimizing errors, and ensuring that operations are conducted in an approved manner. Another way of looking at internal controls is that these activities are needed to mitigate the amount and types of risk to which a firm is subjected.

Internal control comes at a price, which is that control activities frequently slow down the natural process flow of a business, which can reduce its overall efficiency. Consequently, the development of a system of internal control requires management to balance risk reduction with efficiency. This process can sometimes result in management accepting a certain amount of risk in order to create a strategic profile that allows a company to compete more effectively, even if it suffers occasional losses because controls have been deliberately reduced.

A system of internal controls tends to increase in comprehensiveness as a firm increases in size. This is needed, because the original founders do not have the time to maintain complete oversight when there are many employees and/or locations. Further, when a company goes public, there are additional financial control requirements that must be implemented, especially if the firm's shares are to be listed for sale on a stock exchange. Thus, the cost of controls tends to increase with size.

Internal control comes in many forms, which include the following:

- A board of directors oversees the entire organization, providing governance over the management team.
- Internal auditors routinely examine all processes, looking for failings that can be corrected with either new controls or tweaks of existing controls.
- Processes are altered so that more than one person is involved in each one; this is done so that people can cross-check each other, reducing fraud incidents and the likelihood of errors.
- Access to computer records is restricted, so that information is only made available to those people who need it to conduct specific tasks. Doing so reduces the risk of information theft and the risk of asset theft through the modification of ownership records.
- Assets are locked up when not in use, making it more difficult to steal them.

A key concept is that even the most comprehensive system of internal control will not entirely eliminate the risk of fraud or error. There will always be a few incidents, typically due to unforeseen circumstances or an exceedingly determined effort by someone who wants to commit fraud.

Preventative vs. Detective Controls

Internal controls are typically comprised of control activities such as authorization, documentation, reconciliation, security and the separation of duties. And they are broadly divided into preventative and detective activities.

Preventive control activities aim to deter the errors or fraud from happening in the first place, and include thorough documentation and authorization practices. And the separation of duties ensures that no single individual is in a position to authorize, record and be in custody of a financial transaction and the resulting asset. Authorization of invoices and verification of expenses are internal controls. In addition, preventative internal controls include limiting physical access to equipment, inventory, cash and other assets.

Detective controls are backup procedures that are designed to catch items or events that have been missed by the first line of defense. Here the most important activity is reconciliation, used to compare data sets, and corrective action is taken upon material differences. Other detective controls include external audits from accounting firms and internal audits of assets such as inventory.

Limitations of Internal Controls

Regardless of the policies and procedures established by an organization, only reasonable assurance may be provided that internal controls are effective and financial information is correct. The effectiveness of internal controls is limited by human judgment. A business will often give high-level personnel the ability to override internal controls for operational efficiency reasons, and internal controls can be circumvented through collusion.

References

- Auditing and Assurance Vol.1. The Institute of Chartered Accountants of India. 2011. p. 3.4. ISBN 978-81-8441-135-5
- "Internal Audit Checklists of various processes". Internal Audit Expert. internalauditexpert.in. Archived from the original on 13 December 2013. Retrieved 12 December 2013
- Gilbert W. Joseph and Terry J. Engle (December 2005). "The Use of Control Self-Assessment by Independent Auditors". The CPA Journal. Retrieved 10 March 2012
- Sawyer, Lawrence (2003). Sawyer›s Internal Auditing 5th Edition. Institute of Internal Auditors. ISBN 978-0894135095
- Loeb, Stephen E.; Shamoo, Adil E. (1989-09-01). "Data audit: Its place in auditing". Accountability in Research. 1 (1): 23–32. doi:10.1080/08989628908573771. ISSN 0898-9621. PMID 26859053
- "CONCEPT RELEASE ON POSSIBLE REVISIONS TO PCAOB STANDARDS RELATED TO REPORTS ON AUDITED FINANCIAL STATEMENTS" (PDF). Retrieved 22 July 2011
- Pathak, Jagdish; Lind, Mary R. (November 2003). "Audit Risk, Complex Technology, and Auditing Processes". EDPACS. 31 (5): 1–9. doi:10.1201/1079/43853.31.5.20031101/78844.1

Permissions

All chapters in this book are published with permission under the Creative Commons Attribution Share Alike License or equivalent. Every chapter published in this book has been scrutinized by our experts. Their significance has been extensively debated. The topics covered herein carry significant information for a comprehensive understanding. They may even be implemented as practical applications or may be referred to as a beginning point for further studies.

We would like to thank the editorial team for lending their expertise to make the book truly unique. They have played a crucial role in the development of this book. Without their invaluable contributions this book wouldn't have been possible. They have made vital efforts to compile up to date information on the varied aspects of this subject to make this book a valuable addition to the collection of many professionals and students.

This book was conceptualized with the vision of imparting up-to-date and integrated information in this field. To ensure the same, a matchless editorial board was set up. Every individual on the board went through rigorous rounds of assessment to prove their worth. After which they invested a large part of their time researching and compiling the most relevant data for our readers.

The editorial board has been involved in producing this book since its inception. They have spent rigorous hours researching and exploring the diverse topics which have resulted in the successful publishing of this book. They have passed on their knowledge of decades through this book. To expedite this challenging task, the publisher supported the team at every step. A small team of assistant editors was also appointed to further simplify the editing procedure and attain best results for the readers.

Apart from the editorial board, the designing team has also invested a significant amount of their time in understanding the subject and creating the most relevant covers. They scrutinized every image to scout for the most suitable representation of the subject and create an appropriate cover for the book.

The publishing team has been an ardent support to the editorial, designing and production team. Their endless efforts to recruit the best for this project, has resulted in the accomplishment of this book. They are a veteran in the field of academics and their pool of knowledge is as vast as their experience in printing. Their expertise and guidance has proved useful at every step. Their uncompromising quality standards have made this book an exceptional effort. Their encouragement from time to time has been an inspiration for everyone.

The publisher and the editorial board hope that this book will prove to be a valuable piece of knowledge for students, practitioners and scholars across the globe.

Index

www.ingramcontent.com/pod-product-compliance
Lightning Source LLC
LaVergne TN
LVHW080603210926
848485LV00003B/99